BENEATH
THE TYRANT'S YOKE

Norwegian Resistance *to the*
German Occupation *of* Norway
1940 – 1945

RICHARD S. FUEGNER

Beaver's Pond Press, Inc.
Edina *Minnesota*

ISBN 1-931646-86-4

Library of Congress Catalog Number: 2002112521

Printed in the United States of America

First Printing: November 2002

06 05 04 03 02   6 5 4 3 2 1

Beaver's Pond Press, Inc.

7104 Ohms Lane. Suite 216
Edina, MN 55439-1465
(952) 829-8818
www.beaverspondpress.com

to order, visit midwestbookhouse.com or call
1-877-430-0044. Quantity discounts available.

To my grandson, Ryan,
a young man on the way.

Table of Contents

Acknowledgments

I would like to thank the following persons for their assistance while I was conducting research at the Norwegian Resistance Museum in Oslo. All of them were most helpful: Anne-Karin Sonsteby, archivist; Arnfinn Moland, research fellow/lecturer and director; Ivar Kraglund, curator and deputy director; and Frode Faeroy, research fellow.

I would also like to thank Arne F. Egner, who took time to discuss SOE airdrop operations to the Norwegian Home Forces, staff members at the University of Oslo Library who provided me with additional reference material. I am particularly grateful to Jorgen Hoff-Jenssen, former publisher of an "illegal" newspaper in Kritiansund during the years of the German Occupation, and his wife Nanna. Not only did they provide me with detailed information concerning the clandestine press operation during the war years, but provided me with warm hospitality during my stay in Norway.

I am indebted to Kristian Ottosen, a former member of an intelligence unit in Bergen, who worked closely with the British Secret Intelligence Service during the war, and to his wife, Gerd, for the cordial reception in their home. Mr. Ottosen provided me with much firsthand knowledge of Anglo-Norwegian intelligence operations, which I have incorporated into my book.

My sincere thanks also to Siv Biebel, who translated the bulk of the Norwegian source material, and to Hilde Oliver and Mette Adamsen for additional help in translation.

Thanks also to Dr. Charles Ford for clarification on several points relating to membership in the Norwegian Fascist Nasjonal Samling Party.

I am particularly grateful to Paul Byorth and to Virginia L. Martin for the detailed proofreading, corrections, and suggestions in the final preparation of the manuscript.

Photographs are reproduced with the kind permission of Kristian Ottosen and Jorgen Hoff-Jenssen.

Richard Fuegner
Kirkwood, Missouri
March 2002

Introduction

*If there is anyone who still wonders why this war is being fought, let him
look to Norway.*

*If there is anyone who has any delusions that this war could have been
avoided, let him look to Norway.*

*And if there is anyone who doubts of the democratic will to win, again I
say, let him look to Norway.*

—Franklin Delano Roosevelt (1882-1945), American President, 1933-45

In the fall of 1996, while traveling through Norway with my wife,
Mary, those words struck a responsive chord in me during a visit to the
Resistance museum in Oslo. Although President Roosevelt's words
were not unfamiliar to me, I had never given them much thought before
visiting the museum. But there I asked myself: what was so special
about Norway that the President of the United States should single out
this small Scandinavian country for an explanation—nay, a justifica-
tion—for conducting a worldwide conflict that was to ultimately cost
the lives of over 40 million people?

It was at this museum that I started to seek an answer to that question. As I made my way through the museum observing newspapers,
photographs, objects, and exhibits that highlighted those years of the
Occupation, I began to acquire a greater appreciation for what
Norwegians experienced and what the Resistance actually was: a particular state of mind, a spirit of defiance, and a deep-seated rejection of
the Occupation. It was with these thoughts in mind that the idea of a
book occurred to me that would take the reader back in time to the
Occupation period.

To my mind, behind the numerous forms of memorabilia, were real
flesh and blood, human faces occupying that state of mind, harboring
that spirit of defiance, and fostering that deep-seated rejection. All of
them were, in some measure, participants in a day-to-day life under a

foreign yoke. Much of that life was, as one section of the museum depicts it, "the dreary daily round." But much of it also involved courage and dangerous risk-taking, protracted suffering, and self-sacrifice by countless men and women. I have tried to present to the reader some of both sides of life during the Occupation.

The book is, by no means, meant to be a comprehensive study of the Resistance. It is simply one writer's attempt to describe life under the five-year Occupation for the Norwegian people—ordinary people, many of whom did extraordinary things to preserve a sense of national identity at a time in history when it was in danger of being lost.

One of the joys of writing contemporary history is the opportunity to meet personally with the subjects of one's research. My appreciation and understanding of the Resistance movement in Norway has been enhanced by those persons and by others who have studied this subject in greater detail.

I, of course, take full responsibility for the book's shortcomings, omissions, or inaccuracies.

The Neutrality of the Dove

There is in some men a dispassionate neutrality of mind,

which, though it generally passes for good temper,

can neither gratify nor warm us; it must indeed be granted

that these men can only negatively offend; but then

it should also be remembered that they cannot positively please.

—Lord Greville (1554-1628), English poet

When the German Occupation Forces marched down Karl Johansgate, Oslo's main boulevard, on Tuesday, April 9, 1940, without any prior warning or declaration of war, the citizens of that beleaguered capital were shocked, frightened, and without leadership or guidance. Less than a year earlier in October 1939, one month after Hitler unleashed his Nazi legions against Poland, Norway—along with Denmark and Sweden—reaffirmed its post-World War I record of strict neutrality, but had taken almost no precautions to defend itself. Idealist in outlook, the Norwegian people thought of peace as the natural condition of nations and were therefore psychologically unprepared for war.

The great majority of Norwegians did not believe that they would ever suffer the same fate as Poland and Czechoslovakia. They had no reason to quarrel with the Germans since there were no borders to dispute nor conflicting ethnic or national minority problems. Besides, the Germans had always viewed their Scandinavian neighbor as "Nordic cousins."

Traditionally, Norway had strong cultural and economic ties with Germany. In the fields of education and the arts, and especially in the industrial branches of building and engineering, Norway owed much to German thoroughness and organizational skill, much of which can be traced to the ancient link with the mighty Hanseatic merchants of the Middle Ages who dominated Norwegian trade into the seventeenth century. German tradesmen, craftsmen, and experts on mining, forestry, and glass and iron production introduced working methods in Norway as early as the fifteenth and sixteenth centuries. The 1800s brought a new dimension to the relationship, with a more equal exchange between Germany and all of Scandinavia. German universities, art academies, and museums attracted great numbers of Norwegians. Humanistic research in both Germany and Norway became directed more towards the Nordic past and culture than the Greco-Roman classical world. Literary and musical salons were important cultural meeting places in both Germany and Scandinavia, where one could make new contacts and present one's latest works.

At the turn of the century, Germany exported numerous technical products to Norway, such as telegraphs, cameras, telephones, electrical meters, and printing presses; and many Norwegian engineering students were eager to study in Germany. German tourists came to Norway as early as the 1820s, but it was Kaiser Wilhelm II, a frequent visitor to the west fiords from 1889 to 1914, who really started the tourist stream towards the north. For the wealthiest of the German middle classes, a cruise to Norway on one of the luxury liners became a status symbol, and the possibility of meeting the Emperor was as much of a main attraction as the fiords, mountains, and waterfalls.[1]

World War I had limited contacts between Germany and Scandinavia. It also highlighted differences in political views: Imperial Germany, particularly as personified in the Kaiser, was always viewed to some extent distrustfully. While important sectors of Swedish opinion sympathized with Germany, most Norwegians and Danes favored England and France. Doubtless, such feelings were heightened when almost 50 percent of the Norwegian mercantile marine tonnage was sunk and about 2,000 Norwegian seamen lost their lives as the result of Germany's unrestricted submarine warfare.[2]

Yet, despite the seeds of conflict, which these incidents and Norwegian trade restrictions produced, Norway's neutrality was a reflection of the country's relative immunity to German pressure. In the twenties and thirties among visitors to Scandinavia, German tourists were second only to the British in numbers, although later events were to prove them to be something other than disinterested sightseers.

After 125 years of peaceful existence, pacifism had become deeply rooted in the Norwegian mentality. It was especially predominant in the Labor government formed in March 1935, under Johan Nygaardsvold, a former lumberjack, who promoted a remarkably progressive social policy, but had little interest in foreign affairs and defense matters. What Norway desired from international politics was respect for its wish to be left alone.

Nevertheless, like the other Scandinavian countries after World War I, Norway was an active proponent of the League of Nations, and relied strongly on that body to preserve the peace as a substitute for national defense. Even before the coming of peace, Norway's growing interest in international problems found expression in the Norwegian Society for a League of Nations.[3] Its leader, Fridtjof Nansen, a distinguished son of Norway who earlier had won world fame for his polar expeditions, was later to become the High Commissioner of the League of Nations.[4] He did much to relieve the untold suffering of millions of victims scattered throughout Europe and the Near East during the twenties.[5] It was Nansen's belief that "small states have a peculiar mission to seek out and find the new paths that humanity must tread in order to abolish war altogether."[6]

Throughout the troubled thirties, however, the increasingly evident failure of the League of Nations as a peacekeeping body caused Norway gradually to withdraw from an already half-hearted commitment to the principles of collective security. Thus, under the influence of a strong pacifist sentiment and an almost exclusive concern with the country's internal affairs, Norway's defense posture had fallen into a deplorable state. Yet, until the late 1930s, there seemed to be no lack of arguments to justify a low priority for defense expenditures. War seemed a remote possibility; and even if war came, it was assumed that Norway's neutrality would be affected only economically—not militarily. Trade and shipping would inevitably be affected, but the expectation of a more hostile threat calling for active military measures was a long step, and a step which few were prepared to take.

It was believed that because Norway had emerged from World War I with its faith in neutrality unshaken, that same posture could be maintained in any future conflict between the Great Powers. But the situation on the eve of World War II, while it may have appeared similar to the situation that faced Scandinavia before the outbreak of World War I, was only superficially the same. Adolf Hitler's Third Reich was far more daring and aggressive than had been the government of the Kaiser. If Norway hoped to remain aloof from the struggle, pressures were at work which would sweep those hopes aside.

In 1936, the year in which France and Great Britain refused to carry out League sanctions against Italy when Mussolini invaded Ethiopia, the Norwegian Minister of Foreign Affairs, Halvdan Koht, echoed the sentiments that Nansen expressed in 1919. He stated that "we cannot and will not have in this country any strong military organization."[7]

As peace activists in outlook, the neglect of defenses by the Labor Party was partly attributable to the belief among left-wing politicians that the professional nucleus within the armed forces was a bastion for reactionaries, and they sought to replace the army by a small defense guard. Even then, anti-military propaganda discouraged few volunteers from enlisting.[8] Moreover, it was believed that money spent on national defense was money lost to social services, an understandable concern at the time, in view of the substantial social and economic reforms undertaken in Norway during the depression years. By the late thirties, Norway had one of the most advanced social security systems in the world.[9]

During the inter-war years, numerous professional, cultural, and social meetings took place in Germany in which large numbers of Norwegians had been invited. German professors, scientists, entertainers, and musicians visited Norway to express their friendship in the promotion of a common Aryan culture. After the bewildering shock of German Occupation, however, any feelings of "kinship of race" between the German people and the Norwegians were quickly dispelled. The nation woke up to the realization that a Great Power, with whom the Norwegian people had been on such friendly terms both professionally and socially, had suddenly become a deadly enemy.

After Hitler's rise to power in 1933, when liberal politicians began to realize that military defense might be required in the future, the geographical position and the character of its land mass fostered the dangerous belief that "the country was easy to defend"—a notion which probably refers to the invulnerability of the mountainous hinterland.[10]

Logistically, however, the physical features of the country made the problem of defense intrinsically difficult. The unevenly distributed population of scarcely more than 3 million people was spread over a land mass larger than the whole of the British Isles. More than half the food supply had to be imported, since no more than 3 percent of the total area was arable. Although the country is 1,100 miles long, its jagged sawtooth coastline, which measures nearly 12,000 miles, is lined with high, rugged, mountainous terrain and deep narrow fiords, some extending for a 100 miles into the interior of the country. Throughout western Norway, they provide the normal means of access to the sparsely inhabited farm settlements that lie at the base of the mountains. Only the rolling flatlands of the southeast were at all densely settled; elsewhere the population was confined largely to the heavily indented coastline and narrow valleys that lead into the fiords.

Oslo, with nearly 300,000 citizens, and Bergen, with little more than 100,000, were the only towns of considerable size, the others being mainly small ports with some industry and dependent upon communications by sea more than by rail or road. For so small a population and with poor communications, the cost of grappling with problems of transportation was overwhelming. Since over one-half of the country is covered by mountains and a fourth by dense forests, railroads were few (in the north almost nonexistent) and single-tracked. Roads were narrow, hazardous, and rough-surfaced; shipping routes slow; and air communications (except by seaplane) underdeveloped because of the prohibitive cost of landing-space. Given these features, Norway was in no position to defend itself against a well-armed and highly trained Nazi juggernaut that vastly outnumbered the Norwegians.

As the aggressive tendencies of Nazi Germany became increasingly apparent after Hitler's seizure of the Sudetenland, Norway began to bolster itself militarily. Defense expenditures rose from 34 million kroner in 1935-36 to 58 million kroner in 1939-40, of which almost one-half was an ad hoc expenditure because of the threatening world situation.[11] Yet, in terms of manpower and materiel, Norway was practically defenseless. Transport was largely horse-drawn, and tanks and antitank guns completely lacking. The air force consisted of two separate army and navy branches with no coordination. Approximately 30 seaplanes were located at seven naval coastal stations; 18 scouting aircraft and a total of 6 fighters, were in service on 5 airfields under army command.[12]

Before the war, Norway placed orders in the United States for a large number of high-quality aircraft for both the army and navy air forces. On the day of invasion, however, practically none of what had been ordered had been delivered. Nineteen non-operational Curtis Hawk 75A P-36 pursuit fighters had been sent from the United States, five of which were assembled and the rest still lying on the ground in their crates at the Kjeller military airfield just north of Oslo.[13] The navy was small, designed for coastal defense, and the ports themselves protected by obsolete artillery. At the fiord approaches to the main coastal fortresses at Oslo, Kristiansand, Bergen, and Trondheim, fortifications were equipped with batteries, minefields, lights, and patrol vessels, but were undermanned and with no infantry garrisons to defend against an enemy landing party. The authority to lay minefields was withheld, a shortage of ammunition precluded regular gun exercises, and in April 1940, some of the searchlights were away in Sweden for overhaul and modernization.[14] On the day of invasion, 13,000 ill-trained and ill-equipped troops were under arms, of whom nearly one-half were in the northern half of the country.[15]

This unpreparedness was underscored by Norway's reliance on the traditional aid and almost automatic protection by the British Navy for the defense of its coasts, a presumption that ruled out any German invasion by sea. The disarmingly candid statement by Norway's prime minister in 1908 that "we trust in the British nation" had much truth in it then, but was far more applicable to the situation on the eve of the World War II.[16] Norway, as well as the major Allied countries, were to learn in the spring of 1940 of the futility of allowing their armed forces to diminish in peacetime and then to use them, inadequate in personnel and equipment, for tasks well beyond their capabilities.

The Cunning of the Serpent

Neutrality is no favorite with Providence,
for we are so formed that it is scarcely possible
for us to stand neuter in our hearts,
although we may deem it
prudent to appear so in our actions
—Caleb Colton (1780–1832), English clergyman

In the spring of 1939, Norway, in the face of impending war clouds, reaffirmed its neutralist stance so that it might be more readily respected, and refused to enter into a Scandinavian defense agreement, even after aligning itself with Sweden by refusing Hitler's offer of a non-aggression pact. Unlike Denmark, which as a neighboring country to Germany felt its position more difficult and accepted the non-aggression treaty, the Norwegian government wanted to maintain an independent position outside all European alliances. It was an offer that might seem attractive to nations that were anxious to keep out of war, but Norway realized that the non-aggression treaty Poland and Germany had concluded had been regarded as the beginning of a German orientation on the part of Poland. Norway felt that acceptance of the German offer might be interpreted in the same way.[1]

And it was only a half-year later that Germany, by its attack on Poland, was to prove what kind of respect it had toward such treaties. According to Foreign Minister Halvdan Koht, the government could not imagine the idea of a German attack against Norway. He stated, "At the time, I was convinced that Germany would shortly be at war with the Western Powers, and I did not wish my country to be bound to Germany by any particular ties."[2] During the last two days of August, the foreign ministers of the Scandinavian states met for the last time in Oslo and renewed their declaration of strict neutrality.[3] Before the ministers of the other countries could get home to their respective capitals, Germany had invaded Poland. War was a fact.

Unlike the annexation of Austria and Czechoslovakia, and the conquest of Poland, the plan to occupy Norway and Denmark did not originate in the mind of Hitler, but rather was the brainchild of officers of the German Navy, specifically Grand Admiral Erich Raeder. In fact, it was the only military act of aggression in which the Navy played the decisive role. It was also the only one in which the Armed Forces High Command (OKW) did the planning and coordinating. Neither the Army High Command and its general staff nor the Air Force were ever consulted until the plan was almost completed.[4] Many believed that the largely passive naval strategy in World War I had been a failure; essentially defensive in character, its purpose was to deter the Allies from offensive operations in the vicinity of German territory.

Postwar naval critics of this strategy considered it to be a waste of naval power, as it meant defending positions that were never attacked. The severe restrictions laid upon the fleet enabled the Allies to establish a distant but watertight blockade around the Central Powers— Germany, Austria-Hungary, and Turkey. Against this development, the lack of imaginative prewar planning had even blunted the effectiveness of the submarine. And although it had at times shown itself to be effective, strategists began to realize that the submarine's full potential could only be realized by a more offensive general strategy which aimed at providing operational submarine bases nearer to their hunting grounds in the Atlantic. Thus, past failures could be remedied by a new navy, better equipped with submarines, guided by less orthodox operations, and supported by air strength.[5]

The German Navy had long realized that it had no direct access to the open ocean, and concluded that in any future war with Great Britain, Germany must acquire ports along the Scandinavian peninsula with its open ocean shores, which its own geographical position failed to provide. Strategically, the Germans recognized the importance of the deeply indented fiords and inner passages, which lie between the island archipelagos and the mainland, ideal for the establishment of naval bases along the Norwegian coast. They provided access to the North Atlantic and thereby opened up the ocean to German surface and undersea vessels and aircraft. The Reich could then mount an effective blockade of the British Isles and stave off interdiction by the Royal Navy in anticipation of an Allied invasion of Norway.

An equally important economic consideration was the guarantee of safe passage for German freighters carrying cargo of Swedish iron ore so vital to Germany's war-making capacity. During the summer months the shipments were transported from northern Sweden down the Gulf of Bothnia across the Baltic to Germany, but in the winter this shipping lane was inaccessible because the gulf was frozen. Hence, the ore had to be shipped by rail from the Gullivare ore field in Sweden to the Norwegian port of Narvik and brought down the Norwegian coast by ship to Germany. For almost the entire journey, German vessels could sail within Norway's territorial waters unmolested and thereby escape destruction by British naval vessels and bombers. Germany had no misgivings about the superiority of British seapower and realized that its navy could not yet deal effectively for any length of time with severe surface warfare off the Norwegian coast. It was not surprising, then, that after the outbreak of war in 1939, the German Navy recognized the importance of an occupation of the Norwegian coast and that Raeder called the matter to the attention of Hitler.

Although the Fuehrer recognized the significance of the Scandinavian problem, and the importance of submarine warfare from forward bases on the Norwegian coast in case of a prolonged war, he was at the moment preoccupied with a shorter war based on launching a rapid offensive in the West. The prevailing view in Germany was that Britain and France would pursue a mainly passive "phoney war" role until their economic and military resources would permit a more aggressive struggle.[6]

Raeder, however, pointed to the danger that the British, as a counterstroke to a German offensive in the West, might carry out a surprise landing in Norway and occupy key bases at Trondheim and Narvik. Furthermore, he drew Hitler's attention to the voluminous trade between Scandinavia and England, especially of a number of strategic raw materials such as nitrates, ferro-alloys, and non-ferrous metals, as well as fish products and whale oil. Much of it passed through Trondheim, but left Norwegian waters from various points along the coast. A German occupation would enable exports from Scandinavia to be deflected from Britain to Germany.[7] Nevertheless, Hitler still refused to act on Raeder's Norwegian proposal.

In June, Germany received support for an occupation of Norway from a quite different quarter in the person of Vidkun Quisling, a major in the Norwegian Army and a former minister of defense in the early 1930s who, in May 1933, founded the fascist-inspired political party *Nasjonal Samling*—National Unification. As early as 1930, Quisling, whose name would soon become an international synonym for traitor, sought contact with the German Nazi Party. But despite periodic contacts throughout the thirties with individual members of the Nazi hierarchy, his movement seemed to attract little interest and even less in the fertile democratic soil of Norway, where he was unable to even get elected to Parliament.

In Germany, he established contact with Alfred Rosenberg, the "official philosopher" of the Nazi movement, whose utopian dreams included the establishment of a vast Nordic Empire from which the Jews and other "impure races" would be excluded and which would eventually dominate the world under Nazi German leadership. Quisling took the opportunity to "warn" Rosenberg of pro-British factions in Norway who were intensifying their efforts against Germany and of the danger of Great Britain gaining control of Norway in the event of war. The Norwegian conspirator later met with Raeder and told the Grossadmiral that England would not in the long run respect Norwegian neutrality.[8]

Furthermore, he alleged that a secret agreement between Britain and Norway already existed, that in the event of war, the English would be permitted to land troops near Stavanger and establish a base at Kristiansand on the southwest coast. Quisling thereupon emphasized the danger of such developments. He then stated that his *Nasjonal Samling* Party—commonly referred to by the initials NS—wished to forestall the British action by putting corresponding bases at the disposal of Germany.[9] Quisling's plan was to create a *coup d' etat* by using units of the German Navy with troops on board that would be posted at selected points near the approaches of Oslo, ready to be called in by the new Quisling government. This proposal was called the "political plan," since it called for the occupation of Norway by peaceful means— that is, German forces called in by Norway.

However, in December, after Quisling met with both Hitler and the German military planners, the Fuehrer was skeptical of this proposal.

He preferred Norway to remain neutral, but on the other hand, he could never permit the British to gain control of Narvik, the transshipment port for the Swedish ore. Moreover, Hitler's skepticism of the Quisling plan was based on the presupposition that the majority of Norwegians would assume a hostile attitude, which would create the need for continuous German support and an early military penetration of the country to forestall internal conflict. Thus the political plan was dismissed as unworkable and the proposal went ahead on what was called *Studie Nord,* the coercive alternative for the occupation of Norway.[10]

On January 27, Hitler set up a small working staff comprised of one representative from each of the three armed services to work out a detailed plan for the invasion of Norway. The operation was code-named *Weseruebung* (Weser Exercise) in deference to the Weser River that flows by the German port of Bremerhaven and empties into the North Sea. Copenhagen would later be included in the plan since the conquest of Norway would depend on securing Denmark and its airfields. It was the first campaign in which land, sea, and air forces were employed in close coordination over long distances. The plan was a model of Teutonic thoroughness and meticulous care involving covert preparation, swift execution, and diplomatic deception as to its true objective.

In London, authorities were equally aware of the strategic value of Norwegian coastal waters, and studied the experiences of the blockade during the previous war, not with a view to copying those experiences, but rather of perfecting the system without repeating the many mistakes that had hampered its earlier effectiveness. One way of accomplishing this where the neutrals were concerned was to supplement the traditional "blockade by agreement" with direct action, where British naval power could be brought to bear.[11]

As early as mid-September 1939, Winston Churchill, then First Lord of the Admiralty and a member of Prime Minister Neville Chamberlain's War Cabinet, was acutely aware that the blockade was Britain's principal naval offensive measure and lost no time in trying to implement it. He realized that the Scandinavian peninsula had "immense strategic significance."[12] He recognized the importance of iron ore to the German war effort, and proposed mining the Leads, the inshore channel near the Norwegian coast south of Narvik, to halt the iron ore shipments. The Leads would then force the ships out to the open sea where they would be exposed to interception by British warships. But the British cabinet was reluctant to violate Norwegian neutrality, and the decision to lay the mines was delayed. Despite persistent efforts by Churchill to gain approval for the mining operation in the months that followed, Chamberlain and the cabinet remained adamant and the sanction was still refused.

Meanwhile, the Scandinavian peninsula became the scene of an unexpected conflict when Russia attacked Finland in late November, a situation that aroused strong feelings in Britain and France, and strongly affected the discussions about Norway. The attack was the result of a territorial dispute over the Karelian Isthmus, the cession of certain Finnish islands in the Gulf of Finland, and the leasing of two naval ports as Russian naval and air bases. Despite the willingness of the Finns to concede most of the Russian demands, the talks broke down and less than three weeks later, units of the Red Army crossed the Finnish frontier. The Russian invasion produced worldwide indignation and an appeal by the League of Nations to provide Finland with all possible material and humanitarian assistance. For Britain and France, the conflict held out the prospect of additional action in the developing Scandinavian situation.

Churchill, ever mindful of seizing an opportunity to halt the German war-making capacity by a mine-laying operation, "welcomed this new and favorable breeze as means of achieving the major strategic advantage of cutting off the vital iron ore supplies of Germany."[13] Despite the violation of Scandinavian neutrality, which a minefield operation would involve, the resolute Churchill dismissed all objections to his proposal. "Small nations," he persisted "must not tie our hands when we are fighting for their rights and freedom."[14]

France at this point proposed an even more aggressive plan—dispatching an Anglo-French force to aid Finland. Since Finland could be reached only by going through Norway and Sweden, the force would occupy the Norwegian port of Narvik and seize the railroad that led to the iron mines just across the border in Sweden. A further small British force would occupy the southern ports of Trondheim, Bergen, and Stavanger. Predictably, both Norway and Sweden rejected the Churchillian plan, as they had no desire to be occupied by Allied troops, much less by the Germans. Moreover, the British cabinet refused to authorize the operation without a Finnish appeal for troops. The appeal never came. Instead, on March 13, the Russo-Finnish war ended with Finland's acceptance of the Soviet terms. Thus ended the Allied pretext for an expeditionary force into Scandinavia.

One month earlier on February 14, Britain's lingering doubts concerning the violation of territorial waters were lessened considerably when a British reconnaissance plane sighted a German supply ship, the *Altmark,* proceeding southward in Norwegian territorial waters off the coast of Bergen. Aboard the German vessel were 299 captured British sailors from ships sunk by the German pocket battleship, *Graf Spree,* who were being taken to Germany as prisoners of war. A Norwegian gunboat halted the *Altmark,* made a superficial inspection of the ship, found that it had no prisoners aboard and that it was unarmed, and allowed it to proceed on to Germany. Churchill, who thought otherwise, personally dispatched a British flotilla to enter Norwegian waters, board the German ship, and free the prisoners. On February 16—17, despite protests by Norwegian torpedo boats, the British destroyer *Cossack* entered the Josingfiord where the *Altmark* sought safety. A confrontation took place in which four Germans were killed and five wounded. The sailors were found in locked storerooms and an empty oil tank where they had been hidden to avoid being discovered by the Norwegians.[15]

When the Norwegian government lodged a strong protest to Britain about this violation of its territorial waters, Prime Minister Neville Chamberlain replied that Norway had violated international law by permitting its waters to be used by the Germans to transport British prisoners to a German prison. The *Altmark* incident had shown the unwillingness of the Norwegians to maintain their neutral rights against a German violation, as compared to their opposition to what Britain considered a more justifiable infringement of neutrality. Despite a stiffened British resolve that such a state of affairs could not be allowed to go on indefinitely, immediate action in favor of the mine-laying operation was delayed still further.

Hitler viewed the *Altmark* affair somewhat differently. After hearing of the liberation of all British prisoners aboard the German vessel, he was enraged that the Norwegians would not seriously oppose a British display of force in their own territorial waters. He was also furious over the refusal of the crew members of the *Graf Spee* who were aboard the *Altmark* to resist the Norwegian inspection. The incident showed that the Oslo government was no longer capable of enforcing its neutrality. Clearly, this was the spur that prompted the Fuehrer to press energetically for the completion of plans for *Weseruebung*. On February 1, orders were issued to equip the ships and put all troops in readiness for embarkation. The final top-secret directive was issued on March 1:

> *The development of the situation in Scandinavia requires the making of all preparations for the occupation of Denmark and Norway. This operation should prevent British encroachment on Scandinavia and the Baltic. Further it should guarantee our ore base in Sweden and give our Navy and Air Force a wider starting line against Britain. . . .*
>
> *In view of our military and political power in comparison with that of the Scandinavian States, the force to be employed in "Weser Exercise" will be kept as small as possible.*
>
> *The numerical weakness will be balanced by daring actions and surprise execution.*
>
> *On principle, we will do our utmost to make the operation appear as an occupation, the object of which is the military protection of the neutrality of the Scandinavian States. Corresponding demands will be transmitted to the governments at the beginning of the occupation. If necessary, demonstrations by the Navy and Air Force will provide the necessary emphasis. If, in spite of this, resistance should be met, all military means will be used to crush it… The crossing of the Danish border and the landings in Norway must take place simultaneously. It is most important that the Scandinavian States as well as the Western opponents should be taken by surprise.*[16]

Throughout the months of February and March, while preparations for the invasion were moving forward, the utmost secrecy was maintained. But because of the size of the operation, rumors inevitably began to leak out of Germany and across Europe. Several weeks before the plan was put into effect, the Norwegian government received warnings from its legation in Berlin and from Sweden of a German concentration of troops and naval vessels in the North Sea and Baltic ports.[17]

The Norwegian General Staff had for some time urged the government, without success, to mobilize more troops. Nevertheless, the cabinet and people, like the British Cabinet and people at the time of Munich, were firmly established in the habit of optimistic inaction.[18]

In London, meanwhile, Churchill's bulldog tenacity and the announcement in March by the newly formed French government of Paul Reynaud of its support for the mining operation prompted the British Supreme War Council to carry out the plan Operation *Wilfred*. Both Norway and Sweden were warned that their interpretation of their neutral rights operated to the advantage of Germany, and that the Allies could no longer tolerate this in the face of impending German aggression. They knew that the mining would provoke immediate retaliation by the Germans, and that the unfortunate Norwegians would be the target.

In anticipation of a violent counterstroke of a German troop landing to keep the coastal waters open to traffic, the Allies decided that a small Anglo-French force be sent to Narvik and advance to the nearby Swedish frontier. Preparations were also made to send an expeditionary force to the key Norwegian ports of Narvik, Trondheim, Bergen, and Stavanger to deny these bases to the Germans. This was known as "Plan R-4." because of the Admiralty's preoccupation with the blockade measures and the possibility of conducting successful large-scale naval engagements. However, the operation was abandoned. Orders were given "to deal with any sea-borne expedition the Germans may send against Norway. Only when the Germans set foot on Norwegian soil, or there is clear evidence that they intend to do so, would the military expedition sail."[19] Churchill's plan (approved by the War Cabinet and the Allied Supreme War Council) now reduced to laying mines off the Norwegian coast, was scheduled to begin on April 5. A last-minute postponement, however, altered the date of *Wilfred* to April 8 without the knowledge that a far larger German operation was in prospect despite earlier intelligence reports.

On April 3, the British War Cabinet received information from Stockholm that a German military buildup of assault troops was already on board ships in Stettin and Swinmunde harbors, and a large additional force at Rostock was preparing to sail for Scandinavia. Yet no action was taken. Moreover, Royal Air Force (RAF) bombers on leaflet raids over Germany had noticed unusual shipping activity near the German ports of Wilhemshaven and Kiel. Despite these indications, the warnings were not taken seriously. And on April 5, just four days before the invasion took place, Neville Chamberlain declared in a public speech that "Hitler had missed the bus," a reference to Hitler's failure to attack in the West when the British and French were unprepared—a phrase he was soon to regret. That same day, Oslo received confirmed intelligence that German warships were fast approaching the southern coast of Norway. But the government remained skeptical and still no preparations were taken. On April 6, the British Admiralty, provided with information from a neutral minister in Copenhagen that a German naval force of 10 ships containing a division of troops was scheduled to land at Narvik two days later, notified the Norwegian legation in London, but still, the government did nothing to prepare the country for the invasion which by now was imminent.[20]

As if these reports were not convincing enough, on April 7, British planes strafing a German battle fleet sighted several German war vessels heading up the Norwegian coast. The next day, the British Admiralty informed the Norwegian legation in London that a strong German naval force had been seen approaching Narvik. Not even then did the Norwegian government consider the matter seriously. On the afternoon of the 8th, evening newspapers in Oslo appeared on the streets reporting that a German troop transport, the *Rio de Janeiro*, was torpedoed that day off the Norwegian coast at Lillesand by the Polish submarine *Orzel*, on patrol in the Skagerrak, an arm of the North Sea between the southern coast of Norway and Denmark. German soldiers rescued by Norwegian fishing boats stated that they were bound for Bergen to "defend it" against the British.[21] So on the night of April 8, the Norwegian people retired to their homes with no idea that a massive German strike force was positioned off the Scandinavian coast preparing to occupy their country the next morning, an occupation that would last for five years.

Norway at War 3

Married men often wrote to their wives:
For the children's sake, you know, even
if I should fall—and I hope that will not
happen—then it is better than if I should live
and not be able to answer them
when they get older and ask: "What did you do,
Father, when the Germans invaded Norway?"
—Sigrid Undset (1882-1949), Norwegian author,
Return to the Future

Just before midnight on April 8, 1940, German warships were fast approaching all the main ports along the Norwegian coast. Assault troops and supplies were to be landed simultaneously at Kristiansand on the south coast; Stavanger, Bergen, and Trondheim, the principal west coast ports; Narvik in the north; and Oslo, the capital, where the major build-up would take place. The plan consisted of landing 15,000 troops commencing at 4:15 a.m. on August 9. The attack began at the entrance to the 50-mile-long Oslofiord where the German warships were challenged by the *Pol lll*, a Norwegian patrol boat that sent a communiqué to the Oscarsborg fortress commander, Colonel Birger Erikson, some 15 miles south of Oslo. The *Pol lll* rammed a German destroyer in the fog before being sunk by gunfire. After landing a small force to put the shore batteries out of action, the German vessels proceeded up the fiord in a single line led by the flagship heavy cruiser *Bluecher.*

Meanwhile, at the Foreign Ministry in Oslo, the German emissary, Kurt Brauer, arrived precisely at 4:20 a.m. to present his government's ultimatum to Foreign Minister Koht for total and unconditional capitulation. According to Brauer, "The sole aim of the German military operations is to protect the North against the intended occupation of bases in Norway by Anglo-French forces. The German government is convinced that in taking this action they are at the same time serving the interests of Norway."[1]

The memorandum expressed the expectation that the Norwegian government and people would show understanding for the German action and offer no resistance. But it added that all resistance would be mercilessly crushed by the German forces and result in nothing but useless bloodshed.[2] Koht's reply was unequivocal: "We will not submit. The fight is already in progress."[3]

Indeed it was. Shortly before dawn, as the flotilla was approaching the capital at the ancient Oscarsborg fortress, Erikson gave the order to fire the fort's 28-centimeter Krupp vintage cannons. A devastating salvo hit the *Bluecher's* anti-aircraft control center, followed by a second shell that struck a storeroom containing aviation fuel and setting off explosions throughout the ship. Torpedoes were also launched from the shore and the 10,000-ton cruiser exploded, heeled over, and sunk with the loss of 1,600 men. Some of the Gestapo and administrative officials, who were ordered to arrest King Haakon VII and his ministers and take control of the capital, were either killed or disabled. The Norwegian minelayer *Olav Trygverson* damaged the light cruiser *Emden* and the pocket battleship *Luetzow* was also damaged but not completely disabled.

The survivors of the *Bluecher*, including Rear Admiral Oskar Kummetz, the commander of the squadron, and General Erwin Engelbrecht, the divisional commander of the 163rd Infantry Division, were taken prisoner by the Norwegians, but were released several hours later with the arrival of the German occupation forces. The crippled German fleet turned back temporarily, but later that morning German ships were able to land two battalions of *Wermacht* assault troops some 20 miles from Oslo. They were dispatched to capture the forts and harbor fortifications supported by *Luftwaffe* bombers. At 8:00 a.m., a separate attack was launched against the Oslo civilian airfield at Fornebu, and by mid-afternoon after six companies of airborne troops were landed, Oslo was completely occupied.

The temporary German setback at Oscarsborg provided the necessary respite for King Haakon, the Royal Family, members of the cabinet, and the *Storting* (Parliament) to board a special train that left Oslo at 7:30 a.m. for the town of Hamar, some 70 miles inland. At the same hour, a column of 23 trucks carrying Norway's gold supply from the

Bank of Norway and confidential documents from the Foreign Office left Oslo. This decision to leave the capital was not simply a flight but a wise strategic decision. If the King and government had remained in Oslo, the Germans, with one stroke, would have captured them all and broken down all possible resistance. Nevertheless, their departure left Oslo in a vacuum and its 250,000 citizens bereft of effective leadership, direction, and any organized defense.

At Hamar, while the Parliament and the Nygaardsvold government were deliberating on the future course of the country, a commandeered motorcade of German troops was in pursuit of the recalcitrant King and government. However, they were stopped by an improvised roadblock in a skirmish with Norwegian troops under the command of Colonel Otto Ruge, and the Germans were forced to fall back to Oslo. The Royal Family and government then moved northeast to Elverum, where the Parliament was to hold its last meeting. Here the *Storting* took the most far-reaching decisions that saved the Kingdom of Norway, because it provided for all eventualities, which might arise during the course of the war. Here, the Labor Party was transformed into a national government.

The president of the *Storting*, Carl Hambro, declared that the government had the necessary international authority to make any decisions, even if it had to move to a foreign country. The *Storting* thus laid the constitutional foundation for the government's fight for the liberation of Norway from London.[4] The Germans, having failed to capture the King and his government, next attempted to pacify them by negotiation. German Minister Kurt Brauer, at the insistence of Foreign Minister Joachim Ribbentrop, sent a message to Elverum requesting a meeting with King Haakon.

Meanwhile, the situation in Oslo had changed dramatically. To the consternation of the Norwegian people, on the evening of April 9, at 7:30 p.m., once the capital was in firm control by the invading force, Vidkum Quisling stormed into the main Oslo radio station, and without previous consultation with the Germans, broadcast a pronouncement naming himself as the new prime minister of Norway. At the same time, he granted the powers of government to his *Nasjonal Samling* Party. He proclaimed that all resistance to the occupying power would be not only useless, but a punishable offense and that all official and municipal employees as well as all officers of the armed forces were to take their orders from the new government. Ironically, this treasonable action in the face of widespread opposition by the Norwegian people rallied stunned citizens of all classes to what was soon to become a resolute and protracted resistance that was to continue for the duration of the war.

The following day, Dr. Brauer left Oslo to meet with the King in Elverum. The German envoy, both by flattery and intimidation, sought the King's approval of the Quisling government. He said that resistance would be futile and would result in the useless slaughter of Norwegians. The King explained to Brauer that he could not make a political decision; that was the responsibility of the government. He could, however, influence a decision and when the government assembled, it immediately rallied around the King in refusing to consent to a Quisling cabinet. At 8:00 p.m., the German diplomat telephoned Minister Koht, who, when asked if the refusal meant that the Norwegian resistance to the German invasion would continue, answered: "Yes, as long as possible."[5]

The decision was now final. A country whose government would soon be in exile and which had been less prepared to defend itself in a major conflict than most other European nations, was now mustering the faith and determination to resist a superior aggressor which much larger countries faced with irresolution. On April 10, all the members of the *Storting* returned to their constituencies. All contact between the government and the people was disrupted. The first response to the King's refusal was a German aerial attack on the peaceful village of Nybergsund, not far from the Swedish border, where there were no military objectives other than the King, Crown Prince, and members of the government and their staff who had taken refuge in the woods nearby. While shielding themselves as best they could from continuous bombing attacks—a step ahead of the advancing Germans—and moving farther north into the Gudbrandsdal Valley and then on to Molde on the Romsdalsfiord, the enemy strengthened its grip on the main population centers on the western coast as well as in the south and east.

Kristiansand, the southern port which dominates the north side of the entrance to the Skagerrak, put up considerable resistance to the approaching German fleet on the day of invasion. It was just to the east of this fortified port that the steamer *Rio de Janeiro* was sunk less than 24 hours earlier, giving the defenders the first clear indication of the Germans' intentions. The ships, led by the German light cruiser

Karlsruhe, encountered heavy fog as they approached the harbor at the appointed time, and by the time the fog cleared two hours later, a Norwegian seaplane sighted the group and gave the alarm. The ships were twice driven back by shore batteries and in a third attempt, the *Karlsruhe* nearly ran on the rocks.

Since this port lay well within bomber range of the airfields in northwestern Germany, by mid-morning, *Luftwaffe* bombers were over the forts and the ships gained easy access to the harbor. Shock troops were put ashore. By mid-afternoon all harbor installations were captured, and three other ships arrived safely with reinforcements and supplies. The *Karlsruhe,* in company with a smaller force, then proceeded farther east to the undefended towns of Arendal and Egersund, favorable harbors and railway line heads, which were occupied without resistance. After leaving port that evening, *Karlsruhe* was torpedoed by the British submarine *Truant* and was so badly damaged that it had to be sunk. The remainder of the group steamed safely back to Kiel.

Stavanger, at the southern end of the west coast of Norway, was unfortified and easily taken. Eight miles to the south, at 8:00 a.m., six German Messerschmitt 110s appeared over Sola airfield and bombed the two machine-gun emplacements that were its only protection. That was followed by 10 Junker 52 transport aircraft, which dropped some 120 parachute troops, who easily captured the field. This was Norway's largest airfield and tactically of the greatest importance to the *Luftwaffe* since it could be a springboard for German bombers to attack not only the British fleet along the Norwegian coast but the principal British naval bases in northern Britain. Later that day, a total of 180 Junker 52s landed with two infantry battalions and a regimental staff. Within a few hours the airfield, town, and harbor were secured. The seizure of Sola was not only a principal factor in providing German air supremacy in Norway, but also the decisive factor in halting any attempt by the British to land sizable ground forces.

At Bergen, the second-largest city in Norway, lying about 100 miles north of Stavanger, the German flotilla passed the outlying fortification without opposition. Upon entering the harbor, the cruiser *Koenigsberg* and an auxiliary ship were badly damaged by a battery of guns, but troops from other ships, with the support of the *Luftwaffe,* landed safely without opposition. The occupation of the city and the harbor was completed by mid-morning.

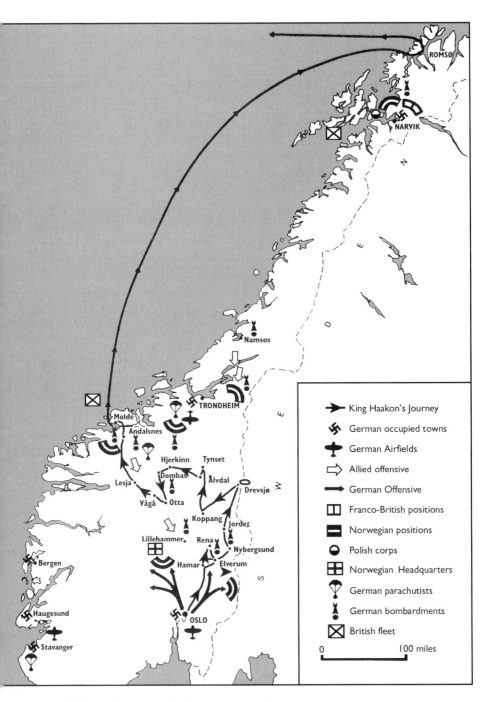

The Day of the Invasion
April 9th 1940

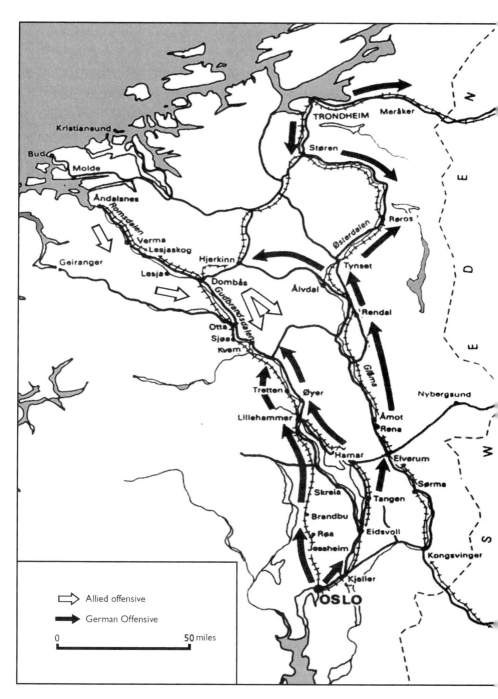

Operations in Southern Norway
April 1940

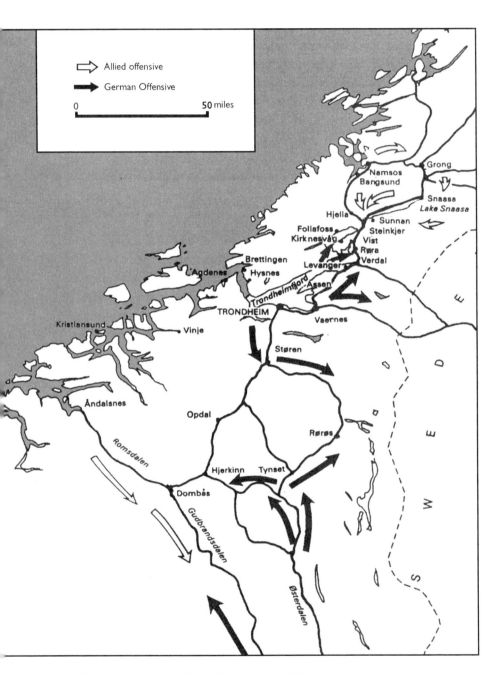

Operations in Central Norway
April 1940

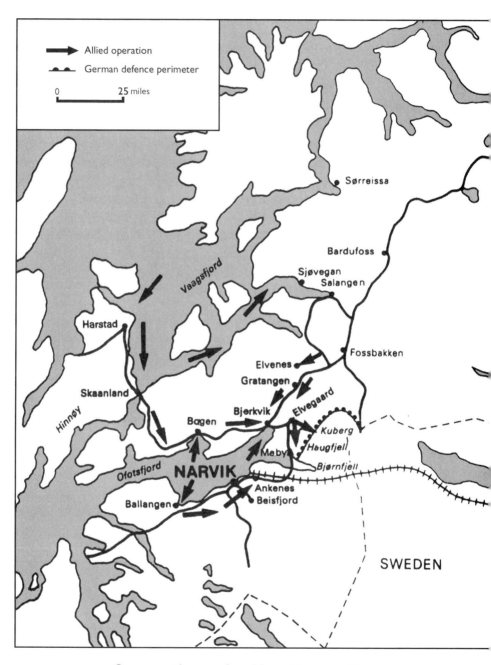

Operations in Northern Norway
until May, 27th. 1940

Later in the afternoon, 12 British bombers attacked the harbor, but the German ships escaped damage. Early the next morning, 15 Skuas of the British Fleet Air Arm returned to Bergen with a dive-bombing attack that scored three direct hits on the *Koenigsberg*, sending the first major warship ever destroyed by enemy air attack to the bottom of the harbor. It was at Bergen that the Norwegians first received direct British aid.

Trondheim, located halfway down the 1,100-mile Norwegian coast and some 300 miles north of Bergen, offered little resistance to the German fleet. Forts on both sides of the inlet defended access to the Trondheimfiord. When the German squadron, consisting of the heavy cruiser *Hipper* and four destroyers approached, batteries from the fort on the one side instantly opened fire. In response, the first German salvo struck an electric cable on which both forts depended for their searchlights, thereby enabling the fleet to put 1,700 crack Austrian regulars of the Third Mountain Division ashore. The city surrendered without resistance, although the Vaernes airfield, 16 miles inland, resisted and was not captured until April.[10]

This superb port that commands Norway's land and coastal sea routes, was strategically important both as an air and submarine base, but hazardous due to its great distance from Germany. Consequently, it was dangerously exposed to British counterattacks and entirely dependent upon the *Luftwaffe* for reinforcements and supplies.

The one remaining port to be occupied was Narvik—the most distant and exposed, and the one that was the most difficult to take. The main coastal defenses of the harbor consisted of two obsolete Norwegian ironclads, the *Eidsvold* and the *Norge*, both dating back to 1900. At 3:12 a.m., the two vessels received the alarm from watch boats stationed at the mouth of the Ofotfiord and prepared for action; but because of foul weather and the possibility that the ships were British, *Eidsvold* sought to identify them first.

When the first of the 10 German destroyers was within sight of the harbor, the ironclad fired a warning shot and signaled for identification. Commodore Friedrich Bonte aboard the lead destroyer, *Wilhelm Heidkamp*, sent an officer in a launch flying a flag of truce to demand surrender. When the Norwegian commander refused, the German emissary left the *Eidsvold* and signaled Bonte, who immediately fired torpedoes that split the ironclad in two, killing the captain and all members of the crew. The *Norge* then opened fire, but was immediately torpedoed and sunk.[6]

By 8:00 a.m., Narvik was completely occupied by two battalions of Nazi troops under the command of Bavarian Generalmajor Eduard Dietl, one of Hitler's most favored officers dating back to the early Nazi street-fighting days in Munich and the Beer Hall Putsch of 1923. The Norwegian local garrison of about 450 men, which was rapidly being reinforced, could still have put up some resistance with the help of its newly constructed pillboxes. Its commander, Colonel Konrad Sundlo, a staunch supporter of Quisling, surrendered to the Germans without a fight, however. Meanwhile, three other German destroyers captured important stores of military equipment at Elvegaard, the regimental depot for the area, about eight miles northeast of Narvik.

So it was that the entire western coast of Norway, from Kristiansand in the south to Narvik in the north, was seized and occupied by the onslaught of the invader. Operation *Weseruebung* had proved a complete success. It was obvious, as Churchill admitted, "that Britain had been surprised and outwitted" by the seizure of Norway.[7]

Now in the far north where German land-based bombers were, for the time being, out of reach, the British Navy reacted quickly to the sudden German occupation and went on the offensive. The stage was now set for a naval battle, the thunder of which had never before startled the echoes in those secluded fiords. On April 10, the day after Dietl's troops disembarked and occupied Narvik, a force of five British destroyers under the command of Captain Warburton-Lee entered the Ofotfiord shortly after midnight. Bad weather that slowed their approach also prevented their early detection. Their appearance in Narvik harbor at 4:30 a.m. was a complete surprise to the Germans. Five of the German destroyers were lying in harbor as the British entered. Two of the five German destroyers, including the *Wilhelm Heidkamp*, were refueling, two were lying at anchor, and a fifth was entering the harbor when the British attacked with a salvo of 15 torpedoes, totally destroying the *Wilhelm Heidkamp* and killing Commodore Bonte. One of the anchored destroyers was hit twice and sank immediately; the remaining three were all damaged. In a second attack, all but one German freighter was destroyed.

Upon leaving the harbor, however, the British ships encountered the five remaining German destroyers approaching from nearby fiords. The German ships were larger and heavier-gunned, and sank one British destroyer and forced the beaching of another on which the British commander, Captain Warburton-Lee, was mortally wounded. Three of the five British destroyers managed to break out into the open sea where, in retiring, they sank a large German freighter loaded with ammunition which was entering the fiord. The remaining German ships were all short of fuel and soon had to return to Narvik.

On April 13, the British, this time with the battleship *Warspite*, a 33,000-ton vessel carrying 15-inch guns and a flotilla of nine destroyers under the command of Vice-Admiral W. J. Whitworth, returned to Narvik, outnumbering the Germans three to two. Once in range, the British sunk one German destroyer, another foundered on the rocks, and a third sank at the quay in Narvik. Four other ships fled eastward up the narrow Rombaksfiord, where all were nearly out of ammunition. By late afternoon, all the German destroyers had been sunk. Admiral Whitworth considered sending a landing party ashore to occupy the town, but anticipating a counterattack by a superior number of German troops, he decided against it.[8]

In fact, General Dietl and his forces had retreated to the hills after it became clear that the German naval strength had been crushed. But when the British warships withdrew without mounting a land assault, Dietl, utterly amazed at the British failure to put ground troops ashore, returned to refortify the town. The following day, Whitworth informed the admiralty that the Germans were disorganized and stunned by the German losses at sea and that a main British landing force assigned to Narvik should occupy the town without delay. Overly cautious, the British Army commander, Major-General P. J. Mackesy, refused to attack, believing that the harbor was strongly held by the enemy with machine-gun posts. He also pointed out that his transports had not been loaded for an assault, but only for an unopposed landing.[9] Instead, he disembarked his contingent of three infantry battalions at Harstad, 35 miles to the north, which was occupied by Norwegian ski troops under the command of General Carl Fleischer.

Despite the arrival of the British troops and the damage inflicted by the formidable power of the Royal Navy, General Dietl's situation was eased somewhat by the weapons and equipment seized from the Norwegian camp at Elvegaard. Furthermore, the cargo and ship's stores from the one remaining tanker that was not destroyed was a welcome relief to Dietl and his seasoned Austrian regulars, who now faced a long and hazardous period of isolation, except by air, from their source of supplies and reinforcements. After the *Warspite* launched an unsuccessful naval bombardment on April 24 to dislodge the German garrison, the idea of an immediate assault against Dietl's forces was delayed. This marked the end of the first phase of the Norwegian campaign. Fighting continued in the Narvik region, but for the next two weeks, the principal theater of operations shifted southward.

Although the fate of Norway was essentially decided on the first day of the invasion, the country's dauntless struggle lasted two months. Before it was over, it would involve not only German and Norwegian troops, but British, French, and Polish ground forces; and it would range throughout the entire country, with two major theaters developing almost simultaneously—one in the south-central part of the country and the other in the far north, where Narvik, although occupied by the Germans, remained a coveted prize of war.

After the German landings had been achieved, the Wehrmacht, under the leadership of Lieutenant General Nikolaus von Falkenhorst, the commander of all German military forces in Norway, faced three principal military tasks.

- Consolidating their position in southern Norway and joining their forces in Oslo, Kristiansand, Stavanger, and Bergen.[10] This was accomplished without much difficulty. In less than a week, the Luftwaffe was established at the Oslo, Stavanger, and Kristiansand airfields, and seaplanes were operating from Trondheim harbor. It was this control of the air that discouraged the British fleet from venturing far south of Trondheim. Thus deprived of landings by British ground forces, and invaded before full mobilization had been ordered, the Norwegians could do little to stem the consolidation of German forces in southern Norway.[11]

- Usher in a rapid build-up of air and ground strength in Oslo, organize a striking force north through Lillehammer and the twin Osterdal and Gudbrandsdal valleys, and link up with units in Trondheim.

- Arrange the means to reinforce Dietl in Narvik, over 400 miles north of Trondheim.[12]

Norwegian troops, under the capable command of Colonel Otto Ruge, put up stiff resistance between Bergen and Oslo, but were beaten back repeatedly by superior German units. Ruge, a peerless organizer who had arranged the defense of Elverum while the King was fleeing from the pursuing Germans, was promoted to general's rank and commander-in-chief of the Norwegian forces on April 10. His task, to contain the advancing Germans until Britain and France sent reinforcements to aid in stemming the anticipated German offensive, was not an enviable one. Air attacks seriously hindered Norwegian communication and supply lines. Telegraph cables had been cut, telephone lines were being monitored by the Germans, and there were no field radios. Liaison officers had to be dispatched by car, on skis, or on foot. Contact with whole regions of the country—the southwest, the center, and the whole of northern Norway—was lost. Moreover, mobilization centers were under constant bombardment and most weapons depots were already in German hands.

Nonetheless, amidst much confusion, men by the hundreds flocked out of occupied towns and villages to join General Ruge's fighting forces. The roughly 40,000 men—made up chiefly of reservists, retired officers, and raw recruit volunteers, young and old—were poorly equipped and completely lacking any combat experience. These men joined an army consisting mostly of makeshift companies and battalions. Many arrived on trains, in cars and trucks, on bicycles, skis, and even on foot.[13] Nevertheless, Ruge, who had a unique ability to inspire confidence in his men, stressed that Norway was at war and, despite the odds against them, they must be "willing to fight to the last breath."[14]

On April 14, less than a week after the initial invasion, Falkenhorst deployed his troops north of Oslo for the northward push toward Trondheim. Within eight days, the Germans advanced 130 miles from Oslo to Rena in the Osterdal Valley where General Ruge's headquarters were located, and in the Gudbrandsdal Valley. With no field artillery or air support, Ruge, with only 12,000 troops at his immediate disposal, could not restrain the German panzer battalions for long without Allied assistance. But with the assurance from Britain that help would come, Norwegian Resistance stiffened. It was here that Ruge and his force could use the mountainous terrain to their advantage. The narrow valley floors with steep, heavily forested sides provided defensive cover, and the sparse roads and deep April snowdrifts made it difficult for German tanks to maneuver. Troops were deployed at the base of both valleys with orders to slow the German advance by ambushing German patrols, blowing up bridges and tunnels, and blocking the narrow roads with rockslides and trees. But Ruge knew that these were only delaying tactics to slow the German advance toward Trondheim until British reinforcements arrived.

Meanwhile in London, the War Office was moving at a snail's pace, marked by disorganization and a complete lack of coordination among the various military branches. As early as the afternoon on April 9, the first day of the invasion, a telegram from the British government to its minister in Oslo, Sir Cecil Dormer, assured Norway that Britain would "extend their full aid to Norway, and fight the war in full association with them."[15] Yet several days later, Churchill complained in a memo to Prime Minister Chamberlain that "there are six Chiefs of Staff . . . [and] three Ministers . . . who have a voice in Norwegian operations. But no one is responsible for the creation and direction of military policy except yourself."[16] Final decisions came from the War Cabinet on the advice of the separate branches, which operated independently of one another owing to bitter and long-standing rivalries.

Although Narvik was treated as the primary objective for possible counterattack because of its iron ore traffic, Trondheim offered the best approach into the heart of Norway. After urgent, repeated appeals from General Ruge to make that port city the focus of their relief effort, London authorities reassembled their expeditionary force for a ground invasion. Fearing that a direct attack on Trondheim from the sea would be too dangerous because of German air attacks, the British sent two brigades to less-conspicuous ports that were still held by Norwegian forces. On April 14, advance parties made a northern landing at Namsos, some 80 miles northeast of Trondheim. The other was put ashore on April 17 at Andalsnes, 100 miles to the southwest. The main landing forces followed these in during the next few days.[17] The two forces were to launch an assault on Trondheim by a combined pincer attack.

On April 19, the British brigade code-named *Mauriceforce*, under the command of Major General Sir Adrian Carton de Wiart, was ashore at Namsos. Reinforced by three crack battalions of mountain ski troops of the French Chasseurs Alpins, the Allied troops joined forces with Norwegian forces, but lacking field artillery, antiaircraft guns, and air support, their base of operations was attacked night and day by German bombers. The following day, Namsos was heavily bombed by German aircraft, setting the town ablaze and severely damaging the port facilities, which blocked the further landing of supplies or reinforcements. That night, Carton de Wiart reported to the War Office that unless enemy air activity was severely restricted, he had little chance of carrying out any further operations. Four feet of snow offered no concealment from the air, and his troops, lacking antiaircraft guns, were under constant air bombardment. Bombing continued on the April 21, and the following day, to make matters worse, the Germans were able to increase their bombing offensive by operating out of the Vaernes airfield just east of Trondheim.

On April 20, another brigade, commanded by Brigadier General Harold de Riemer Morgan and code-named *Sickleforce*, landed at Aandalsnes, the southern arm of the pincer movement, with instructions to push northward toward Trondheim. But after meeting a Norwegian unit at Dombas, a rail junction 60 miles to the east, Morgan was contacted by General Ruge and advised that a heavy concentration of German infantry supported by artillery and tanks was massing for a new assault below Lillehammer. Morgan realized that a Norwegian collapse and German breakthrough would leave the British stranded in unfamiliar terrain, wedged between the German garrison at Trondheim and the advancing German troops from Oslo. So without waiting for confirmation from London, Morgan reluctantly abandoned his original mission and ordered his force to move 80 miles south to Lillehammer, where the first engagement of the war between British and German ground troops took place.

When the British forces arrived on April 21, the Norwegians were shocked at the unmilitary bearing of their British Allies. Instead of fully equipped professional fighting men capable of matching the oncoming Germans, most of the new arrivals were half-trained, half-armed, territorial battalions comprised of recently mobilized reservists. Still worse, they were not prepared for winter warfare. Ill equipped and unskilled in the use of skis or snowshoes, they were incapable of operating tactically at all. Even the Regulars, who gave a good accounting of themselves, lacked the tanks and artillery for stemming an advance for which the Germans were now bringing in reinforcements.

Shortly after the British troops arrived, the Germans attacked. The crescendo of battle increased all around. Without critically needed air support, and under constant pounding by *Luftwaffe* planes, the British infantry were quickly outflanked, forcing Morgan's entire line to fall back. After a 24-hour battle, Lillehammer fell, and the British and Norwegian troops were forced to retreat 140 miles up the Gudbrandsdal Valley. For two days, a rear-guard action was fought, but the pincer strategy against Trondheim was an abysmal failure. For days, in hills along the Gubrandsdal, British detachments were scattered, and many of the separated British soldiers—hungry, exhausted, and confused—wandered aimlessly, hoping to escape capture by the Germans. A few reached Sweden; some reached the coast and escaped to Scotland in Norwegian fishing boats; but most of the battle-weary men were rounded up by the Germans.

On April 24, the French Fifteenth Brigade, commanded by Major General Bernard Paget, landed at Aandalsnes, hoping to stem the German advance in the Gudbrandsdal. Together with the remaining soldiers of Morgan's brigade, Paget had fewer than 3,000 men to hold a defensive line unless reinforcements arrived, but he had no illusions about the precariousness of his position. Ruge had assigned a few Norwegian ski detachments to Paget's force, but without artillery and no air support, he could not hold out for more than two days. German air attacks on road and rail lines continued throughout the increasingly long hours of daylight and in the deep snow of Norway's seemingly endless winter. Against a German spearhead of 8,500 motorized troops, supported by tanks, artillery, and dive bombers, *Sickleforce* could do no more than fight a series of delaying actions. By April 28, the British High Command was resigned to the failure of the Trondheim campaign, and the decision was made to evacuate both Namsos and Aandalsnes.

The *Sickelforce* evacuation took place on the nights of April 30 and May 1 when French troops and what remained of General Morgan's brigade embarked on British cruisers and destroyers from the devastated still-burning port of Aandalsnes. At sea, no further losses were suffered. The previous night, King Haakon, the Royal Family, members of the government, and General Ruge embarked at Molde, 25 miles northeast of Aandalsnes, aboard the British cruiser *Glasgow* and were taken to Tromso, about 100 miles north of Narvik, where the war was still raging.

Mauriceforce was not so fortunate. At Namsos there had been no fighting on land since April 23, and British ships successfully removed the entire force on the night of May 2-3. But the ships were pursued by German bombers throughout the day, sinking two destroyers. Thus, a superbly equipped *Luftwaffe* had virtually defeated a numerically superior yet impotent British navy in supporting an overseas invasion of ground forces far removed from Germany.

Nevertheless, the Norwegians were still determined to show their resilience against overwhelming odds. On April 16, at Hegra, 28 miles east of Trondheim, the Norwegian Third Artillery Regiment, under the leadership of Major Holtermann, improvised a local defense on its own at an obsolete fort cut out of the rock of a hill, and equipped with four outdated field guns. His troops consisted of volunteers who had just joined up, some of whom had to be turned away for lack of weapons.

Holding out against repeated attacks, the garrison became a symbol of successful Norwegian defiance, attracting to itself German forces, which might have been used elsewhere.[18] The stouthearted troops, bombed and bombarded, had beaten off all attacks. Food was running out, and water was being collected from the dripping rock ceiling. In the end, many of the 190 men who were still holding out were down with pneumonia with one nursing sister from Trondheim to attend to them when the Allied evacuation of central Norway forced the Norwegians to surrender on May 5. The garrison closed ranks, sang the national anthem, proclaimed, "God save the King and Fatherland," and then dispersed.[19]

With the departure of Allied troops from Aandalsnes and Namsos, all of the cities and main towns of central and southern Norway had been irretrievably lost. The Germans had cleared the whole route from Oslo to Trondheim, so that further resistance served no strategic purpose. Yet Narvik still remained the coveted prize for both the British and the Germans, and for one critically important reason: to gain control of the railway route that ran from Narvik into the Gullivare iron ore fields in northern Sweden. To cut this route had been, from the start, a principal aim in British strategy. Yet, after two weeks of fighting to the north of Narvik, the British and the Germans were both at an impasse. General Mackesy's troops, slowed by the terrain and weather, made very little progress.

But General Dietl's forces were no better off. His troops were near exhaustion and he realized that unless reinforcements arrived immediately, he would be unable to hold his position. The ever-imperative Churchill, pressing for action, sent the following message to Lord Cork, the Admiral of the Fleet: "Every day that Narvik remains untaken, even at severe cost, imperils the whole enterprise."[20] Accordingly, on May 3, after a further reconnaissance of Narvik, Lord Cork requested a build-up of Allied forces.

For the first time in the campaign, the Allies had reason to be guardedly optimistic. In late April, the Allied troops in Narvik totaled some 25,000 men by the arrival of three battalions of French Alpins, commanded by General Antoine Bethouart, followed by two battalions of the Foreign Legion on May 6. Three days later, a Polish brigade of four battalions arrived, whose fighting abilities had yet to be tested, since they had no experience in mountain warfare. In defense of the ground forces against German air attacks, 48 heavy and 60 light anti-aircraft guns were allocated.[21] Lord Cork's naval force had also been increased after his arrival in Norwegian waters by the battleship *Resolution*, and on May 6, by the aircraft carrier *Ark Royal*, whose Skua fighters were desperately needed for air support.[22]

Although the size and condition of the German forces defending Narvik was uncertain, it is estimated that General Deitl's Mountain Division had 2,000 men, which had presumably doubled to 4,000 after absorbing the destroyer crews that survived the naval engagement on April 13. It is also unknown how many losses were sustained by the earlier naval bombardment and the other fighting on the extended front.[23] The cession of hostilities in central Norway facilitated an increase in German bomber attacks from aircraft now based in Trondheim and a build-up infantry strength by paratroopers. But the Germans experienced many difficulties. Although the number of German aircraft far exceeded those of the British, they lacked the number of long-range

Junker 52s needed to supply the overland advance from the Trondheim area. Troop positions were widely scattered to minimize transporting them through melting mountain snow, and supplies had to be dropped close to them. The aircraft they did use were hampered by the weather because poor visibility often restricted air operations.[24]

On May 11, General Claude Auchinleck arrived in Narvik to replace the overly cautious General Mackesy as commander of the air and ground forces, now called the North-Western Expeditionary Force. Its mission was to capture Narvik, destroy Dietl's force, and establish military control of northern Norway. But by the time the Allied build-up had reached its peak, its strategic value had been radically changed by the German offensive in France and the invasion of the Low Countries on May 10. At this juncture, a new British government was formed, and Churchill was appointed the new prime minister. Narvik was reduced to a minor theater of war, and as the Allied situation in France worsened, authorities in London began to see the futility of maintaining such a large force in so remote an area, the outcome of which was uncertain at best. To make matters worse, General Auchinleck was now faced with a new threat. General Valentin Feurstein, in command of the Second German Mountain Division at Trondheim with supporting troops from a regiment of the Third Mountain Division, was mobilizing his troops to move northward to reinforce Dietl's force in Narvik.

On May 10, Feurstein's forces proceeded on the long and arduous route to Narvik, through the coastal towns of Mosjoen, Mo, and Bodo. Despite delays caused by road obstacles placed by the Norwegians, and poor roads separated by fiords requiring transport by ferry, the Germans covered 90 miles in four days across country that the Allies believed impassable. As they approached Mosjoen, some 90 miles north of Namsos, two British Independent Companies, commanded by Colonel Colin Gubbins, joined by two Norwegian companies, ambushed 60 German cyclists leading the German advance, killing most of them.[25]

But the action was simply a delaying tactic; by midday the German pressure drove the Allied force back.[26] By a daring amphibious operation, Feurstein, who was less than 200 miles south of Narvik, sent a company of mountain infantry to the ferry at Hemnesberget, 15 miles west of Mo, cutting off the retreat of British forces at Mosjoen, and forcing their evacuation by ship north to Bodo. The geographical conditions of the area between Mo and Bodo made serious delaying actions—to say nothing of a counteroffensive—very difficult in the face of German air power.

On May 13, General Auchinleck assumed command. He decided to divide his forces by diverting three British battalions in the Narvik area to stem the enemy advance from the south, which was making disturbingly rapid progress. General Bethouart was left with the responsibility of leading the main assault on Narvik. The attackers consisted exclusively of French and Polish troops in conjunction with the Norwegians. The Norwegian Sixth Brigade had been fighting Dietl's forces since May 6 in the mountains where conditions were harsh, and both sides suffered from severe exposure to the elements.

By May 21, Dietl's men were approaching complete exhaustion. Despite the arrival of two paratroop companies on May 23 and 25, he was still short 1,500 to 2,000 men for the strength needed to hold out. His men could hardly be persuaded to move from one position to another, and were falling asleep even under machine-gun fire.

Nor were the Norwegians any better off. They were without warm food and their only shelters were holes dug out of the snow. Ammunition and rations carried by packhorses had to be carried by the men for four or five miles up slopes that were too steep for the horses. Signal cable sank during the day into the snow, then froze and could not be moved.[27] Delaying operations and skirmishes involving units of the First Irish Guards, Second South Wales Borderers, and four of (now promoted) Brigadier Gubbins' Independent Companies slowed Feuerstein's vanguard as it continued north.

Furthermore, Dietl's force had been pushed back from Narvik east along the ore railway to the Swedish frontier. The establishment of the military airfield at Bardufoss, 50 miles north of Narvik, further strengthened the Allied position. The airfield was put to operational use for a squadron of Hurricane and Gladiator fighters. Under cover of naval bombardment, one battalion of Norwegian troops and two of the Foreign Legion crossed the Rombaksfiord, and by noon on May 28, the German garrison was driven out of Narvik. The harbor was extensively damaged, as were the railway and the ore-handling plant, the result of seven weeks of naval bombardment and attacks by ground forces.

Conditions had improved dramatically for the Allies in the north, but was deteriorating even more rapidly in the west. The *Wehrmacht* had advanced to the Channel Coast at Dunkirk and the Blitzkrieg against Belgium now prompted Churchill and the War Cabinet to call for the evacuation of all British troops from Norway. Narvik was not essential as a naval base, and to hold it much longer would be an unaffordable drain on Allied resources. Accordingly, on May 24, nearly four days before the attack on Narvik, the Prime Minister called for the withdrawal of all Allied forces from Narvik after its capture to meet the supreme test if and when an invasion should be attempted against England. But timing was a crucial factor. According to Churchill, the capture of Narvik had to be achieved "to ensure the destruction of the port . . . [*and railway to Sweden's ore fields*] and to cover our withdrawal."[28] The decision to evacuate was concealed from General Ruge and the Norwegian forces until June 1 for security reasons lest it should somehow be leaked to the enemy before the convoy of ships was en route to Britain. The secret was well kept; it was not until June 8 that Dietl became aware of the Allied departure and re-entered Narvik.

The evacuation of 25,000 troops took place between June 3 through June 7. It was a rigorous and time-consuming operation since many of the men were located at smaller embarkation points among the fiords, imposing a heavy burden on the already extended fleet in Norway. On June 8, 1940, King Haakon and his government boarded the cruiser *Devonshire* at Tromso, where it sailed to England. Throughout this period, British countermeasures were taken to ensure a safe evacuation. Aircraft from the carriers *Arc Royal* and *Glorious*, which arrived on June 2 to cover the embarkation, bombed German troops and communications, including the German airfield at Bodo in the south. Gladiators and Hurricanes at the Bardufoss airfield were in action until June 7, when they were flown to the carrier *Glorious*, a feat the more remarkable in that Hurricanes had never landed on a carrier deck.[29]

On June 9, General Ruge, disappointed that he was unable to make a final assault to drive Dietl's forces into Sweden, remained to demobilize his Norwegian troops. The following day, an armistice with Dietl was negotiated, thereby ending all ground hostilities in Norway. Later, Ruge gave what reassurance he could to his listeners from the town of Tromso at the only free broadcasting station left in Norway: "The first chapter in our struggle for freedom is over, and we have a dark time to face now in a conquered land. But the war continues on other fronts—Norwegians are joining in the struggle there. The day will come when you can raise your head again."[30]

Afterthoughts on the Campaign

The conquest of Norway was an important victory for Hitler and a humiliating defeat for the Allies. Yet in comparison with later campaigns in Europe, Norway was to have no direct influence on the future course or outcome of the war. But there were lessons to be learned from the two-month campaign in Norway, perhaps the most fundamental being that no outside nation should become embroiled in areas of conflict where it is highly unlikely to succeed.

Throughout the seven months of the invasion, British policy toward Norway was marked by vacillation over what to do in all of Scandinavia, from mining the territorial waters to more direct action in support of Finland. This indecision stemmed from a national complacency rooted in the erroneous notion that a numerically superior British fleet at Scapa Flow was enough to keep Germany from landing ground forces on the west coast of Norway. This belief was underscored by the failure of the British to take seriously the numerous reports of German naval activity throughout the winter months, many of which reported an imminent invasion of Norway.

This false confidence and irresolution has been explained by a "war of nerves" within the Admiralty. In fact, two days before the invasion, the commander-in-chief of the Home Fleet remarked that "all these reports are of doubtful value and may well be only a further move in the 'war of nerves.'"[1] It was believed that the German fleet was heading for the open sea rather than actually transporting an expeditionary force. Yet had the intelligence in possession of the British been correctly interpreted and evaluated, and the fleet taken to sea at once, the German expedition might at least have been brought into action before reaching its objective.

Unlike the German strategists who realized that success depended upon the close co-ordination of the three separate services, the British Navy, while proposing action that must inevitably involve the other services in Scandinavia, played down the effort to send them there in force. Since the campaign in Norway was the first occasion in which land, sea, and air forces fought a combined action, the inevitable difficulties of command should have been worked out in advance by the implementation of a joint command structure. But as Major-General J. L. Moulton, one of the foremost English military experts on the Norwegian campaign, has stated, "Like Chamberlain deluding himself that pomp and ceremony would impress the power-hungry dictators, Britain believed that at sea, if nowhere else, she could teach 'em.'"[2]

Ironically, the British based all their planning before the invasion upon the supposition that it would take the initiative by a sea strategy. This turned out to be a defensive action—a serious oversight that would have easily been corrected by a more thorough examination of enemy intentions. Before the invasion, little thought seems to have been given to how Britain would react if Germany seized the initiative.

Nevertheless—despite the failure to train and prepare an adequate number of land and air forces for deployment in Norway; despite an ignorance of climatic conditions and a lack of detailed knowledge of harbors, landing space, and storage facilities, particularly in the central and northern reaches of the country; despite the mistake of sending inexperienced territorial troops to accomplish impossible objectives; and despite the failure to provide the artillery, tanks, and weaponry needed to face a fully equipped and highly trained *Wehrmacht*—the Allies decided to commit themselves to a campaign that was a prescription for defeat.

Unquestionably, the decisive factor was the superiority of air power. The *Luftwaffe* was able to hold the Allies at bay in southern Norway so that reinforcements could be landed in Oslo and Stavanger. Control of the air also increased the effective striking power of the ground forces by the continuous bombardment of Allied troops and positions. The predominance of German air power was demonstrated in practically every aspect of the campaign, including these:

- conducting reconnaissance activity

- landing reinforcements

- providing food and munitions to troops in forward areas, particularly for the garrison at Narvik

- rendering the Allied bases at Namsos and Aandalsnes unusable

- using paratroopers, albeit in few places

Even the mere presence of the *Luftwaffe* in Norwegian skies was enough to produce a chilling effect on the Allied ground forces as well as the civilian population. The Allied response to all this was mainly ineffective. Distance was a severe handicap, and the shortage of British home-based bombers precluded all but a few scattered attacks on German-occupied airfields in Norway since the already modest but growing RAF was unable to spare enough fighters to provide adequate "cover." Almost all of the air force was assigned to support the British Expeditionary Force in France; in addition, the Air Ministry's main concern was the air defense of Great Britain itself.

From a tactical standpoint, *Weseruebung* was a remarkable success. The German acquisition of naval and air bases along the 1,100-mile west coast perimeter of Norway facilitated the German launching of air and submarine operations against Allied shipping. Especially deadly were the U-boat attacks, which seriously weakened the Allied position in the North Atlantic, particularly the convoy approaches to Murmansk, the one vital link to Russia. Moreover, Germany gained control of the bitterly contested iron ore route after the reoccupation of Narvik, even though Germany's conquest of France was soon to provide an alternate source in the Lorraine ore fields. Finally, German national pride and prestige were greatly enhanced both within the armed forces and among the civilian population by the defeat of a superior naval power. That power had been neutralized by a well-coordinated strategy on land and in the air, tested and proved successful at the operational level.

The casualties sustained in the campaign on both sides in men and weapons were roughly comparable. The British lost 1,869 men on land and approximately 250 men died or were lost at sea. About 530 French and Polish officers and men were lost in the Central and North Norway theaters; and 1,335 Norwegians were killed and wounded, not counting prisoners.[3] About 400 Norwegian civilians were killed, 4,000 buildings destroyed, and 300 bridges blown.[4] The Germans lost a total of 5,296 people, either dead or missing. As for aircraft, 242 planes of the *Luftwaffe* were destroyed, of which one-third were transport aircraft, and 112 RAF planes.[5]

At sea, the Germans suffered much more severely than the Allies. In addition to the heavy cruiser *Bluecher* and two light cruisers, *Koenigsberg* and *Karlsruhe*, 10 destroyers were sacrificed—half of their entire strength. Six submarines and one torpedo boat were sunk; the pocket battleships *Scharnhorst* and *Gneisenau* were torpedoed on return to Germany, and the warships *Luetzow, Hipper*, and *Emden* were also damaged in sea engagements. At the end of June, German naval forces were reduced to one heavy and two light cruisers and four destroyers. The British Navy's major casualty was the sinking of the aircraft carrier *Glorious*, the day after the evacuation from Narvik; the cruiser *Effingham* was destroyed and the cruiser *Curlew* was sunk; three other cruisers were damaged. The French and the Poles each lost one destroyer, and one French cruiser was seriously damaged. With few exceptions, the small craft of the Norwegian Navy were lost or fell into German hands. The large and highly significant Norwegian merchant fleet, however, was added to the Allied cause for the prosecution of the war.[6]

In trying to understand Norwegian responsibility in the events preceding the invasion, the historian has the sometimes dubious advantage of hindsight, which often prompts oversimplification. This can too easily lead to erroneous judgments or, at best, partial truths which, fail to provide a complete understanding of the issue in question. A common criticism of the Nygsaardsvold government, which was heard from all classes of the Norwegian population, was its resentment over the refusal to provide adequate defense.

To be sure, British vacillation and indecision were accompanied by Norwegian laxity and unpreparedness. Mobilization was confused—untrained soldiers had to face German tanks and aircraft with obsolete field guns and small arms. Minefields were not laid out. Communications broke down. There was no well-planned defense of the airfields. Implementing these measures could not have turned defeat into victory, but could have delayed the German incursions, thereby giving the British time to come to their assistance. Many bitter words were spoken in Norway during this unequal struggle, and still harsher ones when the defeat sank into people's consciousness. But what of the national mood *before* the invasion?

Norwegian attitudes were complex and often contradictory. Along with a widespread hatred of Nazism went a rejection of great-power politics, which tended to brand *all great powers equally culpable.*[7] Fear of involvement in the war was accompanied by a belief that Norway was relatively free from the danger of attack owing to Great Britain's naval supremacy. And as the reputed Norwegian historian, Olav Riste, has stated, "however weak, inefficient, short-sighted or clumsy the government's action may at times have been, it should also be recognized that they were inspired by an honest and burning desire to remain at peace with other nations, and they were supported by an overwhelming majority of the Norwegian people."[8]

A century and a half of peace reinforced by Norway's successful effort to avoid involvement in World War I had, in the Depression-torn 1930s, brought about an open hostility between large segments of the working class and members of the Norwegian army, who were criticized for their elitist disposition and conservative politics. Moreover, nothing in Norwegian policy entitled other powers to a massive violation of its territory under the pretext of international law. Understandably angry over Churchill's desire to mine the territorial waters, however justified from the Allies standpoint, and harassed by reports of an impending German invasion, Norway believed itself caught between Scylla and Charybdis in its desire to maintain its neutralist stance.

As to the lack of foresight for which the government stands criticized by the chain of events, it should be remembered that the entire nation—not unlike the United States a year and a half later at Pearl Harbor—was both mentally and physically unprepared for war. But as Foreign Minister Koht in his analysis of the campaign one year later ruefully remarked, "Unfortunately, in international politics, the cunning of the serpent is still indispensable beside the simple-mindedness of the dove," a lesson as old as the art of warfare and one the Allies and the Norwegians would not soon forget.[9] This small Nordic nation which desired only to live in peace and to carry on its own way of life—devoted to social justice, economic progress, and international understanding—was entering the darkest period in its long history.

Under Nazi Rule

Clouds of doom were all around us,

Ill we stood the test,

When the ninth of April found us

In the battle pressed.

Freedom's claims are sternly stated,

Mercilessly made,

And too long we had debated

Where to look for aid.

—Nordahl Grieg (1902-1943), "The Ninth of April," from War Poems

On April 10, 1940, the day after the invasion began, rumors of impending Allied air raids spread feverishly throughout the city of Oslo. Although the attacks never materialized, teeming throngs of the population took to the streets. The scene was chaotic. Buses, trams, and trucks were crammed with men, women, and children struggling with their belongings; masses of people on bicycles and on foot rushed to leave the city. *Aftenposten*, Oslo's largest newspaper, had managed to publish a four-page edition announcing the invasion, the departure of the King and government, orders for general mobilization, and plans for the complete evacuation of the city. However, on the following day, all newspapers and radio announcements were in German hands. No one was allowed to leave without a military pass, and all who had left the city were ordered to return.

The Germans wasted no time in occupying the major arteries of Oslo. Guards with machine guns and hand grenades were stationed at every pier, the railway station, the Parliament building, the university, and at checkpoints along the street. Many were bivouacked in the parks, posted outside office buildings, riding the trams, and monopolizing the best restaurants and cafes. Oslo's newest hotel, the Continental, was taken for officers' quarters, and troops were barracked in the National Theater and at every hill of the Palace Park. Initially,

German military regulations were not severe except those regarding Resistance activity. Proclamations were posted on buildings every-where, declaring in large bold letters *Skutt Blir Den Som*—"Shot will be the one who, . . . " followed by this list:

- gives information to the enemy

- conceals arms

- fails to show respect for the Reich

- joins an illegal organization[1]

The astonishment, uncertainty, and sense of outrage that Norwegians felt in the wake of the invasion was intensified by their general detestation of the Quisling *coup d'etat*, which the people repu-diated with open ridicule: intellectuals and the upper classes snubbed him, labor leaders mocked him, and public officials refused offers of high government posts. When Quisling ordered all Norwegian ships to sail to German, Italian, or neutral ports, more than 80 percent of the merchant fleet—the world's fourth largest—were on the high seas or moored in foreign ports. One thousand twenty-four vessels refused to return home, and all put their crews at the disposal of the Allies.[2]

The widespread opposition to Quisling's proclamation was a clear sign that chaos was threatening. He had never at any time commanded the allegiance of more than a negligible number of supporters. When the Germans discovered that Quisling had no member of the *Nasjonal Samling* Party (NS) in the Parliament, they at first refused to believe it.[3] It was not long before the German High Command realized that the pompous self-proclaimed prime minister could no longer serve as an intermediary between the Germans and the population. Just three days after the government takeover, when Quisling, in a blatant assertion of power fired the Oslo chief of police, the Germans told the dismissed official to take no notice of it. That same evening, the President of the City Council was also told "to ignore it; it doesn't matter in the least."[4]

Thus, on April 15, just six days after the invasion, Quisling and his lackeys were forced from their headquarters in the Hotel Continental and stripped of all further authority. Quisling's resentment was some-what mollified by his assignment to the newly created post of Commissioner of Demobilization, an utterly disreputable title that con-firmed his traitorous activity among the people.

Since the Germans were not yet prepared to take over the government, and the Norwegian government was no longer in a position to act, the Norwegian Supreme Court appointed an Administrative Council. The German military commander, General von Falkenhorst, who initially controlled both military and civil affairs in Norway, granted its authorization. Headed by I. E. Christiansen, Governor of Oslo and the Akershus Province, it consisted of seven leading citizens, including Paal Berg, President of the Supreme Court, and Bishop Eivind Berggrav, Primate of the Lutheran Church of Norway. The Council was formed in response to a need for a Norwegian civil authority in the southern and central regions overrun by the German Army. It had no authority in foreign affairs or defense matters, and therefore no responsibility in the conduct of the war. At the termination of the military campaign, the Council's limited authority was extended to the whole country since there was no longer any unoccupied region. As a temporary arrangement, it was forced to comply with the orders of the occupying power.

From the German point of view, the Council was intended to maintain an atmosphere of normalcy and to prevent any disturbance that would adversely affect the maximum strategic and economic benefits that the Germans hoped to obtain without using a large number of troops that could be better employed elsewhere. So as not to appear as belligerents, German soldiers were instructed to treat the Norwegians well.[5] Before leaving Germany, they were given directives on how to behave toward the populace. They were told that the people had no understanding of the aims of National Socialism and that it was advisable to avoid discussing politics with them. The idea was to win them over by friendliness and flattery.[6] They were told that a hostile attitude would be met with bitter resentment by a robust, independent people with strong nationalistic feelings and a love of freedom.

Unlike the contempt that the Germans exhibited toward the peoples of the Slavic East who, like the Jews, Hitler considered as subhuman, particularly the Czechs and the Poles, the Norwegians were erroneously viewed as "pure Aryans." And as members of the "Germanic brotherhood," they should as far as possible be treated especially well. There were few cases of violence by German soldiers against civilians so long as the latter behaved. In fact, the soldiers were severely punished if they committed violent acts. So also, the exile government in London instructed the Norwegians to remain loyal, disciplined, and obedient as they awaited liberation by the Allies. Nevertheless, watching the seemingly endless numbers of helmeted *Wehrmacht* troops constantly marching through the streets singing *"Dan wir fahren gegen Engeland"*—Next we go to England—only added to the resentment toward foreign dominance.

Within two weeks of Quisling's removal, Hitler issued a decree entrusting the management of all Norwegian civil affairs to *Reichskommissar* Josef Terboven, an old-line Nazi Gauleiter from Essen and president of the Rhine Province. His reputation as a tough street fighter against the Communists during the 1920s contributed to his rise to power within the Nazi Party. His coming foreshadowed a five-year occupation nightmare. As the supreme head of the government in Norway and answerable only to Hitler, Terboven wasted no time in making the German oppression more heavily felt. At the Parliament building where the headquarters of the German High Command was located, the Norwegian flag was replaced by the swastika, and the bronze tablets memorializing those Norwegians who lost their lives in the last war were replaced by a bust of Hitler.

The stage setting was but an early sign of a policy discouraging and intimidating all potential enemies of the Reich. Besides Terboven's own administrative personnel, branches of the *Sicherheitsdienst* (SD), the intelligence service later known for its unraveling of Resistance networks, the dreaded *Schutzstaffel* (SS), Hitler's elite black-uniformed praetorian guard, and the *Staatspolizie,* the dreaded Gestapo, were deployed throughout the country.

During the first four months of the Occupation, the Administrative Council, the Bank of Norway, and all other public organizations, were forced to work together with the German authorities whose aim was to gain greater control of the political, economic, and social life of Norway. In June, the Germans contacted Norwegian political leaders to negotiate a more permanent government—a Council of State, which would replace the exiled government and depose the King. Then, from within, its present members would be replaced, one by one, by those more receptive to collaboration with the Third Reich. Thus would Norway gradually be reduced to satellite status in Hitler's Teutonic Empire.[7]

The widespread feeling of hopelessness throughout the country after the withdrawal of Allied troops from Narvik, abetted by the German conquests of the Low Countries and coupled with the prospect of a harsh military regime in Norway, prompted some Parliament members to yield to the German demands. Acting in despair, when the Allies were at their lowest ebb in the wake of France's capitulation on June 17, the Presidential Board of Parliament appealed to King Haakon to abdicate the throne.[8]

Meanwhile, throughout the country, the people felt lost and isolated, not knowing what to do, believe, or expect. The devastation wreaked by the war had created uncertainty about the future. The mood was one of ambivalence. Many criticized the poor performance of the British troops, which led to a loss of confidence in the Western Powers; others cited the failed defense policy of the Nygaardsvold government; while still others were impressed by the German political organization and economic successes, especially the creation of jobs in Germany. Unemployment was a serious concern to many Norwegians, particularly in those towns and villages, which were reduced to ruins as a result of the damage inflicted by the *Luftwaffe*—towns such as Kristiansund, Molde, Namsos, Bodo, and Narvik. In North Norway alone, nearly 30,000 people were homeless in the autumn of 1940. Bridges, roads, harbor and railroad facilities that were destroyed brought economic life in many areas to a standstill.

Additionally, there was concern over the future of consumer goods, since Norway was far from self-sufficient. Before the Occupation the nation was able to supply only about 45 percent of its needs.[9] And although the government had taken care to accumulate stores of essential supplies in anticipation of a general European war in which it expected to remain neutral, they were quickly diminishing. During the first month of the Occupation, rationing of bread, flour, butter, and fats was introduced and all trade by sea was stopped. For new supplies, Norway was totally dependent upon the Germans.[10] And although they had promised to provide the Norwegians with specified amounts of food and other necessities, the commitment was not kept, partly because of a lack of shipping facilities, but principally due to indifference, spite, and selfishness.

Yet they had no scruples about taking sorely needed products from Norway to supply their own troops.[11] The German practice of butchering cattle and sheep in the pasture and carrying them off for their own consumption created an acute meat shortage in the fall of 1940. Moreover, food products such as fish, eggs, and innumerable other necessities were confiscated and shipped to Germany. Figures show that from April 1940 to February 1941, Norway shipped to the Reich 1,277 tons of coffee, 133 tons of eggs, 5,819 tons of butter and oleomargarine, and 6,382 tons of meats and canned goods. From January 1 to July 1, 1941, the country shipped 3,972 tons of cream, 5,108 tons of milk, and 1,116 tons of cheese.[12]

Those living on farms and in the countryside were not as adversely affected by the rationing in the early stages of the occupation, since they consumed much of what they grew and produced. Yet the Germans, totally indifferent to the needs of the farmer, drafted farm workers for the construction of coastal fortifications, lumbering, and road building. The shortage of farm labor resulted in crops being unharvested and wheat unthreshed until late fall or even later, and a general lowering of agricultural production, all of which added to the struggle to survive. To combat the lack of farm labor, the Germans began to mobilize children between the ages of 12 and 18. Their teachers were ordered to go along and direct the work, and the parents were expected to furnish them with food, clothes, and transportation.[13]

For those living in the cities, such as Oslo and Bergen, halting the import of critically needed food items, coupled with the nation's normal lack of self-sufficiency, soon created a condition of near starvation. Food rationing restricted the amount an individual could receive. People could not always obtain the allotted food essentials on the ration card, since there was no guarantee that the food the consumer was entitled to was even available. Frequently people were hungry before and after a meal, partly because there was not enough to eat, and partly because the unappetizing food was often difficult, if not impossible, to digest. For example, the bread ration which consisted of about nine ounces a day was as indigestible as leather, since it was made from barley, oats or rye of extremely poor quality, and often crawling with worms. Owing to the poor quality of the flour and the shortage of yeast, the dough had to be made sour to make it rise. Many believed that the flour contained sawdust, cellulose, and other adulterations. Frequently a homemaker in Oslo would have to queue-up all night outside a store to get a meager amount of margarine while worrying about the many tasks left undone at home.

As a result of the shortages, people started using a number of food substitutes: Vaseline as oil in foods, butter mixed with starch, whale oil in oleomargarine, young grass mixed with bark and made into bread, coffee combined with chemically treated leaves; and tea a concoction of many ingredients.[14] Eggs, when available, were reserved for the sick, and gotten only by a doctor's prescription. Fruits such as apples, peaches, and plums were harvested to provide the necessary nourishment, but like everything else, the Germans were the first to secure these crops for themselves. Frequently, people would go into the woods to gather blueberries and raspberries and anything else that was edible to keep from starving. Nevertheless, despite the struggles, disappointments, and monotony of everyday life, most people were able to cope. Complaining was considered bad form and tended to weaken morale.

The chief concerns for most Norwegians were the struggle against nazification and the German demand for the abdication of the King. These were issues that touched the hearts and minds of the Norwegian people deeply. King Haakon was a symbol of the Constitution and of everything that Norway stood for. Public opinion from all quarters rallied around him more strongly than ever. It has been suggested that had the Germans hammered on the issue of the British abandonment of Norway and not demanded the abdication of the King, an agreement might have been arranged.[15]

Yet the Germans were unable to understand that for most Norwegians, the soul of Norway was at stake. One could often hear people paraphrase the passage from Scripture: "Better to lose your life than your soul."[16] Members of Parliament were deluged with letters urging them not to submit. Everywhere people wore small flags and produced portraits of the King. On July 8, 1940, the King, in a radio address from London, gave his response to the Presidential Board:

> *I cannot see that the Presidential Board has any constitutional authority for redrafting legal resolutions voted so far by the Storting. On the contrary, it is quite evident that the whole arrangement proposed is*

unconstitutional… The freedom and independence of the Norwegian people is to me the first commandment of our Constitution, and I feel I must follow this commandment and best serve the interests of the Norwegian people in holding fast by the position and the task a free people gave me in 1905.[17]

Nevertheless, despite the King's refusal to yield, talks between Norwegian representatives continued into September without resolution. The Presidential Board had hoped to obtain a freer and more independent position for the Council of State than that of the Administrative Council. And when the board tried to reach a compromise by which the King would resign until the end of the war, when he would automatically resume his duties, the Germans would not agree. The latter revealed their true intentions when they proposed that when seats in the Council of State became vacant, that body, and not the Presidential Board, should appoint the new members. If that proposal had been adopted, the *Storting* would have committed suicide, since the Germans would have filled the Council of State with *Nasjonal Samling* members, thereby legalizing the NS Party. The situation remained at an impasse until *Reichskommissar* Terboven, after consulting with Hitler who would not concede anything, broke off the negotiations.[18]

On September 25, Terboven, in an inflammatory and denunciating speech, accused members of Parliament of agreeing to discussions for a Council of State based upon motives of preserving their own political existence. He declared the King and the Royal Family dethroned, the government deposed, the Administrative Council terminated, and the Parliament dismissed. In its place, a German-staffed apparatus called the *Reichskommissariat* was formed, composed of members of the *Nasjonal Samling* Party (NS). All other political parties were banned. Despite Terboven's support for the NS, he knew that it had no backing from the vast majority of the population. All real power would be exercised by the German authorities.[19] Thus began the German rule of Norway and the struggle to draw the country into the "New European Order."

The Civilian Reaction

5

Today the flagpole stands naked

'mongst Eidsvoll's green-budding trees

But just in this very hour

We know what freedom means.

A song through the land is swelling,

Of victory's hour it spoke,

Though only by closed lips whispered

Under the foreign yoke.

—Nordahl Grieg (1902-1943), "May 17, 1940"

War Poems

Although the majority of the people were determined to behave as though the German presence did not exist in the early stages of the Occupation, small pockets of Resistance were in early evidence. On the morning of April 13, two tenacious young men, Olaf Reed Olsen and Kaare Moe, set off an explosion under the Lysaker Bridge, an overpass and major link between Oslo and its airport at Fornebu.[1] The bridge was vitally important for the movement of *Wehrmacht* reinforcements into the country, and the German reaction was predictable. Von Falkenhorst immediately issued a proclamation that further acts of sabotage would be met by summary executions of the perpetrators and by reprisals against the population at large. On the following day, no less than 200 well-intentioned prominent citizens supported the German announcement by publishing an appeal against exposing the civilian population to reprisals for any form of destructive act likely to provoke the occupying power.[2]

Nevertheless, the Lysaker Bridge incident, albeit an isolated act, was important for several reasons. First, it demonstrated to the Occupation forces that there were people in Norway who were prepared to actively resist beyond the limits of conventional warfare. Second, the German reaction revealed the anxiety of the invader at the prospect of not having to fight a small army, but rather an entire nation.[3]

Throughout the summer and early autumn of 1940, a spirit of passive resistance was beginning to simmer throughout the country. Initial enmity took the form of spontaneous acts of what Resistance historian Henri Michel called "'prickly xenophobia,' the instinctive aversion to the presence of the foreigner, particularly in a position of superiority."[4] One of the first signs was a "cold shoulder policy," which reflected a natural urge to do *something* to express one's state of mind. There was the refusal to understand the language of the German occupiers and consequently, the apparent inability to obey orders, give directions to German soldiers on the street, or serve them in cafes and stores. On one occasion, a woman met some German soldiers on the street who asked her the way. "Do you mind if I answer in English?" she responded. When they had agreed to this she said: "I don't know," and left them.[5]

The non-acceptance of the Occupation was often humiliating to the Germans' pride. After Terboven had commandeered the elegant residence of Crown Prince Olav a short distance from Oslo, he invited a well-known actress to a reception there. She declined the invitation, giving as her reason that she never accepted an invitation when the host and hostess were absent.[6] And when another recognized Norwegian personality was sitting alone in a restaurant, having a cup of coffee, a German officer approached her and asked if he could take a seat. When a Quisling supporter who was nearby told her to answer, she replied: "I cannot see why he should ask me if he may take a seat when they have taken the whole country."[7]

It was not uncommon to see local patrons leave the premises or the trams when a German soldier or collaborator appeared; and tram conductors showed their loyalty whenever they came to one of the many King Haakon Streets by shouting, "His Majesty King Haakon Street." In Oslo, authorities posted notices warning that demonstrative acts were punishable offenses: "It is regarded as a demonstration to change places when one finds oneself beside an NS member or a German, or to refrain from sitting beside an NS member or a German, when this would otherwise be natural."[8]

Contrary to what one might expect by the conditions created by the Occupation, such as severe stress, frayed nerves, and confused minds, the average man or woman drew on mental and spiritual reserves: calmness, common sense, endurance, and optimism. Although life for the most part was dull and uneventful, there were major disruptions at times. One of the most unsettling conditions borne by the Norwegians was the German demand for housing. Invariably, the German higher-ranking officers sought residence in the more select homes; equally disturbing were the German "boarders" who had to share kitchen and bathroom facilities with the homeowner. Protests by the owner could possibly lead to his loss of the entire house. However, some of the "renters" were so harassed by the owners' unpleasant attitude that they simply moved out.

Generally speaking, Norwegians and Germans moved on separate levels and seldom spoke to one another since friendly attitudes could easily be misinterpreted by both Germans and fellow Norwegians, who might mistake one for a Nazi sympathizer. Since the main function of the Resistance was to provide an alternative society with its own distinct social code of behavior, fraternizing with the enemy was discouraged at all costs.[9] The punishment doled out to any member of Norwegian society who was known to associate with such a person was called "shunning." Shunning was one of the strict *Jossing* [Patriotic] Codes, which demanded that all NS members or anyone associated with them be rebuffed or ignored and treated like traitors. Loyal Norwegians considered *Jossing* an honorable designation. It meant a patriot, but was a derogatory term when the Nazis used it.

In accordance with police regulations, blackened shades or blinds were required on all windows, and occupants of any homes where light could be seen entering from outside were subject to heavy fines. During the summer months, when daylight extended well into the evening, citizens were required to remain in their homes and forbidden to look out the windows under the threat of fines or even worse penalties. The Germans confiscated the buses and trucks, and doctors were among the few permitted the use of cars. Public transportation consisted of overcrowded streetcars and rundown trains, which prompted many city and suburban residents to walk or bicycle longer distances. Self-imposed restrictions were put on everyday activities.

In the winter months, there was little satisfaction in taking walks in the evening as no streetlights were lit and there was always the risk of bumping into Germans in the dark. Couples were discouraged from frequenting their favorite cafes and restaurants, since the Germans often made it unpleasant to go there. Even little children returning from school on dark winter nights (which started at 3:00 p.m.) were affected by restrictions. With no streetlights and no light coming from the windows of homes, children would stumble and fall or get lost in the dark. Worried mothers would go out looking for their children with flashlights that only permitted a light that was so faint that it was of no real assistance.

The focus on the home, where families regained their inner strength, was an essential feature of the Occupation. And since the movies, theaters, and concert halls were gradually being converted into forums for Nazi propaganda, the home suddenly became the focal point and meeting place for friends and neighbors. Guests often brought sandwiches and the hostess would offer ersatz coffee or rose hip tea. Frequently they would gather around the radio to listen to the Norwegian news broadcasts from London. When the Norwegian national anthem was played over the air, family and friends would rise and sing in unison: *"Also we, when we are called, will join the fight for peace."* The meaning: We will join the war to fight. In the early stages of the Occupation, the home, fortified by a pervasive patriotic spirit, was the place where much of the Resistance activity was planned and discussed.

As an antidote to the changed environment created by the ubiquitous Germans, jokes and irrepressible ridicule provided some consolation to the Norwegians. A few examples:

- Question: "Why did Hitler buy a deep-sea diving suit?"

  Answer: "He needed it to inspect the German Navy."

- Question: "Why did Hitler buy a 12-volt radio?"

  Answer: "That's the only way he can get England."

- German officer to a churchwarden: "Do you have room for some hundred soldiers?"

  Churchwarden to German officer: "Certainly. We can find room for all of you in the churchyard."

- Norwegian: "I would rather work for 10,000 Germans than for one Englishman."

  German: "Delighted! And what is your job?"

Norwegian: "I'm a gravedigger."

- Quisling (entering Hitler's office with arm extended in a Nazi salute): "I am Quisling."

Hitler: "Yes, but what is your name?"[10]

Lacking any defense and convinced of their own superiority, the Germans and their Quisling supporters were easily offended by this derision, and as the months dragged on, the morale of the German Army began to decline. Many of the soldiers longed for home, especially the older ones who were influenced by the peaceful Norwegian democratic way of life, or affected by the Norwegians' cold-shoulder treatment. A few women fraternized with the Germans, but the majority rebuffed their self-proclaimed "protectors." One German officer who had taken part in the Polish campaign said that it was bad enough to see the furious hatred in the eyes of the Poles, but it was even worse to face the cold contempt of the Norwegians.[11]

The demoralizing effect on the sensibilities of the Germans and their collaborators that such conduct caused was well-expressed in John Steinbeck's novel, *The Moon Is Down* (1942), in which a German officer scorns the attitude of the people of a village in an anonymous occupied country: "These people! These horrible people! These cold people! They never look at you. They never speak. They answer like dead men. They obey, these horrible people. And the girls are frozen."[12] This work, which one Norwegian critic praised as the epic of the Norwegian Underground, brought a voice from the free world which not only expressed the admiration the Norwegians evoked abroad, but more significantly, lent encouragement to a growing spirit of defiance at home.

Resistance was further strengthened by the rhetoric and courage of a few of the more outspoken patriots such as the highly respected journalist-poet, Nordahl Grieg, whose emotional influence was an enduring appeal to his countrymen.[13] So also the well-known doctor and public figure Johan Scharffenberg whose rallying cry for truth and justice encouraged others to an increased patriotic fervor: "This spiritual tutelage from people not superior in character or intelligence is like slow strangulation. If this is going to be our condition in Norway, then I must again seek comfort in the maxim: *Vivere non est necesse*— *to live is no necessity*."[14]

It was not long before inscriptions and various forms of graffiti appeared everywhere in endless and unpredictable ways. Patriotic and anti-German symbols could be seen on walls of homes and store fronts, defacing propaganda posters, in parks, etched in the snow, on clothing, and even on bare skin of the more conspicuous patriots. Red woolen caps topped with the symbolic British bullseye were frequently worn, as were medallions with the motto, "All for Norway." The monogram H7 for King Haakon VII, usually inscribed within the V-for-Victory sign and made famous by Prime Minister Churchill, flourished everywhere. Paper clips were worn on coat lapels and cuffs as a sign of "keeping together"; a wooden match in the breast pocket was a sign of "flaming hate." All these symbolic gestures helped keep the spirit of Resistance alive in the minds and hearts of the Norwegian people.

Soon after the Terboven tirade of September 25, the uncertainty and despondency that had plagued the Norwegian people since April 9 now gave way to a nourishing spirit of defiance in which the stage was set for a test of wills between nazification and resistance. The most caustic reaction to Terboven's speech came from a Labor newspaper editorial in Stavanger on the west coast of Norway. Headlined in bold print was the clarion call to stand firm: "No Norwegian for Sale!"[15] For the great majority, the line was drawn. However long and difficult, no matter the sacrifice, resistance was the only course of action.

The first effort toward the formation of a nationwide Resistance network was started in Oslo by a number of journalists, trade unionists, and leaders from the academic and business communities who joined together in a "Norwegian Front." The R-Group, as it came to be called, played an active role in the autumn of 1940 and in 1941. When the NS was exerting pressure on those in public service to join the party, the pioneer resistance organization sent out a directive to those civil servants encouraging them to stand fast and not to yield. It was arranged into two groups: propaganda and organization and information. The propaganda group started two publications, which served as internal organs of communication for the leaders of the Resistance and as a source of information for the clandestine press. It also provided reviews of the situation at home and abroad, as well as instructions for keeping up the struggle.[16] Additionally, financial support was provided to a number of illegal newspapers in different parts of the country.

The R-Group was not intended to direct the Resistance, but rather to contact Resistance people who were willing to organize their districts and establish contact with the Norwegian government-in-exile. Although contacts were made through various channels with individuals, no extensive district organizations were in fact established.[17] In October, a system of connections was started to link the R-Group with its district contacts partly through reliable railwaymen, bus drivers, and crewmen on coastal steamers, and partly through people who traveled frequently and were suitable as couriers.[18]

Meanwhile, the NS initiated efforts to swell the ranks of its party membership in the hope of forming a national government that would ultimately unite itself with Germany and take a more active role in the "New Order." On October 4, the *Reichskommisar* issued an ordinance in which public servants who refused to cooperate with the NS would be dismissed from service. The leading figure in the NS was A. V. Hagelin, acting minister of Home Affairs and Quisling's second-in-command. Hagelin was a Norwegian businessman who, after a long residence in Germany, returned to his native land to play a major part in the nazification effort. In mid-December, he issued a more compelling demand for loyalty from all civil servants to the NS and the German *Kommissariat.* "Failure in any way will be treated as action against the State, to be visited with drastic penalties."[19]

This situation caused grave anxiety and posed a difficult moral dilemma. In the spring of 1940, before the German invasion, the estimated membership in the NS was only about 3,000.[20] Promises of good jobs and economic privileges attracted several thousand agitators, opportunists, and other self-serving elements within the country. According to one observer who studied the NS members closely,[21] those who were middle-aged or elderly joined the party partly because of a lack of intelligence and good judgment; partly because of easy money, power, and a chance to avenge real or imagined defeats before the war; or because they lacked the backbone to stand up to the pressure and propaganda of the Germans. Many of the younger men and women who joined the NS, however, were influenced by parents or relatives, or they were looking for adventure and a "cause" that they could belong to. In their opposition to Bolshevism and the Resistance, they subjectively believed that they were serving the cause of justice. Able to see the one side, they were easily enticed into becoming the willing tools for an unscrupulous leader. But by autumn, the number grew to only about 20,000 out of a population of over 3,000,000 people.

Since not enough Quislings were available to fill the various municipal appointments, those Norwegians already holding public office were expected to give active support to the NS. Those who refused would clearly be recognized as patriots, but would risk the danger of reprisals. The forces of the Resistance realized that those who did refuse and faced dismissal needed some assurance that they and their families would not be left helpless and completely alone. Consequently, financial aid was provided by obtaining subscriptions from every member in some threatened branch of public service. Additionally, funds came from private sources and, covertly, from the government via the Norwegian Legation in Stockholm.[22]

Conversely, public servants who agreed to remain at their posts would be required to enforce German and NS laws and regulations and risk being viewed as a collaborator by their own people. Some chose to work with the authorities in the hope of simply easing or modifying the German regulations. Others, however, took government posts to gain access to information helpful to the Resistance such as uncovering informers within Resistance networks, alerting those in danger of being arrested, and disclosing enemy troop movements and the location of military or industrial sites for sabotage activities. Those who chose to cooperate with the Underground in this way risked the possibility of prison, torture, deportation, or death.

Apart from this risk, these people's families suffered social disapproval because others, knowing where they were employed, naturally assumed they were Nazi sympathizers. Each individual had to decide for himself or herself whether or to what degree practical cooperation should be shown to the occupying power. In short, an individual was alone with his or her own conscience: preoccupied with personal or family worries and feelings of impotence, individuals found the decision not an easy one. As conditions worsened later, the decision to act became increasingly easier. Nevertheless, this dilemma was in fact basic to the whole Resistance movement and remained until the end of the Occupation.[23]

To recruit members to the NS, numerous public meetings were held, but attendance in most cases was small. Frequently, crowds would gather in the meeting room, but would leave singing the national anthem or "God Save the King, " when the speaker arrived at the podium. At other times, he would be jeered, or the gathering would simply be boycotted. Efforts to draw people into the nazification program were met by demonstrations of various kinds. Large masses of people gathered on national holidays and at memorials. On King Haakon's birthday, thousands of people carried flowers to show support for the exile government as Quisling supporters grabbed the flowers out of the demonstrators' hands. When Quisling appeared at public events, he was booed and pelted with eggs, and when he appeared in the royal box at the Oslo National Theater, the entire audience left.

There were also demonstrations in the cinemas. In Trondheim during a film of the bombing and destruction of Rotterdam, the viewers booed and whistled until the lights were turned up. A German colonel stood up and tried to reason with the boisterous crowd to no avail. Losing his temper, he ordered everyone to leave.[24] At another theater, the Nazis showed a film of the unloading of German ships at a dock in Oslo, conveying the impression that the Germans were bringing their own supplies to Norway. Suddenly a man in the audience rose and shouted: "Stop! You're running the film in reverse." The audience was collectively fined.[25]

In many towns where German propaganda films were shown, the cinema was boycotted. Citizens of Stavanger, Trondheim, and Lillehammer refused to attend any films for weeks at a time. There was also bitter resentment toward bands of Quisling troublemaker youths who would enter the theaters without paying. When patrons did attend, their behavior during newsreel films was so unruly that the NS issued orders forbidding all demonstrations. "Demonstrations were defined as laughter, meaningless applause, i.e., clapping at the wrong places in the film, stamping with the feet, whistling, coughing, and harking, i.e., an expressive Norwegian term for clearing one's throat," wrote historian Jacob Worm-Muller.[26]

In May 1941, leading actors at the Oslo National Theater were called in by the Germans and threatened with dismissal unless they gave radio performances. Their refusal was supported by a sympathy strike by actors throughout the country, which lasted for six weeks despite arrests, fines, and threats of other kinds. The strike had the support of the public and was, to a great extent, responsible for intensifying the attitude of the ordinary citizen in the street.[27]

People used other forms of aversion. They would leave their place of work for hours, and even for days; streets were empty; some people refused to perform work or carry out orders, which were compulsory special orders or just normal day-to-day functions. Arrests and threats of deportation not only failed to discourage demonstrations, but bolstered resolve at all levels of society and from all parts of the country. For the Germans and the NS, many of these infractions were minor or inconsequential; but nevertheless, were irritating and provocative sources of frustration. The authorities were not always certain as to how severely they should react. But collectively, these peccadilloes clearly indicated a brewing spirit of revolt by a proud and patriotic people who were moving from stubborn acquiescence to active resistance, leaving the Germans and their Quisling supporters with the unmistakable impression that they were living in a hostile environment.

By late summer and early fall, solidarity was reinforced by the increasingly restrictive activities the NS imposed on the people. NS refused to allow reception of news from the outside world by placing severe censorship on the press and radio. It did not allow Norwegians to gain access to foreign books and magazines except those from Germany. It published new and restrictive laws and proclamations. In short, the NS tried all public methods to force compliance with its rule.

A further effort to systematically nazify the Norwegian people was the attempt to gain control of the whole complex of voluntary professional organizations made up of doctors, dentists, farmers, fishermen, engineers, lawyers, trade unions, and sportsmen to exert influence on the whole population along lines dictated by the *Nasjonal Samling* Party. When full mastery was achieved, the parliamentary system would be dissolved and replaced by a State Parliament (*Riksting*) based on a corporation system similar to that of Fascist Italy. Norwegian Nazi authorities would control these institutions, thereby bringing pressure on the members. Because many people were more deeply and personally involved in private voluntary organizations, which promoted their own special interests and were at variance with those of the NS, a storm of protest and boycott from widely differing groups and associations met this maneuver.

Of even greater concern was the awareness that if this political goal was achieved, Quisling and the NS would enter into a peace agreement with Germany. If this were to happen, it would likely mean Norway's entry into the war on the side of the Germans and the conscription of Norway's youth to war on the enemy's side. To prevent this was the principal object of resistance, the red thread in every phase of the struggle almost to the last day of the war.[28]

One of the earliest objectives of the NS was to target the youth of the nation by organizing the various sports associations into a new "Norwegian Athletic Association" requiring NS Party membership. Yet when the provisional board insisted on two basic principles—no interference in the affairs of sports and no introduction of party politics into such matters—the NS refused to accede and attempted to restructure Norwegian sports along Nazi German lines. This provoked a nationwide sports strike in which some 300,000 young athletes participated.[29] Despite intense Nazi pressure, the strike lasted for the five-year Occupation. When Nazi-controlled athletic events were held, very few competitors took part, and except for very few spectators, the events were boycotted.

The NS also made attempts to gain control of the agricultural workers by amalgamating the various farm organizations into a Farmers' Guild, an initial step in the formation of the Quisling "corporate union." In November, the national committee of the Norwegian medical association, by a vote of 35 to 2, refused to join the nazified Doctors' Guild or to give a declaration of loyalty to the "New Order." Soon afterwards, four doctors were dismissed on political grounds.[30] Similarly, when the president of the Norwegian Nurses' Association was fired by the NS, the directors and practically all of the 3,700 members resigned in protest. The president was replaced by a woman in the NS who was formerly refused membership because of a lack of proper training.[31] These were but introductory episodes in what was soon to become a head-on confrontation between the NS and the population at large.

In mid-November, the Supreme Court, the one remaining independent branch of the Norwegian government, came under attack by the NS Minister of Justice Sverre Riinaes who issued a decree reserving for himself the right to appoint or dismiss jury members, assessors, and court clerks. In fact, one of the Supreme Court justices, Emil Stang, was arrested without the benefit of a trial. The following month, Riinaes lowered the retirement age limit for all public officials from 70 to 65, which took effect immediately. This was simply a tactic to stack the courts with Quisling supporters, since many of the judges were well within retirement age. The Supreme Court responded with a letter to the Justice Department denouncing the decree as an attack on the independence of the law courts, a violation of the fundamental principles of Norwegian law, and a contravention of the Hague Convention of 1907, which stated that the laws of an occupied country should be respected by the invading power.[32]

Reichskommissar Terboven responded with a letter stating that the court had no authority to express its opinions on matters that he or NS justice officials decided upon. On December 21, the members collectively resigned in protest. The Nazi reaction to the judges' refusal to officiate any longer resulted in the arrest of the chief justice and one of the other justices, but the Bishop of Oslo intervened and they were released. A new Supreme Court was then formed, composed of inferior lawyers who supported the decrees of the *Nasjonal Samling* Party.

News of the Supreme Court's resignation was immediately made public by means of underground news sheets, the distribution of handbills, and reports on the BBC Norwegian News Service. For the Germans and the NS, the matter was more of a defeat than a victory since it was a clear indication of the futility of any further attempt to gain support for the Nazi regime.

Throughout the autumn and winter of 1940-41, conditions grew worse, and unrest became more violent. Expressions of national feeling and disdain toward the Germans and their NS sympathizers frequently led to unprovoked confrontations between law-abiding citizens and the *Hird*. Under the sign of the sun cross—the NS symbol which replaced the swastika—the *Hird* was made up of gangs of a young, lawless rabble of every description, many of whom were recruited from prisons. These Quisling storm troopers, uniformed in dark blue ski outfits, were the NS elite guard. They created an atmosphere of fear and brutality, which many people found less easy to endure than the systematic terror of the later war years. It was reminiscent of Germany in the 1930s at the time of the Weimar Republic when Nazi brownshirts wreaked havoc in the streets without interference by the police. The following are but a few of the officially recorded cases.

- In October, members of the *Hird* broke into the Oslo Business College, threatened the principal, and beat one of the students.

- On another occasion at the same school the following month, they forced their way into a classroom during a class and attacked the pupils, using their fists, a length of rubber hose, and iron tables and chairs as weapons. The teacher and principal were also severely beaten.[33]

- In December, a 16-year-old youth was kidnapped in the Oslo Town Hall and taken to a cellar where he was given 15 lashes with his belt because he had been seen a few days earlier wearing a paper clip in the lapel of his jacket, an emblem of national solidarity.[34]

- A similar situation involved the chairman of the Trondheim Student Association, who was repeatedly beaten for refusing to post *Nasjonal Samling* placards.[35]

The lawlessness of the *Hird* made it quite clear that the new rulers were determined to discourage any signs of resistance in its attempt to impose the New Order. To make matters worse, the NS Minister of Police, Jonas Lie, issued a circular to the police advising them to join the party:[36]

The *Hird* are the political soldiers of the *Nasjonal Samling* and must be strongly supported in their struggle to put the ideas of NS into effect. A good relationship and real collaboration must be established between the police and the *Hird*. Naturally, it must not occur that a member of the *Hird* be arrested by the police, except if he has committed a crime. If the *Hird* or any member of *Nasjonal Samling* are insulted or exposed to terrorism, their answer is a direct action against the attackers—a circumstance which is recognized as free, on principle, from punishment in Paragraph 228, third section of the Penal Code. If the police find reasonable grounds for a complaint of the behavior of the *Hird*, these complaints are submitted to the Police Dept., which then has to discuss the question with the National Leader of the *Hird*.[37]

It was now clear that the forces of law and order were being replaced by a state-supported systematic rule of terror. Nevertheless, many police who joined the NS believed they were helping their fellow countrymen because they were keeping dangerous party members from occupying those same positions. Many ran grave risks to provide help to arrested compatriots and to those in the Resistance. But as the pressure of nazification continued with the misuse of power by the NS and the barbaric activities of the *Hird*, this was not enough. There was a need for a well-organized united home front.

In January 1941, representatives from several organizations met to consider how to deal with the pressure exerted by the NS for membership in the party, but nothing came from the discussions. However, when meetings resumed early in May, it was agreed to lodge a common protest to *Reichskommissar* Terboven, condemning all of the Nazi decrees which contravened international law, Norwegian law, and a common Norwegian sense of justice. The letter was signed on May 15 by leaders of 43 national labor, business, cultural, legal, church, and educational organizations in Oslo representing some 750 workers. The reaction was predictable. The NS and its principal newspaper, *Fritt Folk*, threatened those who had signed the protest. And on June 12, the Gestapo arrested three of the signatories, in support of the NS. On June 18, Terboven summoned the organizations' leaders to a meeting in the Parliament building, where they were surrounded by armed police and scornfully rebuked for their action, after which six more signatories were arrested and imprisoned.[38]

The events of June 18 marked a turning point in the history of the Occupation. A number of the protesting organizations, many of whose members comprised the Home Front vanguard, were eliminated by Interior Minister Hagelin. The others, such as the Norwegian Medical Association and the associations of dentists, engineers, and lawyers, voluntarily disbanded when about 90 percent of the officers and members submitted their resignations. A notable exception was the trade union organization, which the Germans had no wish to disrupt since it was essential to the nation's economy and war production. Before June 18, the Civilian Resistance took the form of *open* protests against transgressions of Norwegian or international law, or against demands for loyalty declarations to the Nazi Party by well-known personalities in the Norwegian community. But after Terboven's response to the 43 organizations, it was obvious that all future opposition would have to be organized covertly and conducted by individuals who were not known to the Gestapo and the NS.[39] The organizations would continue to exist underground.

On September 10, 1941, Terboven proclaimed a State of Emergency in Oslo in which threats gave way to a rule of terror. The situation was occasioned by a strike at two large industrial plants—a shipyard and a steel mill—when milk rations which had been introduced two days earlier were withheld from the factory workers. The next day, the strike spread to other workplaces in Oslo, affecting 20,000 to 30,000 workers. The work stoppage was a spontaneous reaction to the oppression the Norwegians experienced after 17 months of tyrannical rule, resulting in pent-up resentment. But the German reaction was immediate. More than 300 workers were arrested, many of whom were subjected to extensive forms of torture by the Gestapo, while others were sent to prison camps. Two young trade union leaders were sentenced to death. A number of other death sentences were commuted to life imprisonment. Many others, including a number of shop stewards, the Oslo chief of police, the rector and several leading professors at the university, and the editor and several leading journalists of a conservative resistance-minded paper were ruthlessly dealt with. Several Resistance leaders who had signed the protest from the 43 organizations in May were rearrested.

Throughout the remainder of the year, most of the leaders and district contacts of the R-Group were either arrested by the Gestapo or forced to flee the country. Lack of experience in clandestine activity led to basic security violations and betrayal by informers and infiltrators, provocations, raids, and forced confessions, all of which contributed to the R-Group's dissolution. By the beginning of 1942, it was replaced by two groups that gradually assumed the leadership of the Civilian Resistance: the Co-ordination Committee (KK) and the "Circle" (*Kretsen*).[40]

One of the principal responsibilities of the KK was the issuance of *paroles,* that is, secret directives that called for a unified attitude in a concrete, operational situation. The parole created the feeling of solidarity essential for the civil struggle. It weakened the most important weapon of the Nazi terror, namely, the isolation of the individual and the dread of standing all alone. The paroles produced a renewed vigor that led to the development of a nationwide underground network at all levels of society. Representatives were selected in the various towns and villages, and a courier system was created so that a joint united front could be established. The KK was formed as an organ of cooperation where the action committees informed each other of Nazi moves and discussed the effects of a directive for the Home Front as a whole before giving it its final wording and sending it out. Meetings were held either weekly or at two-week intervals, usually in the homes of the individual participants.

The principal role of the Circle was to maintain contact with the Norwegian government in London and to resolve misunderstandings and disagreements between factions within the Home Front. It worked in close cooperation with the KK, and served as the executive power for the organizations in their now-clandestine struggle. Yet before it could hope to succeed, it would need the support of a majority of the population. That support was provided when the forces of nazification struck at the very roots of Norwegian life and culture.

The Ideological War—the Church Front

When the authorities permit acts of violence and
injustice, and exert pressure on our souls, then
the Church becomes the defender of the people's
conscience. One single human soul is worth more
than the entire world.
—*Pastoral Letter of February 1941, Bishops of the Church of Norway*

The Germans were not content to maintain control over the external conduct and affairs of their subjugated Nordic neighbor. They viewed the Norwegians—except for the few who had Jewish blood in their veins—as akin to the *Herrenvolk*, the Master Race, and worthy of assimilation into it. With a total lack of psychological perception, the Germans were determined to gain mastery over the hearts, minds, and convictions of the Norwegian people, especially the youth, in order to mold and redirect them toward the goals of National Socialism. Nazism, like Christianity, demands the whole of an individual. It is not simply a political movement, but also a religion. An ersatz religion to be sure, which in spite of its nihilistic lack of principle, has a firm core in its paganistic worship of power.[1] And since the Christian church is the repository of moral values and ethical standards so alien to Nazi ideology, it was readily understandable that the church was also targeted to play a role in the New Order.

In Germany throughout the 1930s, the resistance to nazification by the churches came from a minority of pastors and an even smaller number of worshipers.[2] Not many Germans lost much sleep over the quarreling of the various Protestant sects or over the arrest of a few thousand pastors and priests. What really impressed them were the glittering successes of the Fuehrer in ending unemployment, creating prosperity, and restoring Germany's military might.[3]

Not so in Norway. After Terboven had "deposed" the King and government and dissolved all political parties except the *Nasjonal Samling*, church leaders quickly recognized that nazification involved a complete revolution and that the church would not be immune to attack. On October 28, all of the various Christian congregations set their factional differences aside to form a "Joint Christian Council for Deliberation" to declare their faith in Christian unity and their determination to defend their beliefs.[4] The declaration was significant because it laid the foundation for a common church front, a militant catalyst, and a rallying point that retained the support of the overwhelming majority of the people. Religious convictions were deeply imbued in the hearts of the Norwegian men and women, and any attempt to eradicate them would be met with defiance. These feelings were well-expressed by the Evangelical Lutheran Church's primate, Bishop Eivind Berggrav, who, with deep-seated and unfailing patriotism, called for a strong united front.

> *God's kingdom in our country, that is the country's future. God made us Norwegian just as he gave you and me our own special peculiarities, our own special dispositions. It is in your soul that God meets you. He will not put you in uniform and destroy your individuality. He will save you and liberate you. Thus is Norway created by Him, and thus will He save Norway and make the Norwegians a medium for His song of open-heartedness the world over. We stand together now. All Christians in this land are now facing in the same direction: help comes from God.*[5]

Ragnar Skancke, the Nazi Minister of Church and Education, realizing that an open attack upon the church was sure to create an explosive reaction, acted slowly. The first challenge from the Nazis came in the form of a request that the intercession for the King, Parliament, and government be removed from church prayer in radio broadcasts. This was an attempt to gain control of all religious programming for the purpose of using the church as a vehicle for Nazi propaganda. Since the church leaders did not find it propitious to lock horns with the state authorities over the prayer issue—they could afford to wait—reluctantly they agreed after Skancke dropped his demand for the substitution of a prayer sympathetic to the NS regime.[6] Nevertheless, the omission of the King's name from the radio services had the psychological effect of attracting the thoughts and prayers of the people more strongly than ever to their revered monarch.

Hostility increased, however, when Jonas Lie issued a decree abolishing the clergy's Oath of Silence, whereby any clergyman who refused to divulge a matter heard in strict confidence when called upon to do so by the police was threatened with imprisonment.[7] According to church law, whatever was disclosed with the assurance of privacy between a priest and parishioner was a sacred trust and inviolable by anyone, most of all by secular authorities. To violate this "Magna Carta of Conscience" was to strike at that which was most hallowed in the church. The bishops could no longer stand quietly by in the face of a state authority that not only used force to obtain compliance with unjust civil laws, but was allowed to attack the divine authority of the church. The time for waiting was over.

The church offensive began on January 15, 1941, when the Norwegian bishops sent a letter of protest to Skancke in which they indicted the NS for supporting violence and for its contempt for the fundamental principles of law and justice. The letter spoke for full religious freedom. The bishops made particular reference to specific cases of systematic violence practiced by the *Hird*, whose brutalities were as severe as those of the Gestapo; the forced resignation of the Supreme Court because the freedom of the courts was abolished; and the abrogation of the sacred Oath of Silence. The letter emphasized that the violence perpetrated by the *Hird* was creating a spirit of hate among the people, especially among the youth. If such things continued systematically, the church would no longer feel that it had any basis for guiding the conscience of the people insofar as respect and confidence in the law of the land were concerned.[8]

Several days later, Skancke replied to the bishops' letter. He contended that the NS stood for order, justice, and peace, and that the alleged incidents of violence would be investigated. (They never were.) In regard to the Oath of Silence, Skancke claimed that the oath had never been absolute and that the growing unrest in the country justified its repeal.

When the bishops received Skancke's unsatisfactory reply, they sent a pastoral letter along with the Nazi minister's response, to all the congregations. In their condemnation of the NS regime, the bishops demanded that the state accept its obligations to administer justice impartially and effectively. Concerning the unrest and anxiety that were becoming more and more evident, they asked: *"Can the Church sit quietly on the sidelines while the Commandments of God are being set aside and while many other events are taking place which dissolve law and order?"* The 50,000 copies of the pastoral letter that were circulated clearly expressed the voice of the church and were endorsed by all of the Christian denominations in Norway.

When Nazi authorities discovered that the pastoral letter was being distributed throughout the country, they ordered the police to confiscate all copies. And although they succeeded in obtaining about 20,000 copies by raiding the printing plants, the Norwegians were able to covertly reproduce "illegal" editions on stencils and pass them to neighbors and friends. Moreover, despite an order forbidding the letter to be publicly read in the churches, many clergymen nevertheless read it out loud to their congregations.[10] Public opinion had been mobilized and resistance to nazification was growing stronger and stronger.

In early March, Skancke made yet another effort to control all religious broadcasts by placing all radio programming in the hands of the Propaganda Department of Culture. A special office was set up to censor any religious material that did not conform to the "new spirit." This action alienated more than 99 percent of the Norwegian people. The result was a very effective boycott of the Nazi-controlled Oslo radio by the clergy in which all ministers participated, except for the few Nazi clergymen. And when the Nazi Department of Church and Education ordered the clergy to confine all preaching to "purely eternal and constructive aspects of the Gospel," they flatly refused. They rightly interpreted the Nazi order to mean that the church was being told to withdraw from the unpleasant realities of life and to disappear into the distant world of theological enlightenment. But the church could not practice political neutrality where conscience was in any way concerned.[11]

In June 1941, when Hitler attacked the Soviet Union, the NS regime saw this as an opportunity to demand from the church a proclamation to the Norwegian people to support a "holy war" against godless Bolshevism. Patriotic church leaders recognized the Nazi "crusade" as a deceptive scheme to distract the Norwegian people from their oppressors and thus entice them to support Germany in its war with Russia. This proclamation was refused collectively by the bishops at an episcopal meeting in Oslo. In their reply, the church leaders declared that the NS demand "represented an unpermissible and dangerous mixture of religion and politics . . . that the Norwegian people were at war, and that the appeal would, under present conditions, only serve to incite civil war."[12]

The Nazi press was quick to respond to the bishops' rejection. After suffering the humiliation of the 43 organizations' protest just one month earlier, *Fritt Folk* waged a major campaign against the bishops. Bishop Berggrav was the target of a series of attacks in which he was accused of supporting the forces of Bolshevism. Yet despite the numerous diatribes leveled against the church, its leaders remained firm and unshakable, realizing that compromise would be tantamount to surrender.

Nevertheless, the Nazis continued to draw the church into the political arena and the crisis continued. The small number of Nazi preachers made every effort to persuade the people, even using the Bible as a propaganda tool. One such preacher used the passage describing Christ's cure of the 10 lepers to suggest that the present-day lepers were those who suffered from "English sickness." He then asked his listeners whether they had thanked God for sending the Germans to save them from this leprosy; and for sending them Quisling, who saw the "treachery" of the King and government, and sacrificed his health for the well-being of the Norwegian people. Finally, he asked his listeners whether they thanked God for the fact that Norwegian boys were found who were moved by a "spiritual impulse" to sacrifice their lives to save their people from Russian godlessness.[13] Sermons such as this only served to increase the widening gap between the church and the NS regime. The atmosphere became so tense that a crisis could be expected at any moment. That crisis was not long in coming.

On February 1, 1942, the Norwegian flag was raised over Akershus Castle (a seventeenth century historical site overlooking the old Oslo harbor) and the Parliament building in Oslo to proclaim that Norway, once again, had its own government. But the occasion was not one for Norwegian rejoicing. For on that day, Vidkun Quisling was proclaimed minister-president of Norway. This sudden elevation of the arch-traitor from relative obscurity was attributable to several factors. Despite the humiliation two years earlier when the Germans removed him from power, Quisling remained committed to increasing the ranks of the *Nasjonal Samling* Party, which, by January 1942, had reached a membership of nearly 40,000. Furthermore, he had the backing of his long-time friend, Alfred Rosenberg, who was able to persuade Hitler that the Norwegian Fuehrer not only supported the German war effort in its struggle against Bolshevism, but would, if granted the authority, mobilize Norwegian men for that purpose.[14] Hitler agreed, recognizing this as an opportunity to facilitate the incorporation of Norway into the Greater Germanic World State. Thus, by the approval of the Supreme Court, which was now packed with NS justices, the so-called Act of State elevating Quisling to the office of minister-president was declared constitutional.

While the ceremony at Akershus Castle was taking place with great flourish, another event, equally significant, was occurring at almost the same hour in the city of Trondheim at the famous Nidaros Cathedral. The highly respected Dean Arne Fjellbu, known for his condemnation of NS policies, had earlier been instructed by the Nazi Minister of Church and Education to open the cathedral that morning to one of its own ministers in order to celebrate the "Act of State at Akershus" at 11:00 a.m. The dean reluctantly postponed his own church services until 2:00 p.m., at which time over 1,500 churchgoers and practically every preacher in the Trondheim area arrived before the Nazi police were able to bar the huge assembly outside from entering. The massive crowd, without any evidence of unruliness and despite the brutally cold winter weather, remained outside singing religious and patriotic songs until a bishop came out to ask the crowd to leave without incident. When the clergy protested, declaring that the police had violated the law by interfering with freedom of the church in preventing congregation members from attending services, Skancke simply replied that the service constituted a demonstration against the Quisling Political Party.

Less than a week after assuming his new office, Quisling issued two decrees, which struck at the very core of Norwegian life: the family. The first pronouncement stipulated that all children between the ages of 10 and 18 years must be enrolled in the *Ungdomsfylking*, the Norwegian model of the Hitler *Jugendsamband*—Youth Service Association. The children would be required to "do service" in the organization. The law did not specify the nature of the work, however, or when or where the service would be performed. Presumably, Quisling's intention was to make the law appear somewhat harmless, so as not to incur the wrath of parents. But he miscalculated. Parents became infuriated at the prospect of their children being taken from home and remolded in the Nazi pattern.

Just two days later, a second decree was issued that was equally acrimonious. All teachers were now required to join the *Laerersamband,* the new Nazi Teachers Association whereby they would be compelled to readjust their teaching to conform with Nazi ideology. Those who refused membership would be dismissed and sent to labor camps in northern Norway or elsewhere.[15]

The bishops, already angered by the events at Trondheim, assembled at Oslo on February 14 and responded immediately to the new decrees in a letter to Skancke:

> *The basic relationship between parents and children is a dispensation of the Creator, a God-stressed relationship which prevails inviolable and sacred for all homes.*
>
> *The responsibility and the right which therein are given to the home, are therefore unconditional and indissoluble. At the baptism of a child the responsibility for the bringing up of the child is placed upon the parents. The children's school is a mutually arranged means of aid in this upbringing and the first paragraph of the school law states that the school's purpose is to assist in giving the children a Christian and moral education.*
>
> *The homes and the church have therefore also a right to share in determining the policies of the school, and the parents have in certain circumstances a right to take their children out of school. The school has no authority against the baptismal obligations nor against the Fourth Commandment.*
>
> *Every father and mother also holds full responsibility for how they have permitted others to take part in forming their children's character, faith and conviction. This conscientious responsibility places not only a duty on the parents, but also gives them an inviolable right.*

In the same way, the Fourth Commandment, "honor thy father and thy mother," is for the children not alone a duty, but a right given them by God. A good home's inner freedom has always been a foundation pillar in our society and no one can by force break into a home and create antagonism between parents and children without God's commandment being trampled under foot.

In all this, the church and the parents stand inseparably bound by their conscience and by God's command. He who would attempt to force the children out of the parents' bonds of responsibility and to disrupt the Divine right of the home, would at the same time be forcing the parents to the utmost act of conscience. Every father and mother knows that they one time will stand answerable to the Almighty for how they have brought up or let others bring up their children. Here they must obey God more than man.[16]

Minister Skancke's response to the bishops' letter attempted to justify the Quisling position by arguing that "obedience due to civil authority is all embraced in the estate of fatherhood and extends beyond all other relations. . . . As the highest authority of a people, the State has the greatest responsibility for, and the greatest right over, every single citizen"[17] In other words, the state is supreme.

The affair at Trondheim Cathedral, coupled with the two recent nazification decrees, were too much for the bishops to bear. They would continue to preach the Word of God and attend to the spiritual needs of their congregations, but to continue administrative cooperation with the Nazi Department of Church and Education would be a betrayal of a most sacred trust and a surrender of the church's rights to the state's injustice. Thus, on February 24, 1942, the bishops submitted their resignations to Minister Skancke. Quisling reacted immediately by forbidding them to perform their spiritual functions, removing them from their bishoprics, and ordering them to report daily to the police.

Several days later, Quisling summoned Primate Bishop Berggrav to his office where he tried to extract a confession from him admitting that the Bishop and Paal Berg, Chief Justice of the Supreme Court, were chiefly responsible for overthrowing the first Quisling government following the arrival of the Germans in April 1940. In fact, it was the Germans themselves who lacked confidence in Quisling and who wanted him removed. Berggrav simply collaborated in the formation of the Administrative Council that replaced the short-lived NS regime. The Bishop, therefore, refused to confess to this false accusation of "illegal" political activity. Quisling, realizing that the bishop could not be prosecuted on purely political grounds, merely shouted, "You deserve to have your head chopped off." "Well, here I am," answered the Bishop.[18] Quisling stripped the Bishop of his title to office and confined him to house arrest at his summer cottage near Oslo. There he remained from April 1942 until April 1945, when he was freed by members of the Resistance. He then went into hiding until the day of liberation less than a month later.

In the wake of the Bishops' resignations, members of the clergy were exposed to numerous forms of maltreatment: police interrogations and hearings, dismissals without explanation, censoring of sermons, NS members spying upon preachers and reporting conversations, arrests, confiscation of property, threats of deportation, and even threats of the death penalty.[19] Thus on Easter morning 1942, more than 90 percent of the nation's 1,200 pastors and clergymen, in a united action, resigned their offices.

An embittered Quisling reacted by asserting that the resignations by the preachers were unconstitutional and a strike against the government. Yet, despite the harsh realities to which they were subjected, the churchmen remained steadfast in their determination to preach the Word of God. As reports of abuse and incarceration spread, the people's bitterness intensified. The Quisling government was deluged with petitions from all parts of the country demanding that the persecutions be stopped. The protests were too numerous to be ignored; and when a compromise was attempted, the church unanimously rejected it. As the collective conscience of the nation, the church continued to protest against the intrusion by Nazi authorities upon itself, the schools, parents, and children.

In June 1942, the church issued a Free Church Manifesto establishing a Temporary Church Leadership that would function in spite of the dismissals and other usurpations by the state. The manifesto listed the circumstances and events which led up to the final break with the

Nazi Church Ministry; stressed continued opposition to the government's interference and aggression against the church and other social organizations; and urged pastors and ministers to continue their proper functions in collaboration with the rightful bishops of the church.[20]

Uncertain as to what action to take against the inflexible church leaders, Quisling consulted with Skrancke and the Minister of Domestic Affairs, after which he announced the dissolution of the Temporary Church Leadership. Nevertheless, the church continued to function. In desperation, Quisling turned to Hitler, who simply told him to leave the church alone.[21] Presumably aware that no amount of pressure would force the church to submit to the New Order, the Fuehrer did not wish to encourage additional provocations that would further antagonize the unshakeable Norwegian people. Always fearful of an Allied invasion of Norway, he was concerned with maintaining order and stability so that additional troops would not be required to step in. Although the personal abuse, arrests, imprisonment, prohibitions, and confiscation of property continued almost until the end of the war, the church, in crisis after crisis, never wavered in its determination to thwart the nazification efforts of the German and NS authorities.

The Ideological War on the School Front

There comes a time when force attempts to subdue the mind.
It is then that the true humanist recognizes his role. Refusing to give in
he opposes brute strength with another, invincible power: that of the spirit.
—André Gide (1869-1951), French author and critic

It was not purely by chance that the schools and the church were united in the ideological struggle against the Germans and their NS collaborators at one and the same time. In Norway, the two institutions have always had a close relationship—the schools were church schools—and were regarded as the pillars of Norwegian society. Thus it should have come as no surprise to the German and NS authorities that the schools would be as zealous as the church in resisting the pernicious influence of Nazism. Nevertheless, with a naïve lack of psychological perception, the Nazis tried to impose their *Kultur* upon what they expected to be a more impressionable younger generation. The Norwegian youth, however, were as contemptuous of the new rulers as were their elders. With few exceptions, the youngsters were openly fearless and defiant of the Germans and their Norwegian collaborators. Even the younger children created various symbols, insignias, and gestures to demonstrate their loyalty to the King and their revulsion of Nazism. They would frequently jeer the soldiers or turn their backs on a German patrol marching down the main street of a Norwegian town. Those children who sympathized with the Nazis, either because of parental influence or by their own choice, were ostracized by their more patriotic peers and sometimes beaten.[1]

During the first month of the occupation, the Germans requisitioned the school buildings as barracks for German soldiers and later, after Hitler invaded Russia, took over additional buildings to be used as hospitals to handle wounded German soldiers returning from the Eastern Front. The shortage of school buildings forced the students in the majority of cases to attend classes in private homes; and in some communities, youngsters attended classes in shifts or in buildings in outlying areas.[2] When classes resumed in the fall of 1940, the NS radically reorganized the schools. The Central Advisory Board and the local school boards were abolished and replaced by NS school inspectors whose job it was to investigate the operations of the various educational institutions. In October, when the teachers were requested to sign a pledge to work for the New Order and counteract all efforts by pupils, parents, or others to oppose it, the five teachers' organizations responded: "I hereby declare that I will remain true to my teaching vocation and to my conscience and that I will carry on my work following those instructions rightly given me by my superiors."[3]

In February 1941, the new Nazi curriculum was introduced into the schools, and all textbooks were revised and purged of all material that varied from the New Order. And in May, an order was issued that German was to replace English as the nation's second language. Consequently, all English language books were replaced by German texts. In the field of religious instruction, a Nazi catechism was introduced. Its explanation of the Fourth Commandment is typical of the "new mentality."

"If Norway is to become a good home, everyone must know his responsibility. Consideration for the nation must be put before all other considerations. Social interest must have preference to self-interest. But above all, we are obliged to show obedience to the Fuehrer and the administration. To oppose the authorities and the State is to oppose the order of God, and this leads to punishment."[4] Although the primer was endorsed by Minister Skancke, the bishops did not approve it and the text was not used in the schools.

In November and December, the school inspectors introduced two new regulations. One stipulated that it was the teacher's duty to devote time to instructing the students in understanding the New Order; and the second ordered that two recently published books be made the basis of a study of Nazism. Additionally, a picture of Quisling and a *Nasjonal Samling* poster were to be displayed on a wall in all of the schools, and teachers were expected to read *Fritt Folk*, the official NS newspaper.

Yet all of these attempts to draw the teachers and students into the nazification program came to naught. Members of Norway's five teachers' organizations distributed circulars among the teachers themselves urging them to stand fast and to remain loyal to their country and true to their profession by refusing to sign any pledge that promoted Nazism. The teachers were urged to "Remain firm. . . . Remember that if we stick together, we are invulnerable. Whoever fails will suffer a stigma for life. Our honor and conscience are not for sale, and they are indispensable in our work for Norwegian youth. Another day will follow this one, and then any weakness of character will be regretted."[5] Contempt for Quisling was often shown by refusing to display his picture in the hall or classroom; and when the NS school inspector entered the room, the youngsters would frequently show their disdain by singing patriotic songs.

Unrest was heightened further when the Nazis staged an elaborate Hitler Youth Exhibition in Oslo in preparation for the introduction of a Nazi Youth Movement in Norway. When high school students refused to attend the exhibition voluntarily, Nazi authorities ordered them to march there in classes with their teachers. Some classes marched through the Exhibition Hall with lowered heads, but the vast majority boycotted the exhibition. Many of the students, including young children, marched up to the Royal Palace and shouted, "Long live King Haakon," and sang other patriotic songs.

Members of the *Hird* retaliated by breaking into the schools and beating up teachers and even young children. These attacks on the school front were interrupted by school strikes in Oslo supported by teachers, parents, and children. Strikes were also declared in Bergen, Trondheim, and other towns.[6] The rectors of the schools agreed to end the strikes after the Germans threatened to use the schools as barracks (those that had not already been requisitioned), but also on condition that parents would not be required to sign a declaration of loyalty to the Quisling authorities on behalf of the students. The authorities agreed, and the schools were reopened without any compromise by either the parents or the students.[7]

The real test of wills for the teachers began in February 1942, after Quisling demanded compulsory membership in the *Laerersamband*—the Nazi Teachers' Association—which required all teaching to be brought into conformity with Nazi ideology. In Germany, this had succeeded far beyond the Nazis' wildest expectations in the creation of a new type of human personality. This personality held a Nordic mythological pre-Christian view of life, believed in an Aryan master race, was filled with racial hatred for non-Aryans, worshipped the Leader, and carried out the duty of informing on relatives, neighbors, and friends.

Under no circumstances could the teachers countenance such a prospect in their own country. Less than three weeks after the Quisling decree, the NS Department of Education was flooded with thousands of letters of protest from the Norwegian teachers. In March, letters from between 100 and 200 parents poured into the department in support of the Teacher Front.[8] Within two months, approximately 90 percent of Norway's 14,000 teachers resigned from the *Laerersamband,* making it ineffectual.[9]

Nevertheless, the teachers paid dearly for their refusal to comply with the new directive. On March 20, more than 1,100—one in every 10—were arrested and pressured to retract their protest.[10] Many were confined at the Grini concentration camp near Oslo, and a large number were sent to the Arctic in North Norway. Unaccustomed to the hard labor and brutal treatment to which they were subjected, many suffered from exhaustion and numerous indignities from which there was no relief.

Seven hundred arrested teachers from eastern Norway and around Bergen were transported to a military training ground near Lillehammer after a grueling 14-hour train ride in open coal cars without food. The teachers were ordered out in the middle of the night 10 miles from their destination and made to march the rest of the way. Those who collapsed were whipped or kicked up and ordered to proceed. After reaching the training ground, they were given a slice of bread for breakfast and then put through a series of exhausting physical exercises, drills, and marches. Those who lagged behind or hesitated were made to crawl on their stomachs through ice, water, snow, and slush with hands tied behind their backs. Some were given the task of carrying snow on a table fork or on a broom handle, scrubbing an article with their bare hands, or moving wood piles back and forth. All of this to break the spirit of the group.[11]

A few gave in when the situation became unbearable. These were principally widowers and those with sick wives and responsibility for small children. But the great majority remained firm. Nowhere was the refusal to yield more eloquently expressed than in the following scene at one camp, which must have served as a powerful inspiration to others.

The prisoners were all paraded outside the barracks occupied by the Germans in charge of the camp. The first man to be called in to sign the statement of apology was a sickly, rather elderly teacher who had sole responsibility for a flock of children. The others had let him know that there would be no reproaches if he signed. He dragged himself up the steps in an obvious state of collapse, which was painful to watch. Two or three minutes passed, and then he came out on to the platform at the top of the steps a completely new man. Standing in front of all 600 men, he clenched his fists and shouted: "I bloody well didn't sign!" Then he went back to his place, and after that it was not easy for anyone else to give way.[12]

On April 12, 1942, 500 of the arrested teachers who refused to sign retractions at the camp were herded into cattle trucks and sent to Trondheim. There they were packed in the cargo holds of an old coastal steamer, the *Skaerstad*, built in 1904 and designed to carry no more than 250 men. They were sent 1,600 miles north to Kirkenes in Finnmark near the Russian border. For many, the voyage was more than flesh and blood could bear. There were no sleeping quarters, practically no light, no fresh air, and only two toilets. The food allotted, which consisted of a dab of butter, a loaf of bread, and some coffee every third day, was scarcely enough to keep a person alive. Numerous forms of illness broke out: pneumonia, prison psychosis (a form of insanity), stomach ulcers, asthma, bronchitis, malaria, and dysentery. Although the only doctor on board was a member of the NS, conditions were so awful that he joined the teachers in protesting the inhumane conditions and beastly treatment of the prisoners.[13]

Besides the German maltreatment, there was the risk of being sunk by Allied torpedoes or mines, a constant fear. When the vessel reached Kirkenes, the teachers were ordered to perform heavy manual labor on German military projects, loading and unloading ships and digging trenches on practically a starvation diet. Inside barbed-wire fences, the majority were housed in a cold, leaky stable with an earthen floor and subjected to such intolerable living conditions that many died. Those who survived, however, were unyielding.

A few reports smuggled out of Kirkenes and into Oslo were communicated to the Norwegian Legation in Stockholm, which disclosed to the world at large the appalling conditions and unspeakable treatment to which the teachers were subjected. In Norway, despite the ban on demonstrations, an incensed citizenry staged protests throughout the land, which led to a strengthening of morale at a time when a renewed spirit and sense of dedication to the cause of liberty were desperately needed.

This was most notably exemplified when local subcommittees and communication networks suddenly arranged for financial assistance for some 10,000 protesting teachers, whose salaries were withheld in March and April 1942. The families of incarcerated teachers were also provided for, particularly those in Kirkenes who were not released until the following November. Most of the money came from the government-in-exile in London, which sent several millions kroner to the Home Front. The Resistance also collected funds from private individuals, mostly in Oslo. Those teachers who were receiving an income voluntarily set aside 2 and later 5 percent of their salaries for a common fund.[14] And when those who were still fence-straddling were told of the courageous stand taken by the teachers, it became increasingly difficult to remain uncommitted.

Clearly, the voyage to Kirkenes resulted in a victory for the people of Norway, albeit at an exceptionally high cost. If the well-planned protest by the teachers had failed, the Civilian Resistance might easily have been in jeopardy. In fact, it provided the inspirational stimulus to the Norwegian people in a most critical period of the Occupation. In those first six months of 1942, both Germany and Japan were victorious throughout all of continental Europe and the Far East respectively, and the Allies suffered one defeat after another. Liberation of the occupied countries seemed a remote possibility, and the morale of the subjugated peoples was at an all-time low. Thus, it was nothing less than remarkable that the teachers at this juncture could inflict such an unconditional ideological defeat upon Nazism in Norway. *There can be no doubt that the Nazi attempts at mobilizing Norwegian children for purposes of nazification more than anything else solidified the Home Front.*

After two-and-one-half months of humiliation, forced resignations, loss of pay, torture, and other forms of maltreatment, it was obvious to the authorities that nothing was going to break the solidarity of the teachers. On April 25, 1942, the decree ordering the dismissal of teachers refusing to join the Nazi Teachers Association was repealed. In May, the schools were reopened and the teachers were gradually released from prison. Teaching was still fraught with difficulty, however, and conditions worsened as the war worsened for the Germans. Although teachers were no longer required to be members in the association before they were allowed to teach, lists were kept of those who attempted to influence others against the New Order and those who refused to return to work. This created a shortage of teachers, even though Nazi teachers, who were totally unfit for their jobs, filled some vacancies. And with few exceptions, the vast majority of Norwegian parents refused to permit their children to attend a school taught by a Nazi regardless of whether he or she was German or Norwegian. Consequently, classes were held in private homes. And when teachers were arrested and imprisoned, ministers would sometimes take over the instruction.

Similarly, the Quisling Youth Service Association was repudiated by all patriotic Norwegians, who recognized it as a subterfuge for enlisting boys in the army to fight for Germany on the Eastern Front. The Underground saw it as a breeding ground for children to be trained as spies in their own homes, and called on parents to be particularly vigilant. Despite threats, arrests, and bribes, the Germans met with little success in attracting adherents into the Nazi movement and concluded that it was not worth enforcing. Never before had parents, students, teachers, and churchmen been so closely bound in a common cause as they were during the Occupation.

The German determination to infuse Nazi philosophy into the minds of the youth was not confined to the elementary and secondary schools. It extended to and cut deepest at the university level. From the very outset of the Occupation, the feeling of the vast majority of students was collectively expressed by the University Student Association in a pledge to oppose nazification whatever the cost. Nevertheless, in the autumn of 1941, threats were made against several professors who had signed the protest of the 43 organizations the previous May. And during the State of Emergency when Terboven let loose the six-day wave of terror, the rector of Oslo University and three professors who were not sympathetic to the NS Party were dismissed and replaced by NS members.[15] But when the Nazi candidate for president of the Student Association received only 11 votes, it was obvious to the authorities that Nazism would have no place in the university curriculum. In retaliation, the acting minister for the Department of Church and Education, Ragnar Skancke, announced that the students' special committee was no longer to be elected, but rather a new committee was to be nominated by the department.[16]

Early in 1942, a secret action committee was formed among the teachers and students, and a key question was whether the university should be closed. The Germans and NS wanted to keep it open and run it according to their own dictates. For many, the reign of terror and particularly the death sentences that were carried out during the State of Emergency the previous September were a recurring reminder that the same fate awaited those who challenged the Nazi rulers. To know how far actions could be carried out without provoking reactions from the enemy was a difficult problem, which the Resistance leaders had to face throughout the Occupation. Although many of the students were chiefly concerned with completing their studies, others were engaged in illegal resistance and intelligence gathering and needed the university as a base; still others were interested in publishing illegal newspapers within the university to make clear that institution's stand against nazification. The school remained open.

In the autumn of 1943, when the NS Department of Education issued a regulation that 25 percent of students were to be admitted on criteria other than their grades, it was obvious what was meant by "other criteria." Furthermore, when a new admissions regulation was announced that no association, club, or assemblage except the NS would be tolerated and that no one outside that body would receive aid or scholarships, 3,000 students voiced bitter opposition. The various school faculties categorically rejected the proposed regulation and created a line of resistance that placed the university alongside the Supreme Court, the church, and the parents and teachers.

Then came the real crisis. On November 28, 1943, a fire was set in the university auditorium. Some leaders in the Home Front believed that it was a Nazi provocation: a Norwegian "*Reichstag* fire." Regardless,

Terboven used the incident to inflict a direct blow against the students. Two days later, the Gestapo, with the aid of 300 SS detachments, closed in on all the male students. Throughout the day and the following evening, German police on motorcycles and in cars rounded up students at control points in the center of Oslo and apprehended them where they lived. Altogether more than 1,100 students were arrested. About half were subsequently released, however, while the remaining number, about 700, were sent to a "retraining camp" in Germany.[17]

Besides the University of Oslo, other institutions of higher learning were targeted for nazification, but were no less resistant in their struggles to remain free and independent. When the rector of the Oslo dental college was dismissed and replaced by a man totally unqualified for the job, the entire faculty resigned, as did those of the School of Pharmacy after the requirement was made that 25 percent of the student body must be members of the *Nasjonal Samling*.[18] The conduct of the educators was most eloquently expressed by Dr. Didrik Seip, President of Oslo University, who, after his release from a German concentration camp at the end of the Occupation, had this to say:

> *A dictator can close universities, but he cannot put out the light of reason, he cannot obscure the clarity of thought, and he cannot halt the drive to desire that which is right. Today our hearts are filled with happiness and thanksgiving that our university has carried on through want and slavery to a free status in a free land and that it can continue unhindered to work out the tasks which await it.*[19]

The Struggle for a Free Press

What gunpowder did for war,
the printing press has done for the mind.
—*Wendell Phillips (1811-1884), American reformer, abolitionist, & orator*

The fight against nazification was not started or directed by any central command. The spirit of resistance that emerged in this small Scandinavian kingdom manifested itself in defiance, self-sacrifice, and high-minded idealism that developed at various levels and on many fronts. People from all walks of life and locales, young and old alike, endeavored to withstand the pressure of Occupation both individually and collectively. Yet for many, if life was to be bearable, one needed confirmation of one's secret hopes. Thus it became necessary to listen to everything that was forbidden. For an increasing number of Norwegians, it was vital that they receive secret encouragement and disregard the publicly controlled press—a press, moreover, that on the day following the invasion, printed such headlines as "Germany Takes Norway Under Her Protection," or "The German Entry Is an Answer to England's Mine Fields."

Under normal conditions, newspapers were certainly read, and to a great extent believed. But censorship completely destroyed its credibility as far as news and commentaries were concerned. During the first two years of the war—1939-41—while Germany was victorious, the Nazified press could print a stream of triumphant—and often true—war bulletins that the Norwegian people least of all wished to read. It was quite another matter when news from the London BBC sowed doubt concerning the truth of the Germans' officially statements and in its commentaries contradicted the claims and views in the official flood of announcements.[1]

In the fight to shape public opinion, the voice from London cannot be overrated. Unlike the German propaganda apparatus, the BBC was remarkably accurate and largely contributed to lifting up the morale of the ordinary Norwegian from desperation to hope. Every evening behind blackout curtains and closed shutters, families would gather in silence around the radio and, amidst the audio distortion, search for the correct wavelength frequency to receive the muffled, indistinct news from across the North Sea. German efforts to jam the London broadcasts were often successful, but their propaganda had one drawback: Too many Norwegians had the opportunity to observe at close range the disparity between the truth and the German version of it. Thus the Germans and their Quisling collaborators lost their expected influence on public opinion.

Nevertheless, Joseph Goebbels, the German Minister of Propaganda, sought not only to control, but to Nazify the press in Norway. Soon it became clear that the aim was to direct the nation toward the German political way of thinking. Only German-approved items could be mentioned. A National Socialist event would be given prominent space in the newspaper, while other events would be toned down or not mentioned at all. For example, the following directive for one day's news edition handed down from the press department in the *Reichskommisariat* read as follows:

- The visit of Reichsminister von Ribbentrop in Rome will have front-page coverage in tomorrow's newspapers.

- Attention will be drawn to the anniversary of the landing of Japanese troops in Java. The reports must be given special attention.

- The commemoration of the Spanish monarchy will not be published to the Norwegian people.

- Distinct attention will be given to the British article from NTB: "England prays for the Bolsheviks."[2]

Forbidden topics included any criticism of the NS regime or German policy at home or abroad, announcements of German officials arriving in Norway, ship arrivals or departures, rationing, news of the enemy, strikes, weather predictions, national holidays, or any mention of the Nygaardsvold government in London. Religious topics, including the dismissal of bishops and other clergy members, were *verboten;* nor could any obituary be printed of persons executed by the Germans even if the cause of death was withheld. Some editors refrained from printing anything favorable to the *Herrenvolk*. Those editors who treated German successes with brevity or failed to say anything detrimental about Great Britain were severely reprimanded. Those who refused to comply with the daily instructions that came from the Propaganda Ministry were immediately arrested and removed.

As early as August 1940, the number of independent newspapers steadily decreased. The Germans stopped some, while many editors decided to halt publication voluntarily instead of allowing their papers to be used as mouthpieces for the Germans. When the regime halted a publication, it was often blamed on a shortage of paper, but more likely it was a punishment for failure to follow a directive. The principal Labor newspaper, *Arbeiderbladet* (Workers Blade), was terminated by the German security police after it published a political report critical of Quisling. The editor was arrested and the premises were taken over by the NS Party paper, *Fritt Folk*. [3]

During the first year of the Occupation, as the war situation worsened for the Allies, newspaper editors frequently found themselves in an ambivalent position. On the one hand, they were required to publish what the German authorities told them to print, whereas the Norwegian public expected them to publish news of the Resistance. Even though the papers were censored, at times it was evaded by placing stenciled pamphlets inside the various newspapers. In the town of Alesund, for example, the local paper reported that NS Minister of Justice Sverre Riisnaes was coming to give a speech and that people were encouraged to attend. At the same time, a conflicting bulletin was inserted in the paper. The result was that no one appeared for the event. Seven people at the newspaper lost their jobs as a consequence. [4] As German censorship became more extensive, the need for a free, unbiased distribution of news grew. Consequently, a broad spectrum of men and women, mostly on their own initiative, pooled their resources to set up their own news organizations.

Contrary to what one might expect, the people who published the clandestine newspapers were mainly inexperienced in the newspaper business. [5] This was obvious by the poor literary quality of the newspapers. Many of those involved in gathering, publishing, and distributing the news had families to support, and since much of the clandestine news work was performed at night, it was possible to work at a full-time job during daylight hours. And unlike the far more dangerous sabotage activity that oftentimes led to severe reprisals, in which the innocent victims would be inhabitants of the town, the illegal press did not ordinarily run that risk. Nevertheless, some were involved in other areas of the Resistance that involved considerable risk. One outstanding example was Max Manus, one of the most highly decorated members of the Resistance. He not only helped organize one of the earliest illegal papers in the country, but was one of the most wanted saboteurs in all of Norway for causing widespread damage to, among other things, German shipping and harbor installations.

The first illegal newspapers were established in the summer of 1940. (The term "illegal" refers to those publications in conflict with the German directives, not with Norwegian law, and is synonymous with the term "free" press.) At first, in the larger cities such as Oslo and Bergen, copies of small bulletins were distributed separately from the publicly controlled press and passed from hand to hand or circulated like chain letters.

One distinguished observer expressed it this way:

> *On one side was a gigantic propaganda machine, which controlled the press and radio, with millions at its disposal and free access to every imaginable form of pressure and propaganda, such as meetings, parades, concerts, sports rallies, flag waving, symbols, and banners with golden promises—all with the guarantee of power behind them. On the other side were small, persecuted groups, anxious meetings, small sums of money scraped together, and, at least in the beginning, insignificant leaflets challenging the massive mesmerism. The legal and favored was bankrupt, the forbidden triumphant. Legal newspapers could tell readers where one could buy second-hand children's clothes, but the little duplicated leaflet that was pressed into one's hand at a workplace was the true message, which could be believed absolutely.*[6]

Soon the leaflets and pamphlets were replaced by stenciled sheets, numbering in the hundreds, and in some cases, in the thousands. These anonymous, hastily written papers were the beginning of a growing trend within the Resistance.[7] An accurate estimate of the number of illegal newspapers published in Norway during the war is not known. Figures have varied from 250 to 500. Between August and October 1941 alone, as many as 75 papers were established throughout the country.[8] The newspapers never concealed their sources of information. In fact, many publications were named after their source. For example, there was *The London Radio, The BBC Report, Eight-Thirty,* and *Radio News.* Most of these radio-newspapers were established after the order was later given to impound the radios. Thus, the two sources of news were mutually dependent on each other.

The Resistance Movement, as mentioned, was needed to provide an alternative society that could function over a long period of time with its own code of conduct. As the predominant form of non-violent resistance activity, the illegal press saw the formation of public opinion as its most important responsibility. Thus, besides the radio transmissions from abroad, people began to realize the importance of providing the newspapers with additional information concerning circumstances and events within their own country. Information came from secret contacts in municipal government posts and police departments, from tapped telephone and teletype lines, and from the editorial staffs of legal newspapers which leaked news they dare not publish themselves. Slogans and commentary on what was really happening in Norway dominated the first newspapers. One such publication was entitled *Vi vil oss et land* (We want a country). In its first issue, dated October 1940, the editor printed the paper's mission statement:

> First and foremost, we want to prove that the fight for a free Norway continues and will be upheld until we are at last free. Secondly, we want to keep the Norwegian people informed about what is happening in their country. We cannot promise sensational news; we can only distribute the thoughts and opinions that 98 percent of the Norwegian public share. Everyone surely knows the dangers that go with this publication; the number of copies handed out will therefore be limited. We want you all to spread the word and share your copy with your neighbors and friends. . . . The fight for a free Norway will continue, whatever the cost. It boils down to the right to stay alive. We hope that

> *this newspaper will help strengthen your beliefs and we are*
> *convinced that a system based on hate, injustice, and*
> *suppression can never survive. Whether the nights are long*
> *or short, our spirits will show more than ever. The Norway*
> *that we love and cherish will rise once again.*[9]

This newspaper, which existed in both printed and stenciled editions, was so successful that other papers copied from it. Among the themes the paper discussed were Terboven's philippic of September 25, 1940, against the members of Parliament, and General Otto Ruge's farewell speech to his troops at the conclusion of military hostilities in June. It was essential to let the public know that the fight was not over, even though Norway had lost the first battle. The illegal press emphasized that the Norwegian merchant fleet still sailed peacefully under the Norwegian flag.[10] And with the publication of King Haakon's unwavering refusal to the German demand for abdication in the summer of 1940, the circulation of illegal news reached a peak. Not only did the King's defiance lift the spirits of the country, it was seen as a major step toward a more aggressive distribution of illegal newspapers.

After the King's broadcast, the illegal press and the organized Civilian Resistance began working in close collaboration.[11] In November of 1940, an unnamed periodical, later called *The Bulletin*, was published. An internal organ of communication for the leaders of the Resistance as well as the general public, it consisted of speeches and articles from key individuals within the Resistance. Whatever was published in the paper was officially sanctioned by the leaders and therefore considered authoritative.[12] It was extremely important to the Resistance leadership that the press spread directives concerning mass actions and appeals for keeping up the struggle. These directives had to be repeated frequently, as in the following message from the Underground printed in the Kristiansund illegal newspaper, *Avisa*, shows:

> *The Resistance leadership sent out sharpened instructions*
> *concerning guard duty, i.e. the Nazis' use of Norwegian*
> *citizens to stand guard. The Resistance leaders expect that*
> *guard duty will be used in increasing amounts in the*
> *future. The instructions are as they were earlier: No one*
> *must meet for citizens guard duty. These instructions must*
> *be followed regardless of the cost. All battles have their cost*

> *or there would be no battle. We are at war and everyone*
> *must stay at their post, and maintain it. The sabotage*
> *troops in the Resistance have been ordered to show no*
> *respect to those standing guard duty.*[13]

Some of the papers were directed toward specific groups and professional organizations, while others were aimed at a more general readership. Among those in the former category was *Fri Fagbevegelse* (Free Trade Unionism), first published in January 1941. The principal organ for the trade unionists, it was published by Resistance leaders in the labor movement. The writing was decentralized and took place in different trade union offices after hours; printing took place on a duplicator in a private home, and between 400 and 500 copies were run off.[14]

In the autumn of 1941, the Germans ordered the confiscation of all radio receiving sets from the Norwegian citizenry, except those of NS members. The Germans had seized the radios of Jews the previous year. The order had largely resulted from an expanding underground press whose primary source of information came from the Norwegian language bulletins of the BBC. The confiscation was clearly an admission of failure by the Germans in their futile attempt to discourage all contact between the people and the lawful exile government in London. Moreover, it was self-defeating on the part of the Nazi Propaganda Ministry, since it would not only prevent the Norwegians from listening to the BBC, but also prevent them from listening to the Nazi-controlled state radio.

Most of those who owned radios handed them in, but people's strong desire to keep in touch with the "voice from London" prompted many to hand in only the shell of the radio and retain the operating parts. The more ingenious constructed their own receivers. And since possession of a radio was an offense punishable by fines and imprisonment and by death in the following year—a large part of that ingenuity consisted of camouflage and concealment. Receivers were hidden in such ordinary objects as a chopping block, a camera, a business directory, a flat iron, and a sofa leg. Others were cleverly disguised in vacuum thermos bottles, empty varnish cans, and other containers of various shapes and sizes. One innovator converted a record player into a two-tube radio receiver when the turntable was rotated and a headset was attached. Another concealed his radio in a simple birdhouse that hung on an outside wall. The exact number of illegal radios is not known, but it is estimated that approximately 1 percent of the Norwegian households disregarded the German directive and kept their radios.[15]

The Norwegians were most interested in the war news, which included speeches by Allied leaders and military developments in both the European and Pacific theaters. And since not all the news was optimistic, it was equally important to relay the bad and cautioning communiqués to maintain the credibility of the illegal newspapers. One such *caveat* appeared in *Avisa*, October 11, 1944:

> *General Eisenhower's Central Command has sent the following warning to Norwegian ships: The Germans, as a result of their great loss of ships, have great difficulty with transports from Norway to Germany and back, and they are using all they can of larger and smaller ships for such transport. They are very desperate now because it is of vital importance that the Germans continue their Occupation of Norway. The Central Command has earlier sent warnings to the Norwegian ships about sailing along the Norwegian coast and that they now do so at their own risk. This warning is now expanded and sharpened and all boats that sail along the Norwegian coast, both large and small, will be open for attack because the British blockade has now been sharpened.*[16]

The German authorities were painfully aware of the importance of the illegal press. They watched with anxiety and later with alarm at the proliferation of newspapers that sprang up all over Norway. Not only did they read the illegal press, they sent exact translations of what was written in the newspapers to Berlin.[17] One German report in the summer of 1942 underscored the influence of the illegal press when it stated that "acting as a support to the Norwegian Resistance fighters, the illegal newspapers play an important part. They spread news from the emigrated government in Britain and give advice as to how the Resistance group should move next."[18]

The Occupation was in its third year in 1943, and, not surprisingly, the war was beginning to tax people's spirits and their will to follow the Home Front directives at the cost of personal sacrifice. Conditions in Norway were worse than ever. Arrests based on the most trivial of charges, terror as a basic instrument of Occupation policy, and food shortages were but some of the more despicable iniquities to which the Norwegians were subjected. In such an environment, it was of the utmost importance that the illegal press continue to function.

During the second half of 1943, a Central Board of Press was established to help the publishers increase the efficiency of the newspapers throughout the country and expand their circulation. Under this new central organ, a chief of press was appointed by the Coordination Committee to find suitable locations for new businesses, supplying them with equipment and other supplies that were needed, and for arranging the finances to keep the papers operating. Sometimes the national press management even took the initiative to establish new newspapers.[19] By the fall of the year, the illegal press was printing approximately 500,000 copies a month.[20]

In Oslo, the Norwegian Postal Service alone was distributing approximately 25,000 illegal issues a month, without the Nazis finding out, even though the service was controlled by the Nazis.[21] On one occasion, a postal worker was arrested and questioned by a member of the Gestapo, who unexpectedly had come upon a stack of papers. "Tell me what is going on in the Postal Service. Five minutes after I leave at night the place is filled with *The London News.* I discovered this one night when I had forgotten my gloves and had to go back. I waited and left two hours later, but it [the paper] doesn't appear until I have left the building for good."[22]

A large number of postal workers who worked on the railways had the opportunity to circulate illegal papers, which they concealed between the bags of mail and deposited at various stops. Moreover, workers in numerous occupations—union workers, seamen on coastal steamers, and even bus, truck, and taxi drivers—helped circulate the papers.

Nevertheless, the Germans, with the help of informants who had connections with the Gestapo, waged a concerted effort to expose the illegal press network. Among the large number of editors, distributors, and fellow workers apprehended was Chief of Press Herlov Rygh, a well-informed and highly connected link between the Home Front leadership and the press, who helped edit the biweekly *London News.* Partly through infiltration in the network and partly through Gestapo interrogation, which frequently involved torture, the Germans were successful in reducing the effectiveness of the illegal press. One widely circulated paper, *The Whispering Times*, a supplier of news to local papers all over the country and to other smaller newspapers, was exposed by a Gestapo informant, which resulted in the arrest of a large number of people.[23] In February 1944, another series of arrests took place after several newspaper offices were raided. In the period of one week, editors, printers, and distributors of most of the illegal papers in Oslo were arrested. Rygh's two successors, Petter Moen, editor of *The London News*, and Viggo Aagaard, who edited *London Radio*, were also apprehended.[24] Both were subjected to brutal interrogation and imprisonment. In a letter which he smuggled out of prison, Aagaard wrote:

> *I was of course driven straight to the [Viktoria] Terrace, where for a full week I was treated quite severely in regular examinations. It was something of a strain, you know, but I think on the whole I can say that I managed it. 1) "Sonderbehandlung," i.e., the attempt to break me down as I received it, consisted partly of the following: arm twisted behind my back; repeatedly lifted up by my hair so that tufts fell out, pressure on the cavities behind the ears; ears twisted (bloody for three weeks afterwards); blows on the head with all sorts of instruments, flogging with heavy ropes and blows with iron rods over the entire body. Result: a completely black body. Threat of 2) castration by drunken interpreter with knife, actual attempts at the same with baton, jumping and stamping all over the body—and much more which I do not care to mention. Altogether there were eight men at it, and on one occasion—the worst—all of them at once.[25]*

As one who stood up to torture better than most, Aagaard was able to conceal his job as a press chief and that he associated with some of the largest illegal papers in the country; nor did he betray any of his fellow workers.[26]

Nonetheless, the collapse of the press in Oslo was a severe setback for the Civilian Resistance, since most all of the important illegal papers were eliminated. Reconstruction of the press network was no easy matter. Precautions had to be taken so that the system safeguarded not only the line between the newspaper staff and the individual paper, but also between one paper and another, so that if the Gestapo managed to destroy a particular paper, the others would be safe. The task of rebuilding the network was given to Paal Brunsvig, an associate of Herlov Rygh, who fled to Stockholm after Rygh's arrest. Brunsvig returned to Oslo, where he set up a system of contacts and managed to establish a network, so that by the end of the summer of 1944, arrangements were made for contacting approximately 20 papers in the Oslo area.[27]

Despite the confiscations and arrests which continued after a paper was stopped, new editors and new papers emerged within a few days to resume publication. Thus the illegal press continued to play a dominant role as the link between the Norwegian people and the Resistance organization. Thousands of men and women participated in gathering, producing, and distributing illegal newspapers. Throughout the five-year Occupation period, the Germans apprehended between 3,000 and 4,000 persons for their involvement, and of those arrested, 212 died, of which 154 were either executed or died under torture.[28] Their tireless efforts were largely responsible for upholding morale under the most adverse conditions. In the midst of defeat, illegal newspapers had great psychological effect as a sign that the fight had not yet ended, but had now begun in earnest.

The Illegal Press in Kristiansund

In these times we fight for ideas
and newspapers are our fortresses.
—*Heinrich Heine (1797-1856), German poet*

Author's Note: The following chronicle is based upon the war memoir of
Jorgen Hoff-Jenssen, the co-editor of Avisa, *the illegal newspaper published*
in Kristiansund North during the years 1942-45, and a personal interview
with the author. Hoff-Jenssen resides with his wife, Nanna, in Fetsund, a
suburb of Oslo, Norway.

Not long after the radios were confiscated in the fall of 1941, news services were established at secret listening posts in many towns and villages.[1] The transmissions from London were committed to writing and later published for much wider circulation in these services. After receiving and compiling the news, it had to be collated and stenciled or printed. This not only required large stocks of paper, carbon, ink, and envelopes, but also cumbersome typewriters, duplicating machines, and hand-operated presses, which were frequently old and worn out and not always easy to acquire or conceal.

Ordinarily such activity would be rather commonplace and uneventful. In the atmosphere in which the clandestine newspaper work took place, however, with the ever-present risk of discovery and arrest, the activity was real drama. There was the worry of not finding a suitable location for the equipment secure enough to not call attention from outsiders. In most cases the equipment was hidden in private apartments, cellars, attics and various kinds of secret compartments.

An even more dangerous aspect of the illegal press operation was the distribution of the news. Early in the war, many of the papers were sent out by mail in envelopes with false return addresses, but postage made this very expensive, particularly if it involved a large circulation. In most cases, the papers were handed from one person to another by people who knew each other well. Sometimes the messengers were persons who had regular delivery routes, such as milkmen or mailmen active in the Resistance. But most of the papers were delivered by couriers, often by women, who concealed the news in shopping bags, handbags, or among other personal belongings.

Frequently, the deliveries involved what seemed like endless walks in the cold under the cover of darkness; carrying manuscripts and messages in briefcases or sacks. They were dropped in mailboxes, concealed in packages, shoes, and even in the clothing of children; and then back again with more papers to be delivered. This entailed considerable risk because, if arrested while in possession of a bundle of papers or even a single issue, there was nothing the person could do to avoid the penalties, which were often quite severe. The young men and women upon whom this covert activity mainly rested were ordinary people to whom fear was no stranger.

One such patriot was 24-year-old John Marius Hansen, who lived in Kristiansund North, a small town on the west coast some 400 miles north of Bergen. Bounded by weather-beaten rocks pounded by the sea, Kristiansund was the largest exporter of dried cod. In 1942, it was becoming a covert importer of radio news from London. Before the radios were confiscated, Hansen purchased a used receiving set and began to spread the news from the Norwegian language bulletins. He selected certain places in the town at certain times of the day where several people would gather to listen to the latest news. Later, new meeting places had to be established, a task which was unnerving, repetitive, and especially dangerous, given the possibility of betrayal by unknown Nazi collaborators.

John M. Hansen

The largest news distribution centers were in two houses. One was in Jossingheimen at Jullumgate 9, where as many as 20 men would come from various sections of town and gather in a room so small that not everyone could fit inside. The other place was in Brushuset, in a very small confections shop. Several of these distributors had their own contacts whom they would visit each night. Afterwards, those they met would spread the news to others throughout the town.

Not surprisingly, as the German authorities anxiously watched the proliferation of the illegal news throughout the country, more drastic measures were taken to bring this unforeseen development to a halt. In October 1942, a new decree was issued from the Quisling Ministry and the German SS in Oslo, and posted on walls in towns everywhere.

- Anyone who hereafter illegally is in possession of a radio apparatus is sentenced to death.

- Everyone who tells or brings rumors of the news which come from someplace other than Berlin or Oslo is sentenced to death.

- All who listen to such rumors without immediately reporting it to the police are sentenced to death.

- This decree becomes effective immediately.

Jorgen Hoff-Jenssen

Undaunted by this new directive, the intrepid Hansen continued disseminating the London broadcasts. He soon realized, however, that the news could be circulated in written form by printing it. For this work, he obtained the help of a co-worker, 21-year-old Jorgen Hoff-Jenssen, who was also receiving, recording, and distributing the news from abroad. He was also well-known to the Germans. In December 1940, Hoff-Jenssen was arrested by the Germans for circulating "libelous" material about Hitler and the *Wehrmacht*, titled the "Laughable News for Norwegians." He was sentenced to eight months in prison, six of which were served in Glasmoor, outside of Hamburg, Germany.

Every part of the news publication process presented the amateur journalists with questions involving editing, printing, and distributing resulting from a shortage of equipment. A local publishing firm provided paper, stencils, ink, and envelopes. Subscribers were requested to make contributions of five crowns or more for the survival of the newspaper and for the editors, provided the finances. But strict precautions had to be observed. No money was to be sent by mail, but rather was to be given to the delivery person in an unmarked envelope.

Because of the Nazi regulation which now meted out capital punishment for the production, distribution, and reception of an illegal paper, extreme caution was to be exercised by those receiving the news since such news could be a provocation from the Germans. The provocation was an attempt by the Nazis to infiltrate the illegal press by establishing bogus clandestine newspapers with names that were similar to already established illegal papers. Although the pretense was usually transparent to the subscribers, people could not be too careful. Anyone who received a newspaper that looked suspicious was told to contact a person that one could trust as knowledgeable and able to provide information about the newspaper in question. Those papers were delivered with a certain code word. As was to be expected, some refused to receive the news. Such persons were to send a signed letter to the editors, which would be burned immediately to avoid possible detection by the authorities in the event of a raid.

The publishing operation was set up at the Fosna A. S. clothes-manufacturing factory where Jenssen worked at night as a security guard. Using one of the factory typewriters at night in the office, the editors printed numerous copies with the use of carbon paper while the reception of the London news continued, as before, at Hansen's home. The first copies of the *Jøssingposten,* as the newspaper was first called, was published August 30, 1942, and distributed by the editors to their regular contacts in town. Soon it became clear that this printing facility was far from acceptable, as discovery was a real possibility. For security reasons it was advisable, but not always easy, to move the operation. They quickly realized one of the cardinal axioms of Resistance activity: anything clandestine is temporary. This was a constant concern until the end of the Occupation.

In January 1943, Hansen reluctantly moved his equipment to the basement of the family apartment at Fosnagata 28c where the radio had been hidden. News was still spread by word-of-mouth, but gathering so many people together at a certain time and place night after night put them at grave risk and was a real source of anxiety to Hansen and Hoff-Jenssen until the resumption of publication. The basement had a very small storage room, a portion of which had not been excavated when the house was built. They called it "The Hole," and it was no more than 40 inches from ceiling to floor. Two small men only had room to maneuver when the radio and typewriter were placed on a rock shelf which leaned out from the floor and up to the ceiling. The Hole, which was enclosed with Masonite panels to absorb the sound from the radio and the typewriter, had to be enlarged enough to allow the men to work inside. A hole was placed in the floor and in the wall behind a plug in the Hansen apartment, which allowed a wire to be dropped down to the basement where it was laid along a piece of trim and concealed with cement. The entrance to The Hole looked like a normal wall, but a simple maneuver divided the wall and allowed people to enter. An ever-present worry was how well their security precautions would hold up in the event of a raid. They harbored no illusions about this if the Germans or the NS were to follow any suspicions they might have. Nonetheless, it gave them enough feeling of security to continue their work even if it was a false feeling—and they knew it was false.

Hansen was able to obtain a simple hand-operated press for stencils in an 8.5"-x-11" format. When necessary, the news would be printed on both sides or on several pages. At times, the stencil would curl up and sometimes crack or tear, all of which contributed to their frustration. Their equipment consisted of the radio, typewriter, the press, ink, paper, and stencils. It was in The Hole that the first stenciled copies of the newspaper were produced. For reasons of security the name of the paper was changed to simply *Avisa* (News) so that everyone who read it and those who heard about the news in this way knew *which* news people were talking about. Moreover, if someone should mention it to outsiders, which, of course, did happen, they could easily have been referring to one of the town's legal newspapers.

Now that the news from London was being published, it was no longer necessary to memorize it, moving the fronts and lines of attack on a mental map until unknown towns and rivers fit together with what they heard and understood from earlier reports. They had previously relied on their memory of real maps that they studied daily, and used to form the reports in their minds that they carried to others orally. They used abbreviations, two-letter words and signs which only they understood, to copy the news from abroad. Hence, the paper was the result of good memories and good notes.

Hansen received the news at 6:00 a.m., and Hoff-Jenssen listened to the evening news from London. The two broadcasts were collated, edited, and transcribed to a stencil for publication. The absence of heat on cold winter nights as the men crouched to produce the news from 6:30 to 9:00 p. m., when the work was finally finished, brought on colds. The constant fear of discovery by the Nazis added to the anxiety and tension associated with this activity. As soon as the printer's ink was dry enough, the newspapers were taken upstairs to the Hansen apartment, and with the help of the family, the delivery people would be given several copies to distribute that night to trusted persons throughout the town. This was one of the most threatening aspects of their work.

Delivery had to occur as quickly as time allowed, and on dark winter evenings when the streets were quiet and empty, a single delivery person could not help but be conspicuous to anyone observing from inside a building. Earlier, German soldiers and officers could be seen returning to their barracks after evening coffee at the cafes; but later in the night, *Streif*, that is, unexpected patrols, were a constant source of fear to the news carriers. And to be questioned for *Shein*—the order to show an identity card or permit—while carrying 30 or 40 newspapers under one's belt, the dreaded, "What do you have there?" would result in a body search and probable arrest and interrogation by the Gestapo.

In March 1943, the printing press was moved to a hospital where Hansen worked for the next three months. He lived in a room on the top floor where his equipment was secretly stored in the wall of his room. The news from London was brought there where it was now printed. In the evening, the on-duty doctors and nurses sat in the dining room where they received the latest news. If it was especially good, there was jubilation, and occasionally "a tear of happiness fell into the nurse's cup of coffee." *

At several different times, Jossingheimen was used as the principal location for distributing the newspaper. The distribution center was a critical factor in the overall press operation. A large amount of com-

*A Norwegian expression meaning good news shared with someone over a cup of coffee.

promising material was usually situated there, and discovery by the Gestapo was always a possibility. Although most of the time things ran smoothly, one frightening incident gave grave cause for alarm and almost led to the immediate demise of the operation.

One morning while 10 of the newspaper workers were sorting and folding the newspapers for distribution, a sharp knock came at the door. Since no other staff members were expected, the men were momentarily paralyzed by fear. When the door was opened, a German officer was standing in the doorway. He simply asked if a tailor lived in the house. When he was told that no such person lived there, he left immediately. Later, as the men were completing their work, the same officer reappeared at the door. This time, the men were convinced that the tailor never existed. Frantically, Hansen and a co-worker gathered the papers in a bundle and rushed up the stairs to the second floor. The frightened worker immediately demanded that they burn the papers, but Hansen disagreed. A moment later, the young boy went into the hallway and darted back to the room where Hansen had taken the newspapers and cried out, "Burn them, burn the newspapers. The house is surrounded." He had seen two German officers down in the hallway and, returning to the room upstairs in a state of panic, he started to jump out the window, but Hansen managed to stop him. As it turned out, the Germans had been told that a tailor did indeed reside there. Yet after suspiciously looking around the house before leaving, one of them queried, "Are all of these your brothers?" One of the men answered "Yes," to which the German responded, "They certainly are unusually busy."

In June, the operation was again moved back to The Hole in Fosnagata 28, where the newspaper was circulated throughout the town. It became a barometer of optimism among the people, and was well received by the leaders of the Underground. When the number of copies printed had increased substantially and the news did not arrive early enough for its readers, Hansen's sister, Mary, offered to distribute the paper by concealing it in the legal Salvation Army paper, *Krigsropet* (War Cry). She would hide the *News* in milk buckets or grocery baskets, a cleverness that stood in contrast to her appearance of a withdrawn innocent girl. Her efforts succeeded without incident for many months.

During the Christmas season 1943, frightening rumors were heard that Hansen and his workers were being watched and that a raid was being planned at the Hansen home. It was then decided to move the editing and press operation to the top floor of the trade union quarters in Vagen, known as Handverkeren, not far from Hansen's home. This arrangement also had its dangerous aspects. The post office was located on the first floor and meetings and other gatherings took place on the floor where the editing work was done. A code word and other signs were arranged to be used when the room was otherwise occupied and in case of unexpected events. Frequently, when steps were heard on the stairway during the reception of radio transmissions, Hansen and others were forced to hide the radio in the ashbin of the chimney and appear as though they were engaged in other innocuous activities. Feelings of insecurity were ever-present: people whispered, rumors spread, and friends warned of possible discovery. Finally fear mounted to a fever pitch, and the decision was made to move the operation again.

There were always moments when a German SS officer or a known Nazi collaborator would be on the street and appear to be walking directly toward one of the Resistance members with the worst possible intentions, only to hurry past and allow one to breathe again. On one such occasion when the editing staff of *Avisa* had just finished printing the weekend edition in the Handverkeren, John Hansen walked outside when he suddenly saw the notorious Norwegian informer, Henry Oliver Rinnan. He was the leader of the traitorous "Rinnan Gang," which had been responsible for infiltrating Resistance groups. More than a thousand Norwegian Underground members were subsequently arrested, tortured, and consigned to concentration camps or prisons.[2] Many of them were executed or died of maltreatment in German concentration camps. Upon seeing the dreaded Rinnan, Hansen made a confused attempt to change the expression on his face as though nothing was unusual, and the collaborator walked past him.

However, farther down the street, Rinnan stopped Oivind Saether, another worker at the newspaper, who failed to recognize the collaborator. When questioned as to where he had been and what he had been doing in the Handverkeren, his response obviously satisfied Rinnan. When Hansen later explained to Saether who he had been talking to, the co-worker breathed a great sigh of relief. Rinnan himself was later convicted of and executed for killing 13 persons whom he admitted murdering with his own hands, including four members of his own gang whom he no longer felt he could trust.[3]

In 1943, Hoff-Jenssen was ordered by the National Labor Service to Aukra, an island near Molde south of Kristiansund for road and railway building. In June, while being observed giving bread to Russian prisoners, he was arrested and put into prison for eight months, first in Norway at Dombas, and later in Rendsburg Prison in Germany.

Upon his return in February 1944, Hoff-Jenssen wasted no time in contacting Hansen at his home where he found him writing an article for the newspaper. As Jorgen entered his room, Hansen's first greeting was "Sit down and write!" It was not long, however, before Hoff-Jenssen was in need of a recovery period after his imprisonment. Two weeks later, he traveled to a farm at Stjorna for a needed rest. Yet, after familiarizing himself with the situation in that area, he established a news service there and arranged to have *Avisa* sent to Kristiansund once or twice a week. A battery-operated receiver was used to get transmissions from abroad as long as the battery lasted. Meanwhile, the news from London continued to flow out of the attic of the Handverkeren.

In August, Hoff-Jenssen returned to Kristiansund. The following month he and Hansen had once again moved the equipment back to The Hole, where the two intrepid stalwarts, night after night, would be stooped over the radio listening to the overseas broadcast. Frequently they would turn the radio off and strain their ears when they heard the sound of heavy boots marching or of footsteps upstairs. It became a war of nerves. As Hoff-Jenssen stated, "In such a time, I can assure you that the last thread of heroism is blown away. Only pure and unadulterated fright lies inside and it is horrible."

Trepidation was no stranger to others in the illegal *Avisa* news operation. One such worker, Harald Saether, was given an assignment by a member of the Resistance to prepare a map of Kristiansund with explanations of important German fortifications in the city. Certain well-informed persons provided him with drawings, which he superimposed on a large-scale map requiring detailed accuracy. One evening he was scheduled to meet Hansen at his home where he was to complete the work on the map. It was quite dark when he left the machinist school that he attended. Carrying a school satchel in one hand and a roll of covert drawings in the other, he was suddenly stopped by a

German patrol who demanded to see his pass. Calmly, Harald handed over the roll of drawings to the officer while he searched for the pass. Upon presenting the pass, the drawings were returned to the young student, and the German was none the wiser.

Toward the end of the Occupation the clandestine news was sent with the regular mail. One distributor worked at the Transport Commission and another at the Notary Public Office in the City Hall. They were able to acquire duty-free stamps marked with the official NS symbol *Solkors* (sun cross), which was used by all government offices in town. Thus the official state Nazi Party was unwittingly financing the distribution of the illegal newspaper. This method of delivery worked successfully until the end of the war.

From the physical hardship and mental anguish of a civilized people living under barbarian rule, and in the long struggle of reconstruction in the scarred towns and villages of Norway which was later to follow, the following homespun lyric, though a bit roughshod, is but one reflection by an anonymous subscriber to *Avisa* who found in the illegal news a symbol of unity and a source of strength and hope. These verses were later—in the words of Wordsworth—"powerful feelings recollected in tranquility," sent to Mary Hoff-Jenssen, the mother of Jorgen and Gunnar Hoff-Jenssen in appreciation for receiving the truth when German propaganda, injustice, and censorship were the order of the day for five long years of Nazi Occupation:

> *It has been a few remarkable years,*
>
> *Often we knew hunger and pain*
>
> *Uncertainty stood like an enclosing wall*
>
> *And helplessness lay there in hiding.*
>
> *Then it was one of your boys*
>
> *Who came with his newspapers*
>
> *It gave us hope, it gave us faith*
>
> *And feelings of safety in our homeland.*

You have not always had it so easy

Perhaps you momentarily shed a tear

Your thoughts followed your boys from door to door

"Oh, don't let the Gestapo sink their claws into them."

Up out of war and chaos and dread

Shines a memory of hope and of faith

And when everything which caused pain is now forgotten

There lay the good in our hearts hidden.

It will shine and warm us in all the years

It will follow us where we go.

And when I bid farewell to these familiar streets

I will always remember two steadfast boys

Who had their home between these mountains and the sea

For the good memories you gave.

They are young of age this brightening spring

And a bright future they will receive.

When their own home they shall build

They must live there with peace and security.

I wish to close this remembrance with values

That follow them on their journey.

My warmest gratitude for all the times they dropped in

Avisa here was so often a comfort

With their very important illegal news.

10

Anglo-Norwegian Intelligence

The reason why the enlightened prince and the wise general
conquer the enemy whenever they move
 and their achievements surpass those of ordinary men
is foreknowledge of his plans.
—Sun Tzu (Fourth Century BC) Art of War

A unique aspect of the Resistance Movement in Norway was the way in which the older generation was in the vanguard. The government, supported by the people, turned to their elderly King for a continuation of the struggle when, at the same time, certain members of Parliament and the Military High Command—men in their fifties—were prepared to concede defeat. Moreover, it was the elderly bishops, judges, and university professors who spoke out from their pulpits, benches, and podiums, even after the official surrender in the field, and proclaimed that Norway had not been beaten.[1] The complacency which decades of neutrality had induced in the ordinary Norwegian had rapidly given way to a stronger loyalty to the monarch, a patriotic fervor, and a hatred of the Germans which aroused an intense national emotion to resume the fight militarily from across the sea.

Although the clarion call was sounded by a much older generation, the response came from the nation's youth. Thousands of young men in their teens and early twenties left home for Britain to join the Allied forces and carry on the fight from abroad. The exodus began in early May after the occupation of South Norway was completed. Most of the "Englandsfarere"—the name given to those who escaped from Norway to Britain—came from the southwest and northwest coastal regions and the outlying islands, but there were also those who came from eastern Norway. They escaped mostly through fishing communities in coastal smacks, yachts, small steamers, and even dinghies across the North Sea. Most of the vessels sailed to the Shetlands, a string of islands some 190 miles west of Bergen. Others went to the Orkney Islands just north of the Scottish mainland and due west of Stavanger.

Planning for a voyage to Britain could be a complicated problem. For many, despite the continuous stream of refugees who left Norway during the first 12 months, it was not always a simple matter to obtain a serviceable boat or a crew qualified to make such a crossing. The Germans were acutely aware of the increased traffic from the ports and the boats that were disappearing, and the German police increased their activity as a result. Notices were posted in boathouses all along the coast, announcing that anyone who tried to escape to Britain would be shot.[2] Security along the coast and in the larger towns of the west and south was strengthened considerably; and every boat moving along or outside the skerries was required to have a special permit from the German Harbor Police.[3] Any sale or purchase of a boat of any size had to be sanctioned by that same authority. There were those who were afraid to sell a boat to strangers; and those who were willing to sell despite the German restrictions would, in some cases, demand prices far in excess of one's ability to pay.[4] Nevertheless, despite the risks involved, an increasing number of such boats managed to slip out of the fiords past German sentries and set course for Allied ports. In addition to the young men who were anxious to continue the fight, the passengers often included entire families.

Many of those who undertook the journey to Britain did so between September and November after the autumn gales had begun when the seas between Shetland and Norway could be extremely stormy. The fear that many felt when they first confronted the ferocity of the North Sea was enormous. Hundreds experienced hurricanes, heavy fog, extreme cold, and continuous darkness such that they thought they would never see land again. Many were buffeted by storms that capsized their boats and resulted in the loss of lives; many others were carried ashore half dead with seasickness.

During the first two years of the war, approximately 3,500 men crossed the North Sea and about 500 struck eastwards to Sweden.[5] From there many made their way through Finland and Russia and across continents—some to China, India, Turkey, and Africa—before proceeding either directly to Britain or by way of America and Canada. Their goal was to reach the free Norwegian or British forces—Army, Navy, or Merchant Marine—in the United Kingdom so that they could continue the fight against the oppressors. The Norwegian airmen who escaped to Britain were sent to Toronto, Canada, where a new Royal Norwegian Air Force was being formed. It became known throughout the world as "Little Norway," and Norwegian recruits flocked to it from all over the globe.

The influx of Norwegian volunteers who arrived in the British Isles in the spring of 1940 enabled the British government to seek out dependable elements capable of being trained and sent back to Norway. They became part of a clandestine network of trained intelligence agents, wireless operators, saboteurs, and instructors of paramilitary Resistance groups. Unlike the Civilian Resistance, which was shaped by countless variations of civil disobedience—for example, individual acts of passive resistance, demonstrations, protests, and strikes—the Military Resistance was organized as a joint Norwegian-British participation involving operations aimed at the eventual liberation of Norway by throwing off the yoke of Occupation.

Essentially, it consisted of two separate tasks. One was *intelligence work*. This involved gathering and transmitting information to the Home Station at Bletchley Park just outside London, for analysis concerning the strength and movement of German troops, aircraft and naval forces, in support of those making operational and strategic decisions. The second task was the *creation and training of secret operational units* by the newly formed British organization, Special Operations Executive (SOE), whose job was to conduct sabotage and other forms of subversive activity within Norway itself against the occupying power.

After the Germans had gained control over the whole of Norway, a purely Norwegian intelligence service was established in Oslo that functioned later under the designation XU. It maintained contact with the Allies via the Norwegian Legation in Stockholm, which set up a special office for intelligence. XU worked chiefly with defensive intelligence material, specifically, maps, reports, sketches, and photographs for use during a possible invasion of Norway.[6] At its inception, XU was a part of Milorg, the central Military Resistance organization established in Norway at the end of 1940. However, in 1941, XU was taken over by civilian leadership. It was not the only intelligence-gathering organization to monitor the *Wehrmacht* in Norway, but it did become the largest with between 1,300 and 1,500 agents spread throughout South Norway, and an estimated 1,400 ultimately spread throughout

North Norway.[7] Those stations organized in North Norway were located in coastal towns as far north as Tromso, where intelligence information was sent by ferry to Trondheim and then on to Oslo, where it was transported by courier into Sweden.[8] No one ever attempted to assemble the entire intelligence service into one organization, nor was it even suggested, for reasons that remain unknown.[9]

What distinguished the Intelligence Service from other resistance in occupied Norway was that it began working with the British Secret Intelligence Service (SIS) before the Occupation, as early as the winter of 1939-40. It was expanded in early spring in conjunction with a plan for a Franco-British military intervention in North Norway. In the summer of 1940, the first intelligence office was opened in London by the Norwegian Ministry of Foreign Affairs. To accelerate the growth of intelligence circuits, particularly on the west coast of Norway, couriers were sent out by Norwegian authorities in London to locate reliable elements that could form a more coordinated movement with British intelligence.

Beginning that autumn, selected Norwegians in the United Kingdom were recruited for training as wireless operators. Once trained, they were sent either by boat from the Shetlands or Scotland, or parachuted back into Norway, where small intelligence units were formed to work in close collaboration with SIS to provide information about German naval movements along the coast of Norway. Most of the wireless operators stayed close to the sea so that they could easily observe the German ships travelling along the coast. Harsh weather conditions often put a far more severe strain on their covert activity than did the Germans outside the more heavily defended areas. Usually four agents worked together, with two at a time keeping watch 24 hours a day. An example of the speed and effectiveness with which the agents were able to make contact with London was provided by Lieutenant Commander Eric Welsh, head of the Scandinavian Section of the SIS in a note to the Norwegian High Command. The note concerned two SIS agents operating along the coast north of Floro, a small town between Bergen and Kristiansund:

> *This station is providing extremely valuable information.*
> *I refer to a telegram No. 8 dated 5 February 1943: Time of*

observation 1100. Message received at the headquarters in London at 1342. Received in the Admiralty at 1348. Message reported a battleship and three destroyers passing outside Floro headed south. At 1617 a continuing message was received saying that the ships involved were Hipper, Koln, and three destroyers.[10]

As soon as the British were informed of the number of ships, their size and escort, they could decide whether they should make an air attack immediately or wait until the whole convoy was farther along the coast. Norwegian naval officers established intelligence groups with radio transmitters in the larger coastal towns. They soon made contact with other groups that had been organized locally. Messages and reports from these individual wireless stations later formed the basis for military operations throughout the country.

Some of the most difficult and dangerous assignments were performed by those wireless agents who operated from isolated cliffs, caves, and other remote places by the North Sea. Initially, these were Norwegian soldiers who fled eastward from the Varanger Peninsula at the end of the military campaign of 1940 into Russian service, but who returned in autumn of the same year. After the Soviet Union entered the war in June 1941, they acted under the command of the Russian army and were sent from Murmansk and locales well north of the Arctic Circle. Their mission was the same as the SIS agents from Britain. From the beginning of January 1942, six Norwegian/Russian radio groups were put ashore at Varangerhalvoya and in North Troms.[11] Scarcely would a German vessel sail along the Arctic coast without the home station being informed of its size, type, and course within a very short time. However, in July-August 1943, practically all of the Norwegian/Russian groups were discovered by the Germans and eliminated. These groups suffered far more severely than those in South Norway.

Several reasons account for this. Most important was that the Germans dealt more harshly with prisoners who were operating under Russian authority than those who were controlled from Britain. Moreover, many of the agents were located in areas on the coast of Finnmark and Troms where it was difficult to remain concealed from the local populace. Consequently, both gossip and Nazi informers accounted for many arrests in those areas.[12]

Equally significant were those intelligence groups that covered the *Wehrmacht* on land during the German building of *Festung Norwegen* (Fortress Norway). Many Norwegian businesses were drawn into the German war machine and became suppliers of products and services for the Occupation forces. However, the intelligence organization managed to turn this to its advantage by gathering information from those suppliers. Gradually, German fortifications, gun emplacements, aerodromes, and military units were described and their location mapped, while changes and troop movements were recorded continuously and then reported to London. In addition, informers and German cover organizations were tracked down and even penetrated, thereby carrying the silent, invisible war into the enemy's own camp. It was not long before agents throughout the country as well as those along the coast became the eyes and ears of the Allies in northwestern Europe. Nevertheless, discovery by the Gestapo or members of the NS was an ever-present possibility, and the least mistake could lead to torture and execution.

The intelligence organization was composed of people from numerous professions. Industrial workers, farmers, fishermen, workers on German construction sites, doctors, teachers, and members of the police force all played an important role using their various skills in gathering intelligence data for the Allied cause. Additionally there were truck drivers, locomotive drivers, and ferry captains—people who had a legal reason for travelling across country and into Sweden—without whose help it would have been impossible to conduct an effective intelligence service in Norway. All agents, whether they operated radio transmitters, cameras, or simply used handwritten materials, had to conceal their covert activity from their legitimate work activity.

Lacking the knowledge and training required in those first intelligence operations, it was difficult for the inexperienced agents to work clandestinely under the cover of anonymity. This was especially true in the smaller towns, where they underwent the painful process of learning from experience and mistakes, which often proved fatal to those in the field. One common failing of many loyal Norwegians, especially in the early months of the Occupation, was loquacity—the desire to tell one's friends and relatives about some exciting operation just completed.[13] Loose talk and other blunders such as excessive optimism and a lack of knowledge of the Gestapo enabled Norwegian collaborators to infiltrate many of the early intelligence groups quite easily. Since most of the Gestapo did not speak the native language nor know anything of the local culture, informers, posing as "good Norwegians," became their eyes and ears.

The first SIS station to suffer operated out of Haugesund, south of Bergen. The station, code-named *Hardware*, was started in early June 1940, but lasted only eight weeks before being uncovered by a Norwegian informer who was disguised as an "Englandfarer." Out of the 18 people operating the station, 10 were sentenced to death, but were later commuted to life imprisonment. Another transmitting station, *Oldell*, operated in Oslo from July 1940, until March 1941, and sent more than 600 signals before being discovered, not by collaborators, but by a radio-direction finder.[14]

The German direction-finding network was highly efficient in tracking down SIS wireless operators. Messages were first intercepted from a fixed location once the transmitting frequency was established; then, by cross bearings, a "snifter" van was dispatched which localized the position of the transmitter by registering the maximum and minimum strengths of the signal through a rotating aerial. Once the van arrived at the proximate location, the transmitting site was gradually pinpointed. To minimize the risk of being apprehended, operators would reduce time on the air to a minimum and frequently move their stations to a new location. Despite these precautions, some agents were caught in the act of transmitting and killed while operating the telegraph. Others who were captured and unable to endure torture had ready access to a cyanide pill. The loss of an operator was a tragedy, but disclosure under torture was a disaster, since it usually led to a chain-reaction of arrests. This occurred quite frequently.

Many radio stations operated out of huts in inaccessible forest and mountain areas, which were very thinly populated. But even from these more remote areas, a direction-finding plane, usually a Fiesler Storch, could locate a concealed station. The greater exposure, however, was in densely built up areas, particularly in towns, where cross-bearings by two or three direction-finding vehicles were used to localize the transmitting point, thereby reducing the operator's transmitting time to a few minutes or, if at a place that had been localized, to less than one minute.[15] SOE, the sister organization of SIS, was far more successful in evading direction-finders since the agents were frequently ordered to move to a new location after a few weeks. This was thought to be less risky than to operate in the same location for longer periods as most of the SIS agents did.

In January 1941, Norwegian Intelligence was reestablished under the Ministry of Defense ("E"-Office). This office continued to recruit and, together with the British, train new wireless operators from the refugees arriving in Britain. The British had operational control in the field, but cooperated closely with the Norwegians. Essentially there were two kinds of military intelligence: *operational*, which was transmitted to London by radio operators and formed the basis for rapid operations; and *static* intelligence, which originated from groups that transmitted reports by courier, and laid plans for future operations.[16] Static intelligence material sent from Norway dealt mostly with German fortifications, air fields, camps, and military stores. Initially, the British handled it but as the Norwegians gradually acquired officers from different districts in Norway, they were themselves able to handle the material, analyze it, and pass it on to military planning staffs. These Norwegian groups grew up largely on their own initiative, whereas the radio stations were, as a rule, established on the initiative of SIS/FOII (FO II was the London office of Norwegian Intelligence).[17] Although some stations had technical problems, and others were exposed and eliminated by the Germans, the number of both operational and static messages increased dramatically during the Occupation. Throughout the course of the war, the number of SIS stations increased substantially. During the second half of 1940, the number of stations increased from four to six in 1941; to 16 in 1942; to 28 in 1943; to 58 in 1944; and were reduced to 47 in 1945.[18]

A great deal of intelligence information had to be sent out from Sweden simply because there was too much data to send to London from any one station. In those cases, documents were microphotographed and given to a courier who would cross over the border and transmit them to the intelligence office in Stockholm for forwarding to Home Station. Concealment of secret messages and other compromising material was made much easier by microfilming. Information that could fill numerous printed pages would be reduced to a microfilm strip and hidden in such objects as a tube of toothpaste, a hollowed out boot heel, cans of hardened fish eggs, dummy batteries, and home-baked loaves of bread. A microdot no larger than one-thirty-second of an inch could be placed in a hollowed-out matchstick, in a removable cap nut from a water tap in a lavatory on a train going from Norway to Sweden, or fastened to an eyeglass lens—and later enlarged to reveal secret information of up to 500 words in length.

The thought of being arrested and subjected to Gestapo interrogation and torture with such incriminating material in one's possession was an ever-present cause of anxiety. For example, a courier might come to an office on the pretext of discussing the publication of a book with an editor—the real reason being to hand over microfilmed engineering drawings for improving the air defense system at the Sola airfield near Stavanger. When he arrived at the office, he might discover that the contact he was to see was "ill," and in his place was a German civilian (possibly Gestapo) who would ask to see his identity card, and then asked, "What did you really come for, Mr. _____?" A prepared explanation had to be made without hesitation to dispel any suspicion that the German might have. The courier would not know whether the contact had been arrested, and if so, whether under torture he had disclosed the courier's identity.

Significant improvement was made in the intelligence groups that operated later in Norway compared to earlier groups that had lacked experience in covert operations and knowledge of the Gestapo. Still, German penetration of intelligence units continued to occur throughout the Occupation. A number of intelligence agents were apprehended because of infiltrators who would notify the Gestapo in advance of a prearranged rendezvous. Acting in the guise of a member of the Resistance, the traitor would disclose the recognition signal in advance to the Gestapo, and when the signal was exchanged between the traitor and the agent at the rendezvous point, the Gestapo would move in from concealment and arrest the agent. After the first 10 seconds, the agent would know whether he had been betrayed.

Generally speaking, however, most intelligence groups acquired a talent that rivaled that of the Gestapo. Those amateur agents who survived the first two or three years of the war eventually became quite professional. They knew much more about the Gestapo and knew that, subjected to torture, they might sooner or later be opened like a book.

The guiding principle was that contacts were to hide or flee the area when one of their own had been arrested.[19]

The majority of agents suffered great strain as a result of their clandestine work. There were months of hiding; of moving, for example, from a hayloft in a barn one night to an attic in an all-too familiar neighborhood the next; of irregular sleep; of answering the telephone only to have the person on the other end hang up immediately; the suspense of seeing the same person several times in a day at different places, or of a stranger staring at an agent in a café. These were but a few of the many causes of fear and anxiety that they had to endure; feelings and experiences not ordinarily mentioned in history books.

Quite often intelligence agents trained in Britain were sent back to operate in districts from which they came. Yet these were potentially the most hostile environments, especially one's own hometown, where there was always a greater risk of being recognized. At every instant, the agent had to be on guard. Even in a city the size of Oslo, the agent was likely to meet people he would much rather avoid, and sometimes in the most undesirable places.

A case in point involved an agent who had just returned home after being away for more than three years and was being sought by the German authorities. On one occasion while waiting for a streetcar in Oslo, a young woman came along the platform and stopped alongside him. The woman was his younger sister. On his other side were three Germans. Although he was disguised and wearing glasses, he boarded the first trolley that came along, to avoid being noticed by his sister. Otherwise it could have been fatal if she had recognized him.[20]

A key concern was knowing how to deal with a chance meeting, should it arise, which of course it did. Obviously, the agent would give a false explanation of what he was about. Then he would cut short the conversation by advising the person who recognized him that if the agent or his family were arrested by the Gestapo, he would know who was responsible. In that case, that person would be named as the agent's contact, and would undoubtedly share the same fate. This threat usually proved effective.

Agents who were arrested were often subjected to barbaric behavior by the Gestapo. Every conceivable means of persuasion was brought into play to extract information. Some agents endured torture longer than others. One agent who was arrested in Kristiansand related the following experience:

> *I was picked up from the county jail and taken up to the Archive (Gestapo headquarters). The first question was "Where are you from?" They were interested in the radio operator we were hiding. Then they asked, "Do you know why you are arrested?" "No," I answered. They were pushing me harder and harder. After hitting me a few times they said: "I will show you that there is a certain connection with the rear end and the brain." They buckled me down to a wooden chair, with my head and hands hanging below the seat and chairlegs. They cuffed me. My legs got attached to the back legs of the chair with cuffs. They used a handle, about eight inches long, inside it had a steel spiral with a ball at the end of it. While they were beating me, they kept asking me, "Why have you been arrested?" They beat me from the knee joints up to my neck. The whole time I kept telling myself: "You will not say anything. You will not say anything." And they kept beating me.*
>
> *Afterwards I was commanded to stand with the cuffs on and stare at an X in the wall. After some hours they put me in a cell. Later that night I talked to people I knew, through a hole in the radiator. My cellmates told me a good deal, so the next day I was more prepared for the torture.*[21]

There were those who broke down immediately out of fear or confusion. Evidence was either overwhelming or the prisoner was confronted with others who had already been forced to talk. No member of the Underground who knew of the Gestapo's methods could pass judgment on those who cracked in prison. Some died during torture, others were permanently disabled, and some ended their own lives to avoid enduring further torment. In spite of this, people throughout the country, and in most groups, thought that they could withstand the torture, at least for a few hours. Some of them managed just that, while others succeeded in misleading the interrogators long enough for the contacts to escape.[22]

In January 1941, a network of agents was formed to cover the coastal areas from Stavanger on the west coast to Kristiansand-Arendal on the Skagerrak. It was from the strategically important naval base and port at Kristiansand that all German convoys that went south, west, and north along the Norwegian coast were formed. Consequently, because of the high level of activity at the harbor, Kristiansand became an important intelligence hub throughout the course of the war. From the reports that were sent to London, the course and speed of German convoys could easily be calculated, thereby enabling the RAF to respond with astonishingly good results.

1941 continued to witness the further eclipsing of continental Europe. In April, Yugoslavia was reduced to rubble after three successive days and nights of saturation bombing by 3,000 aircraft of the *Luftwaffe*. It was occupied by 40 divisions of German troops. Later that month, after occupying Rumania, Bulgaria, and Hungary, Hitler's legions, like the terrifying Valkyrie of Wagnerian opera fame, swarmed across the whole of Greece with panzers and an additional 15 German divisions. By the end of April, it was all over except for Crete, the last Greek stronghold, which was taken the following month from the British by an airborne assault of German paratroopers. At sea that month, 600,000 tons of British shipping were sunk by German U-boats and surface raiders. In the Mediterranean, only Gibraltar and the resilient island of Malta remained in Allied hands. Yet despite the German successes, Hitler was soon to experience a major defeat at sea that was not only a triumph for the Allies, but also a cause for elation for the members of a small Norwegian intelligence group, code-named *Cheese*, operating on the southwest coast, since it was that station that initiated the action that resulted in the Allied victory.

Unlike most of the radio stations in Norway run by the SIS and XU, the *Cheese* station was operated by agents of the Special Operations Executive, whose chief organizer was 22-year-old Odd Starheim. Toward the end of May 1941, *Cheese* operative Viggo Axelssen, a ship chandler who provided food provisions for the German ships in the harbor, spotted a large battleship passing Kristiansand and heading west escorted by three destroyers. The message was relayed to Starheim. Despite the presence of direction-finding equipment in the area, it was decided that the opportunity to report what was believed to be the presence of the world's largest battleship, the *Bismarck*, was too great to miss. The message was sent to the SOE Norwegian section in London and passed on to Naval Intelligence, which recognized immediately that this was a message they had been waiting for. For some time, the Admiralty had suspected that the *Bismarck* was hiding in a Norwegian fiord, preparing to launch into the Atlantic. Home Station instructed *Cheese* to send observers northwest along the coast and await further instructions.[23] Thus started the great hunt for the pride of the German Navy, Hitler's trump card, and the one remaining threat to Britain's supply lines.

But while the British were hunting for the *Bismarck*, the Germans in a fever of excitement were searching for the *Cheese* station. Direction-finding vans pinpointed the transmitter to a relatively small area in the Flekkefiord valley, some 60 miles northwest of Kristiansand. The Gestapo cordoned off the area and searched homes and farms for the station.

Another member of the group, Gunvald Tomstad, joined the NS as a supposed collaborator. He owned the farm where the transmission was coming from. But despite the high regard in which he was held by the Germans, Tomstad realized that the farm might be searched. So he removed the transmitter from the attic and from the farm to avoid detection by the direction-finders. When he got a good distance from the farm, he stopped on a plateau, and at the first lamppost, connected the transmitter to a low-tension wire and tapped out a meaningless message to London. He continued communicating until he was sure the Germans pinpointed the new position. Then he disconnected the transmitter, packed it in his rucksack, and returned to the farm. When the Germans moved away and up to the plateau, it was obvious that the ruse succeeded.[24]

Meanwhile, Starheim, a stranger in the area, was in danger of being apprehended by the Germans. With the help of a young member of the group, Sophie Rorwig, who acted the role of his sweetheart, he was able to pass unmolested through sentry posts and make his way across Norway to Stockholm where he was later flown to London.

While Tomstad resumed transmissions to London, the British continued the search for the *Bismarck*. Coastal command believed that the

German warship was bound for the North Atlantic. On May 23, the *Bismarck* and the cruiser, *Prinz Eugen*, were sighted in the Denmark Strait between Iceland and Greenland. The next morning, the two German vessels were engaged by the battle cruiser, *HMS Hood*, and the newly commissioned battleship, *HMS Prince of Wales*. A shell from the *Bismarck* struck a magazine on the *Hood*, enveloping the British dreadnought in a massive fireball before it slid beneath the waves. However, *Bismarck*, reduced in speed by a bow hit from *Prince of Wales*, thereby cutting off access to more than a thousand tons of precious fuel, was unable to detour away from the British fleet. On May 26, the *Bismarck* was further disabled when torpedo planes from the British carrier *Ark Royal* scored a hit that jammed its rudders irreparably. Unable to steer, the German vessel was forced into the wind—directly into the British force. The next day, she was finally destroyed off the French Atlantic coast by a combination of salvos from the British warships *Rodney*, *Norfolk, King George V*, and a *coup de grace* of three torpedoes from the heavy cruiser *HMS Dorsetshire* that sent what was considered the most powerful warship in all of Europe to the bottom of the ocean. Thus ended one of the most dramatic naval actions of the war.

In January 1942, Starheim returned to Flekkefiord with two additional transmitters. Together with Tomstad, whose feigned collaboration with the NS enabled him to remain unmolested by the Germans, Starheim's *Cheese* organization continued sending Home Station reports of German convoys, fortifications, and airfields. Contact was arranged with SOE-Milorg and a network was set up that extended over a vast expanse of south and southwest Norway.

In February of 1943, Tomstad received a telephone call from Kristiansand advising him that he was being summoned by the Gestapo. Realizing that he could no longer conceal his true identity as a double agent working for the Allies, he immediately went into hiding and in due course reached Sweden and England. Throughout the spring, after numerous arrests, reprisals, and the disclosure of information by torture, the *Cheese* broadcast code was broken, and by September, all further plans were cancelled.[25] Yet, no sooner had the *Cheese* station been rolled up than others rose up to maintain contact with London. Groups such as *Swan* (XU), *Aquila* (SIS), *Makir 1* and *2* (SIS), *Haakon* (SIS), *Sandpiper* (Milorg), and *Lola* (SIS) were but a few of the transmitting stations that provided vital information regarding plans for the blowing up bridges, wharves, and other installations.[26]

Throughout the months of 1943 and even into 1944, agents furnished intelligence concerning German preparations in anticipation of what they believed would be Allied landings in Norway, thereby assuring London that the German garrison in Norway would remain unreduced.[27] Additionally, SIS agents in Oslo had moles in the *Wehrmacht* headquarters and in the *Abwehr*, the German Counterespionage Agency. XU even had a source in Gestapo headquarters at the dreaded Viktoria Terrace.[28]

So what was the Intelligence Service's collective effect on the course of the war? Theirs was a campaign without visible fronts, without indisputable victories, and normally, given few exceptions, without sensational data. Aside from the small number of publicized personal narratives compared to the far larger number of unrecorded events in the history of the Resistance, it is impossible to accurately assess the sum total of achievements of the courageous men and women of the Intelligence Service. Nevertheless, those that have been recorded are deserving of special mention. One such chronicle is that of a small group that operated on the west coast in Bergen from 1940-1942. What follows is their story.

Theta—The Bergen Connection

Courage consists not in hazarding without fear,
But being resolutely minded in a just cause.
—*Plutarch (46-120), Greek biographer*

In the wake of the German military successes in the spring of 1940, widespread rumors circulated throughout Norway that the Germans were preparing to invade England.[1] It was believed that large numbers of the invasion force would embark from the west coast of Norway by means of fishing vessels and coastal ships confiscated by the German Occupation Forces. At that time, Jan Dahm, a 19-year-old student at Bergen Technical High School, joined together with a group of friends to construct a radio transmitter powerful enough to reach England. The plan was to establish contact with the Norwegian authorities in Britain and report the departure of the German forces from Norway whenever that might be.

Jan Dahm

A Norwegian collaborator who had somehow heard of the group's intentions, however, informed the German authorities of Jan's activities. While Jan was taking an examination at school, he was arrested by the Gestapo and charged with espionage. Together with 12 other Norwegians, he was sent to Oslo where he was court martialed under German martial law. The prosecutor demanded the death penalty, but the charge was dropped owing to insufficient evidence. In September, Jan returned to Bergen where he was required to report to the Gestapo twice a week. Undaunted by narrowly escaping the sentence of death and by continuous German surveillance, he was determined to carry out his plan.

The members of the group had been care-fully selected. There were the brothers Leif and Rolf Utne, ages 21 and 20, one a medical student and the other a philology student; Bjarne Thorsen, 19, a high school student; Kristian Ottosen, 19, also a philology student; Hagbarth Schjott, Jr., 20, a tailor; and two friends of Jan from the Bergen Technical School, Sigurd Gran Blytt and Jacob Landsvik, ages 20 and 21. The latter was also a telegraphy graduate of Bergen's nautical school. In the summer of 1941, the ninth member of the group and the only woman, Wenche Stenersen, an 18-year-old philosophy student, joined the group.

Bjarne W. Thorsen

Before becoming operational, two main problems had to be solved. A contact with England had to be established, and a safe house for the station had to be found. The latter problem was the easier to resolve. Jan's mother owned half of one of the harbor houses on the quay in the Hanseatic quarter of Bergen called "The Unicorn." One of the storerooms in the rear of the house was particularly suitable for the group's headquarters, hereafter called the "Café." Then it was only a matter of procuring a radio transmitter, receiver, codes, technical equipment, and weapons.

Kristian Ottosen

In December 1940, Leif Utne was selected to go to England via Sweden to establish contact with Norwegian and British authorities and return to Bergen with the necessary equipment. Owing to his low priority status, however, Utne was unable to get a flight to London until the fall of 1941. In the meantime, he received the approval of the Norwegian military attaché in Stockholm for the radio connection between Bergen and England. But because it was difficult to get to England with the few aircraft then available, Utne suggested that another member of the group be sent across the North Sea.

Bjarne Thorsen volunteered to go, but before he could be considered as a credible Allied agent, the London authorities would require tangible evidence of his loyalty. Introductions were obtained from two highly regarded contacts in the Resistance. One of them was Mons Haukeland, the leader of the Military Resistance in the west of Norway, for whom Thorsen had worked earlier as a courier. Additionally, a photograph was taken of Wenche Stenersen and Thorsen together, and a letter written by Wenche to her father, a major in the Norwegian Army who went to Britain at the end of the military campaign the previous year. The letter was photographed and the undeveloped negative was wrapped in paper and placed in a small, hollowed-out screw. If Bjarne were to be apprehended by the Germans and the screw was discovered, the film would be exposed and destroyed when they opened it. If he reached England successfully, the screw would be opened in a darkroom, the film would be developed, and the letter would grant him the authorization he needed to proceed.

Wenche Stenersen

In October 1941, Thorsen departed from the west coast for England on a motor-powered fishing cutter with 35 passengers on board. Four days later, despite appalling weather and periodic engine failure, the small vessel arrived at the Shetland Islands where, at Lerwick, all passengers were interrogated by a liaison officer. After explaining his assignment, Thorsen was sent to London where he met Utne who had recently arrived from Sweden. Together, after cross-examination, the two boys provided, by way of introduction, the names of the Resistance contacts and the photograph and hollowed out screw concealing Wenche's letter. They then outlined the young intelligence group's planned work distribution—namely, who would gather the intelligence data, who would carry out the technical aspects for coding and decoding material, and who would locate the headquarters location. Acting in consultation with the head of SIS Norwegian Department, Eric Welsh, the two stalwart lads initiated a close working Anglo-Norwegian relationship that lasted the duration of the war.

Thorsen was sent to a special training school at a home in Lexham Gardens, where an intensive six-week course in radio telegraphy was given under conditions of strictest security. He was taught how to set up, tune in, and change frequencies; set up an antenna; put received telegrams into code, both in English and Norwegian; insert the necessary security check; and organize a transmitting plan with both day and night frequencies. The Bergen station was given the code name *Theta*.

On December 2, 1941, Thorsen boarded a fishing smack in Peterhead, Scotland. His baggage consisted of a transmitter, a code book, weapons, money, and ration cards. Within 24 hours he was put ashore on the island of Sotra where, by ferry and bus, he made his way to downtown Bergen, where he arranged contact with Jan Dahm and Rolf Utne at the harbor storeroom "The Café." Thorsen wasted no time in providing the necessary instructions in the use of the transmitter, the codes, and so on. After three days, he returned to England by boat via the Shetlands, where he was given additional training with the intention of returning to Norway to continue resistance work there.

The Café had now been converted into a central headquarters, but because of the direction-finding vans, which the Germans frequently used in Bergen, it was never to be used for communicating with London. Behind a worktable, two beds could be lowered to the floor. In addition, there was a desk, photographic equipment for copying couriers' reports, and a tallboy for storing such items as hand weapons, hand grenades, surgical instruments, radio material, spare parts, and tobacco.

The secret storeroom was unique because it was completely unrecognizable. Jan had constructed the door and equipped it with an electric motor driven by batteries. The mechanism was devised so that it did not appear to be a door, and therefore the Germans would not notice it. From inside the room, wires were put through the door and attached to two of the many nails that had been hammered from the outside. Those who knew the method could short-circuit the heads of the two wired nails and the lock would open. As a necessary precaution in the event of an unexpected raid, a cupboard located above a shortwave receiver in the room contained five kilograms of TNT. If the cabinet door was opened, an electrical wire that was attached to a metal handle on the inside would connect to a plug that activated the explosive, and everything, including the room itself, would explode. The wire would be connected whenever members of the group left the room.

Before *Theta* could be made operational, an information system had to be created. A network of contacts consisting of reliable sources in the Customs Service, Harbormaster's Office, the Ministry of Supply, and the Lighthouse Service was established. Kristian Ottosen, who was in daily contact with Jan Dahm via Wenche, coordinated all intelligence. Jan decided which reports—especially those concerning the movement of shipping to and from Bergen—were to be sent to London.

A sympathetic inspector in the Customs Office provided an available room in his home at Tartargaten 18 for transmitting. The room, which was "rented" by Kristian under a false name for security reasons, was well situated high above the street, and was to be one of the most successful transmitting locations in the city. Jan's mother's garden apartment at Ovregaten 5 was also to be used for contacting London and for encoding and decoding communiqués. When the transmitter was not in use, it was kept in The Cafe. Timetables for transmitting and receiving were arranged on different wavelengths; and to avoid discovery, no transmissions could be sent on two consecutive days from the same location. By the end of 1941, the Bergen-London connection was established.

One day, several weeks after returning to England, Thorsen was called out of a weapons class and advised by Commander Welsh that something had gone wrong during a *Theta* transmission. At the time of a scheduled broadcast, after London notified the Bergen station that it was ready to receive, and after several code groups had been sent, another station suddenly broke in asking the operator to repeat certain code groups. The "other" station was obviously not the Home Station or any other British station. It could only be *Abwehr*, German counterespionage, which had somehow discovered the *Theta* frequency, thereby gaining direct access to the London-Bergen timetable for transmission. Unless *Theta* could be advised before its next scheduled transmission in three days, discovery by the German direction-finders was a certainty. Thorsen was immediately sent back to Bergen with a new crystal to advise the other members of the group.

Two days later, after crossing the North Sea again by boat, he contacted both Jan and Rolf and advised them of the *Abwehr* discovery before the next scheduled communiqué. The message was sent from the back room of the Dahms Elektriske in Strandgaten 18. All went well with no requests to repeat the codes. But even if the Germans did crack the code, the British would know it because of the large number of security checks that were put into the system. The group was now aware of the importance of changing the transmitting location more often.

Early in the morning on Saturday, January 17, 1942, Kristian was informed by one of his reliable contacts that the 43,000-ton battleship *Tirpitz* was lying well camouflaged in an arm of the Trondheimsfiord with six destroyers and several U-boats. The *Tirpitz*, like its sister ship *Bismarck*, was considered a potential threat to Allied supply lines between the United States and Britain, and between Iceland and Murmansk. This was the first sighting of the German dreadnought since leaving Wilhelmshaven three days earlier. Although Saturday was not a normal broadcast day for reporting to London, the message was encoded and transmitted: WKBA DE NYN WKBA DE NYN *THETA* CALLING LONDON, *THETA* CALLING LONDON. But London did not respond. Atmospheric conditions were not favorable. Moreover, as the message was being sent, the room suddenly went dark. In Bergen, the electricity, like everything else, was rationed, and at certain times of the day, it was turned off. For the next two days, connections remained unfavorable. Finally on January 23, contact with the Home Station was made and the message was received from the Tartargaten 18 residence.

The importance of the message is evident from a memorandum British Prime Minister Winston Churchill sent to Lord Ismay and the chiefs of staff on January 25:

> *The presence of Tirpitz at Trondheim has now been known for three days. The destruction or even the crippling of this ship is the greatest event at sea at the present time. No other target is comparable to it. The whole strategy of this war, at this time, is connected to this vessel, which is paralyzing four times as many British battleships, not to mention the two new American battleships that are being held back in the Atlantic. I consider the matter of the very highest importance and significance.*

Churchill ordered Coastal Command to bomb the *Tirpitz*, but because of inclement weather and partly because of the angle of protection, the planes were unable to score a hit. After the sinking of the *Bismarck* just eight months earlier, Hitler refused to permit the *Tirpitz* to sail as long as it was within striking range of a British aircraft carrier. Consequently, it was later sent to Altafiord, in the north of Norway, where it was kept as a threat to the Murmansk convoys.

Meanwhile, on February 25, Jan received a message from one of *Theta*'s contacts that a fleet of German warships was operating in Dolviken, south of Bergen. Kristian was sent immediately to identify the ships; however, the ships had left before he was able to reach his destination. But by going to a number of farms in the area from where the ships were sighted, he was able to determine, from what others had seen, the number, the sizes, and the direction in which the ships were heading. The information was passed on to Wenche, who delivered it to Jan. Using the ship silhouettes that Bjarne had brought back from England, all German warships on active duty could be identified. With the help of the black-and-white drawings, Jan was able to recognize the types of vessels, and how well they were equipped with weapons and firepower. The data was encoded and transmitted to the Home Station in London.

When the Admiralty received the message, it concluded correctly that the vessels—a pocket battleship, cruiser, and three destroyers— were heading north on escort duty to reinforce the *Tirpitz*, which was lying in anchor in a side fiord near Trondheimfiord. One of the German ships was identified as the heavy cruiser, *Prinz Eugen*, which had accompanied the *Bismarck* just before the latter's demise in May of the previous year.

The British submarine *Trident* that was operating in the area at the time torpedoed the *Prinz Eugen*, blowing part of the stern away and damaging the steering mechanism, forcing it to dock in Trondheim for repairs. After the attack, *Theta* received the following telegram from Home Station:

CONGRATULATIONS STOP

YOU ARE IN THE MIDDLE OF EVERYTHING STOP

BE CAREFUL AND LIVE LONG STOP

In the fall of 1942, a bold effort was made to cripple the *Tirpitz* by means of a two-man torpedo called a Chariot, which the Navy had perfected. About 20 feet long, it was driven by electric motors. Its crew sat astride it in diving suits, protected by a kind of windscreen, behind which was a luminous instrument panel and controls. On its nose was a large detachable warhead. The plan was to launch two Chariots from a fishing boat and place their charges under the keel of the *Tirpitz*, which was anchored in the Trondheimfiord. But because of an unexpected change in the weather, the Chariots broke free and sank beyond any chance of recovery.

A second attempt was made in September 1943, using recently developed midget submarine minelayers, called X-crafts. Each one carried a crew of four and two 4,000-pound explosive charges. Two of the X-crafts were lost at sea. Another went aground, forcing it to surface, and its crew was taken prisoner. The fourth X-craft did manage to secure two charges of eight tons of explosives under the hull of the *Tirpitz*.

The charges caused such extensive damage to the turbines, main turrets, range finders, and fire control equipment that the ship was unable to return to Germany for major repairs. Some damage could be repaired in Norway, but it was no longer an operational ship capable of being used in combat. The *Tirpitz* was moved to the Arctic port of Tromso, where it was later sighted by a British reconnaissance plane in the fall of 1944. On November 12, a squadron of Lancaster bombers left Lossiemouth, Scotland, and finally succeeded in sinking the German battleship, thereby reducing the danger to Allied shipping in the far North Atlantic.[2]

Throughout the spring and early summer of 1942, a great deal of resistance activity took place on the west coast. One of *Theta*'s main tasks involved photographing German shipping and military equipment. And since the group had no laboratory for developing the film, Kristian had an arrangement with a man known simply as "Petter," who had a photo-finishing shop, to develop the film. One night in June, the Germans, who had somehow become suspicious, searched the shop and discovered some compromising film that Kristian had left to be developed. "Petter," who knew the address of a room that he had rented, was forced to disclose his name and whereabouts after being severely beaten. While searching the room, the Gestapo discovered a typewriter, telegraphy textbook, and a number of maps, as well as a list that requested information about German military equipment and movements.

On June 25, Ottosen was arrested and taken to Veiten, the Gestapo headquarters in Bergen, where he underwent interrogation by an officer of the *Sicherheitsdienst*. He admitted owning the typewriter, maps, and book, but denied any knowledge of the list. "I think we may be able to help your memory," the *Sturmbannführer*, Helmut Klotzer, retorted. On a nod to the four other men in the room, the prisoner was suddenly knocked to the floor and repeatedly beaten with rubber batons, iron chains, and fists, accompanied by yelling and kicking. The blows were struck with an insane intensity that was matched by a scream from the top of the victim's lungs. Either because of the shock from the screaming, or the thought that Kristian would now talk, the sign was given to stop. When he was asked about the list again, he denied knowing what it meant. "*Gut dann mussen wir Ihnen helfen*" ("Good, then we have to help you"). Then it started again.

But as long as he could deny any knowledge of the list, *Theta* would remain intact. Any disclosure would be disastrous for the members of the group. At a certain point, Kristian yelled, "*Ich soll sprechen, Ich soll sprechen* ("Stop, I will speak"). The torture stopped immediately and he was given a glass of water. Cotton was put into one nostril that was bleeding. When asked about the list again, he said, "Nothing. I said I would speak, and so I am right now, but I can't talk about anything more right now. I just said I would speak to stop the beating and kicking." And the beating resumed with even greater ferocity.

After being thrown back into his cell, Kristian was in such intense agony from the blows to his buttocks, back, and feet that it was impossible to sit, stand, or lie down. He was only able to rest on his knees and support himself by placing his hands on the floor. Before his arrest, Kristian had been offered a cyanide pill by Rolf Utne, which he refused. "I will not say anything if I'm caught," he told him. Would he now be able to keep that promise? Would he be able to endure another day of torture? For many members of the Resistance, the loss of their lives was seen as "freedom" if they had been through an interrogation by the Gestapo.

As the faces of those whose lives depended upon his silence passed before his blurred vision, Kristian saw a porcelain cup on the bench, which he broke. Taking the sharpest piece, he opened a vein in his wrist and allowed the blood to stream across the cell floor. Several minutes later, a German guard peered through the peephole in the cell door and

The Illegal Press

John M. Hansen and Jorgen Hoff-Jenssen at the stencil machine printing
the clandestine newspaper.

Interior view of "the Café"

(which the Germans discovered by accident)

1. Equipment for photographing couriers' reports.

2. Hiding place for approximately 10 kilograms of TNT that would detonate on opening the cupboard door.

3. Short-wave receiver.

4. Desk.

5. Heating element for water.

6. Transmitter

7. Electrical panel with instruments.

8. Storeroom.

9. Thompson submachine guns.

10. Coffee table. After the raid by the Gestapo, it was moved to the residence of the Gestapo where it remained until May 1945.

11. Electrically locked door (see photograph following page?) with the following (12-15) components:

12. Wires attached to two nails that went through door. By short circuiting the heads of these two nails (many had been driven from the outside where it appeared to be a boarded-up door), the lock opened.

13. Electric motor driven by batteries

14. Mechanical transmission for drawing out the bolt that locked the door

15. Worktable and two beds which could be lowered for use.

16. Tallboy for storing hand weapons, grenades, surgical instruments, and other materials.

From the outside the door to the "The Café," the secret storeroom of the Theta group in Bergen, looked like a boarded-up door that the Germans would never notice. The inside, however, looked like this. The wires were attached to two of the many nails hammered from the outside and connected to an electric motor driven by batteries. Those who knew the secret could short-circuit the heads of the wired nails and open the door.

A cupboard above a short-wave receiver in The Cafe contained five kilograms of TNT. If anyone opened the cabinet door, an electrical wire attached to a metal handle inside would connect to a plug that activated the explosive.

A telegraph operator transmitting messages from Oslo.

A transmitter used by a Theta wireless operator to communicate with London.

Nr. 29.   "JÖSSINGEN"   1942

En ny forordning er kommet fra det såkalte quislingske ministerium og tyskerne. Denne forordning som er utsendt til alle offentlige institusjoner i landet inneholdet følgende bestemmelser:

1. Enhver som herefter ulovlig er i besiddelse av radioapparat er hjemfallen til dödsstraff.
2. Alle som forteller eller bringer rykter om nyheter kommet fra andre kilder enn Berlin og Oslo, dömmes til döden.
3. Alle som hörer sådanne rykter eller nyheter uten straks å fortelle det til politiet er også hjemfallen til dödsstraff.
4. Denne forordning trer ikraft straks.

Denne siste desperate forordning er for oss et optimismens tegn. Det viser nemlig at vi snart er kommet til slutten av dette forferdelige skuespill. Ingen god nordmann må dog behandle denne forordning med skjödesløshet, og dermed utsette sig selv og de som driver med propagandaarbeide o.l. for livsfare. Man må også nu vise den största forsiktighet ved mottagelsen av hemmelige aviser, da en sådan kan være provokasjon fra nazistenes side. Hvis man får en slik avis som man mener er mistenkelig, skal man straks sette sig i forbindelse med folk man har tillit til, og som kanskje har kjennskje til det illegale arbeide. Hvis det viser sig efter en sådan undersökelse at avisen er provokasjon, må man straks bringe den til politiet. Vi skal i et senere nummer gi en mere detaljert fremstilling av dette, og bringe oplysninger om de aviser man kan stole på. Det er milig at de hemmelige aviser vi sender ut vil utkomme med et visst stikkord. Dette skal vi også komme til bake til senere. Det som nu gjelder er at man gjör sin plikt ved å være ennu mere forsiktig enn för. Snakk ikke nyheter eller andre illegale emner med andre enn folk De personlig kjenner. HUSK DITT ANSVAR FOR KONGE OG FEDRELAND OG DET NORSKE FOLK.

2/11.42. Östfronten: På et dögn har russen gått til 4 motangrep og tyskerne har frafalt mange av sine stillinger i Stalingrad. N.v. og S.v. for byen fortsetter det russiske press. I stillingene rundt Svartehavshavnen Tuapse er tyskerne fremdeles på defensiven. Den påbegynte tyske offensiv ved byen Nalchik har en del fremgang.

Afrika: Den br. 8. arme kjemper nu delvis bakenfor de tyske rekker. Tyskerne har svære tap av mennesker og materiell. Flyvåpenet retter stadige angrep mot forbindelseslinjer, befestninger og transportmidler. I tokter över Middelhavet senket flyvåpenet 2 transp.skip som skulde til Afrika med forsyninger. Jagerfly skjöt ned 2 tyske fly over Biskayabukten.

Stillehavet: Japanerne har under kampene öst for Salomonöiene tapt 2 kryssere, 2 slagskip, 2 hangarskip og 1 destroyer, samt 22 forsyningsskip og transp.skip og 150 fly. Amerikanerne har tapt 1 hangarskip og 1 destroyer samt 22 fly.

England: I flere dager er der drevet storstilte invasjonsövelser i England med styrker fra hæren, marinen og flyvåpenet.

3/11. Östfronten: I Stalingrad har russen hatt ny fremgang og tatt igjen flere kvartaler i fabrikkströkene. I n.v. fortsetter tyskerne å trekke sig tilbake. I Kaukasus har tyskerne trukket 2 div. fra Mostoch, og satt dem inn ved byen Nalchik.

Afrika: Den br. 8. arme har vunnet flere stillinger og tatt en masse fanger. I lommen ved kyststrekningen utvikler det sig nu et voldsomt panserslag. Flyvåpenet har igjen vært i virksomhet og senket 2 skip i Middelhavet. Britiske krigsskip angrep igår fra sjöen bak de tyske stillinger ved Marsu Matruk, og gjorde stor skade ved et kraftig bombardement.

Stillehavet: På Ny-Guinea har nu de australske tropper inntatt den viktige japanske basis Cocoda. Japanerne forsökte å komme til undsetting med store styrker, men det mislyktes fullstendig.

England: Store styrker br. fly var igår over Aberville i nord-Frankrike. Br. krigsskip traff söndag på 2 tyske konvoier i Kanalen, og gikk straks til angrep på dem. Under treffningen mistet tyskerne 7 skip.

Det herkser fremdeles stor uenighet mellem Hitler og hans generaler. Hitler har derfor sett sig nödsagt til å ansette 4 nye generaler og mange generalmajorer.

Copy of the "illegal" stenciled newspaper, Jössingen.
The name was later changed to Avisa—meaning news.

24th January, 1942.

N./572.

To the Norwegian Defence Ministry,

"E" Office.

SHIP MOVEMENTS.

Source: THETA.
Date of Information: 20th January, 1942.
T.o.R. 1155 hours, 23th January, 1942.

The "Admiral von Tirpitz", six destroyers, and several u-boats were lying in an arm of the Aasenfjord, in Trondheimsfjord on the 20th January.

Four of the destroyers have left.

There are one hundred aeroplanes stationed at Vaernes.

150 tons of petrol arrive in Trondheim, via Storleín, together with other stores, every day.

The same applies to Narvik.

Mottatt den...... kl...........
Oversendt den....... Kl.........
....ret - major Nagell
I .... Kl............

A "most secret" memo from Theta, 24 January 1942, to the Norwegian Defence Ministry about ship movements, including the Tirpitz.

The German troop transport Donau aground in Oslofiord. Max Manus and Roy Nielsen, Oslo "underwater saboteurs," used magnetic limpet mines to wreck the ship.

One of a number of railroad bridges destroyed by Milorg saboteurs as part of Operation Concrete Mixer in March 1945.

Gunnar Sonsteby and the Oslo Gang carried out the sabotage at the Labor Office in Oslo (Akersgaten 55) during the work mobilization in May 1944.

An example of industrial sabotage. This stopped production of aluminum that went into airplane production, August 1944

Swedish Kullager ball-bearing factory in Oslo.
(which saboteurs destroyed in November 1944)

Before

After

observed Kristian sitting in a pool of blood. The inmate was pulled by his feet and put in a blanket and carried outside to an ambulance that was waiting. He was taken to a nearby field hospital where he was admitted and his numerous wounds were treated. The worst part was that his eyes were glued shut from the beatings, making it impossible for him to see what was going on around him.

The following morning, the German doctor who examined the patient said, mostly to himself, "What have they done to this boy?" Shaking his head, he said, "How are things like this possible?" Kristian had a high fever, numerous blood effusions, and open wounds that would require an indefinite stay in the hospital. Suddenly, there were loud voices in the hallway and the door to Kristian's room was opened. It was the Gestapo chief and three of his lackeys. They had come to take him back to prison. Despite the doctor's objections, the patient was forcibly returned to the same cell from which he had been taken less than 24 hours earlier. Completely naked, covered in bandages, and with several stitches in his wrist, a wool blanket was thrown over him. He remained in the cell for five days, at which time he was sent back to the hospital where the bandages were removed, and then returned to his cell and more interrogation.

In the days following Kristian's arrest, further examination by the Germans disclosed that the typewriter found in the agent's rented room was the same machine that had been used to make out the list that was the key to the entire investigation. Again he denied any knowledge of the list. Day after day and night after night the beatings continued.

Then one morning, his cell door was opened and a young Norwegian cleaning girl entered with a bucket and a mop. The floor was covered with vomit and blood. The guard ordered her to clean up the mess, but before leaving the cell, she removed a letter from her blouse and put it inside the prisoner's shirt. When he was alone once again, he read the letter. It was from his fiancée, Gerd Kleppesto. In part it read, *I have tried to make contact, but with no luck. But no matter what happens, I'll be waiting for you.*

At such a critical moment in his life, the letter could not have come at a more opportune time. Resilience took over. His will to live had been rekindled and his determination to remain inflexible had been mobilized. One is reminded of the sanguine *Prison Vespers*, which was put to music by the well-known Norwegian composer, Pauline Hall:

> *Despite padlocks and bolts,*
>
> *Thoughts, hope, and longing*
>
> *To those we have left behind*
>
> *Find their way in the quiet night*
>
> *While we here are prisoners.*
>
> *Some day like these thoughts Freedom will break down the bars.*
>
> *Every prison door shall be opened Freedom we shall carry to the north and south*
>
> *Prisoners no more.*[3]

Kristian's absence had placed the other members of the group on alert. Like others in the Resistance, when one of their own had been arrested, they asked the question: How long could the prisoner stand up to the torture before disclosing names? And when he cracked, whose name would be mentioned? It had been eight days since the arrest, but still there was no word about their compatriot. After three weeks of day and night interrogation at Gestapo headquarters, Kristian was transferred to the Bergen District Prison, where one of the Norwegian warders knew of him and of his arrest. One night, after further interrogation, the warder entered Kristian's cell with a coded message and said, "What can I bring out?" "You can go out," came the reply, "and say that I said nothing, and that no one need be afraid as no one knows about *Theta*, about the radio."

When Home Station was informed that Kristian had been arrested, it was decided that the station be closed down until further notice. Two of the members—Jan and Wenche—were asked to report to the British Embassy in Stockholm and from there, Jan was ordered to London to decide what further action should be taken. In mid-August, after his arrival, Jan gave a detailed report of what had happened in Bergen. Toward the end of October, when it had become clear that Kristian had disclosed nothing that would compromise the group and that the other members were still intact, plans were made to reactivate the station as soon as possible. Both Jan and Bjarne, who had also been sent back to England for additional training, were authorized by Lieutenant-Commander Welsh to return to Norway with new equipment, new codes, and a new transmitter. They expected to be back on line by November 8.

At about the same time in Bergen, the Gestapo had ordered a large-scale raid of the harbor houses on the quay. After surrounding the area, 300 soldiers undertook a systematic search of every building by the pier. One of the soldiers who was creeping along the roof of the "Unicorn" had accidentally stepped through some rotten floor boards above The Café and came down through some new material from a recent construction. The Germans then went to the front of the room on the second story porch, but could not locate a door. They entered the secret room forcibly through the roof. Upon hearing of the raid, those members of *Theta* who were in Bergen went under cover in accordance with previously drawn up security procedures. These were wireless operators Jacob Landsvik and Otto Nielsen, Frank Olsen, the caretaker at The Café, Sidden Blytt, Haggen Schjott, and Jan's cousin, Markus Wiig.

Meanwhile, Wenche, who was still in Stockholm at that time, learned about the raid at the Café from an old friend of her father who had just escaped across the border. Upon hearing the news, she went to the British Embassy and asked them to inform London immediately, whereupon a telegram was sent to Home Station. When Commander Welsh received the telegram concerning the raid, Dahm and Thorsen were stopped just as they were preparing to embark for Bergen. Because of the probability of being arrested upon reentering Bergen, they were ordered to remain in England. It was suggested they transfer to the Norwegian Fighting Forces where they enlisted in the Royal Norwegian Navy. It was now certain that the *Theta* station could not be reactivated.

At the beginning of the New Year 1943, Wenche had left Stockholm for London, where she reported for service in a Norwegian Army cross-country skiing company operating in Iceland. Rolf was in training as a bombardier with the Royal Air Force in "Little Norway" in Canada. But the fate of those members who remained in Bergen was less fortunate. After the raid at the harbor, Frank went to Oslo under cover en route to Sweden with false papers, but was soon apprehended by the Gestapo. Jacob Landsvik was arrested three weeks later on the Oslo train station platform. Both men underwent long and rigorous interrogation at the infamous police station, Mollergaten 19, whose reputation for sadistic forms of brutality was widely known. Landsvik was later transferred to Grini Concentration Camp on the outskirts of Oslo. Both he and Olsen were later sent to Natzweiler Concentration Camp on the German-French border some 50 kilometers south of Strasbourg.

Jacob Landsvik

Equipped with false passports, Sidden Blytt, Haggen Schjott, and Marcus Wiig took the train to Oslo where temporary places were arranged for them by other Resistance contacts. From there they managed to cross safely over the border into Sweden where they waited for a plane to take them to England. After crossing the North Sea, Markus joined an engineering unit in the British Army; Sidden and Haggen joined the Royal Norwegian Navy where Sidden became a specialist in the destruction of German mines. Haggen served aboard motor torpedo boats (MTBs) operating out of Shetland.

Meanwhile, Kristian had devised a plan to avoid further torture from the Gestapo by play-acting in such an irrational fashion that he made a convincing pretense of insanity. He wanted to create a situation in which he would temporarily be taken to a hospital where the chance of escape was much greater than escaping from a cell in Gestapo headquarters. At first, he broke the window in his cell with a stool, and then repeatedly threw a table and iron bucket against the wall, thereby making life intolerable for himself and the guard outside his cell. When the guard finally entered his cell, Ottosen started strangling him, until he was restrained by other prison personnel. He was examined by a Norwegian doctor, who diagnosed him as suffering from an acute mental breakdown. After having been given a sedative, he was put into a straitjacket and tied down to a bench. And although he was refused admission to the hospital by the Gestapo, his feigned insanity had put a stop to the interrogations. On September 1, he was transferred to Grini where, after the next two months, his charade came to an abrupt end.

In December, Kristian was sent to Sachsenhausen Concentration Camp, northeast of Berlin, as a *Nacht und Nebel* (Night and Fog) prisoner. These were persons from the occupied countries of France, Holland, Belgium, and Norway suspected of resistance, who were brought to Germany, but in the absence of proof, were not to be immediately executed. Hitler believed that the death penalty for these persons in their native country would inspire too much unnecessary and negative publicity, and thereby create even more anti-German feeling among the population. Instead, those in question were suddenly, and without leaving a trace, secretly sent "under cover of night and fog," to an undisclosed concentration camp where most of them were worked to death.[4]

In the fall of 1943, Rolf Utne returned to England as an RAF bombardier, where he was later transferred to a squadron of Lancaster bombers at Lincolnshire under Australian leadership. During the night of July 17-18, 1944, their target was the oil refineries in Gelsenkirchen in the Ruhr. During the operation, they encountered heavy German anti-aircraft fire and were attacked by German night fighters. Rolf's plane received several direct hits and one of the engines caught fire. An attempt was made to make an emergency landing near the town of Venlo on the German-Dutch border, but the plane exploded in the air killing everyone but the navigator. Rolf was two months short of his 24 birthday, and was the first member of the *Theta* group to lose his life.

In the spring of 1944, Kristian was transferred to Natzweiler where he met Landsvik and Olsen. They were assigned to work in a stone quarry where the death rate was exceptionally high owing to malnutrition and overwork. Prisoners were given a daily ration of thin soup and a piece of bread consisting of 350 grams. The bread was to be divided so that they had something to eat in the morning, at noon, and in the evening, but many of the prisoners ate all the bread in the evening when they returned from the quarry. The weight loss was terrible, resulting in the high incidence of deaths. Of the 504 Norwegians at Natzweiler, 246 died from starvation or overwork.

By August it was becoming increasingly obvious to the Germans that the Allies were on the offensive and moving rapidly through France and towards Germany itself. Very hastily, and in full retreat, the Germans were evacuating their prisons and camps. All Natzweiler prisoners were evacuated to Dachau, which had now became too small to contain all the prisoners from the evacuated camps in both Eastern and Western Europe. Therefore, after the prisoners were registered in Dachau, the SS decided that most of the Natzweiler prisoners were to be sent to various other camps in Germany. Jacob was transferred to Mauthausen, called Gusen, where he worked in an underground factory producing wings for the Messerschmidt fighter plane.

Kristian and Frank were sent to Dautmergen, not far from the Swiss border. Conditions there were extremely difficult. Unfortunately, Frank died in this camp in November 1944. Kristian had contracted frostbite and open blisters. In October he was transferred to Vaihingen an der Enz, a smaller camp between Karlsruhe and Stuttgart. All together, 29 Norwegian Natzweiler prisoners came to the Vaihingen camp during the autumn and winter of 1944-45 where 13 of them died.

By the beginning of April 1945, 16 prisoners had survived. On April 6, a Swedish Red Cross bus arrived at the camp. Throughout the course of the night the survivors were removed by bus and taken to the concentration camp at Neuengamme, not far from Hamburg. They were then transported to Sweden in early April 1945. In Sweden where Jacob and Kristian met each other, they learned of Rolf's death. The two men returned to Norway in mid-summer 1945 where they were reunited with the surviving members of *Theta* who had successfully arrived in Great Britain after their station had been closed down in the autumn of 1944.

Like most other intelligence agents in SIS who collectively covered the entire 1,100-mile coastline of Norway, the members of *Theta* had no contact with the rest of the Military Resistance. Moreover, they had both limited training and experience along with unsophisticated equipment compared to the highly trained and well-equipped German security service. Yet despite these limitations, they constituted a critically important arm of the Resistance by providing Home Station with the intelligence, in varying degrees that enabled the British to neutralize the German fleet operations from Norwegian ports. Their courage, self-sacrifice, and unwavering perseverance in the face of what were seemingly insurmountable odds, serve as lasting testimony to those thousands of agents, both men and women, whose names are not recorded, but whose valor will long live in the history of the Resistance.

The Politics of Sabotage—SOE and Milorg

sabotage (sab/e-tazh); n. [Fr. saboter, to work badly, damage;

sabot & age; from damage done to machinery by wooden shoes],

1. intentional destruction of machines, waste of materials, etc.,

2. intentional obstruction of or damage to some productive process,

> *organized activity or effort, etc.*

3. a) destruction of railroads, bridges, machinery, etc., by enemy agents

> *in time of war;*

4. hence, b) any deliberate obstruction of a nation's war work.

—Webster's New World Dictionary of the American Language

> *(Third Edition, 1997)*

The British Intelligence Service and the Norwegian Intelligence Office acted jointly as early as the summer of 1940 to establish a line of communication for gathering secret information from within occupied Norway. However, the relationship between the two separate paramilitary fighting groups—the British Special Operations Executive (SOE) and the Norwegian Military Organization (Milorg)—followed a somewhat different course. To understand the evolving pattern that this relationship involved throughout the Occupation, it is necessary to sketch briefly the purpose of each of these ad hoc organizations.

Winston Churchill established the SOE in July 1940, to carry out sabotage activity in all of the countries of occupied Europe, and to train secret armies to rise up against the occupying power when the time for invasion came. SOE was divided into two sections: SO1 (propaganda) and SO2 (sabotage).[1] Christened the "Department of Ungentlemanly Warfare," SOE's aim was, in Churchill's words, to "set Europe ablaze" by training saboteurs covertly and sending them behind enemy lines on secret raids to destroy or damage facilities and supplies used or owned by the Germans in the conduct of the war.[2] Derailing trains, blowing up petroleum and oil storage facilities, destroying power stations that provided current to war manufacturing plants, mining roads, cutting telephone and telegraph wires, attacking aerodromes and sinking ships in harbor—all of these activities were designed to force the enemy to guard vulnerable points, thereby immobilizing thousands of soldiers who might otherwise be employed in another theater of operations.

In the summer of 1940, when Britain stood alone in the war against the German onslaught of occupied Europe, SOE officials in London believed that only Norway, Czechoslovakia, and Poland had the moral resolve and the nucleus of a potential military organization needed to create a patriotic uprising that would provide armed support in the event of an Allied invasion. Czechoslovakia was too far by air and land locked, and the terrain offered no accessible reception. Poland was also distant and, because of the stronghold that the Germans had over the country, the invasion could be done mainly by sea transport. Moreover, the number of Norwegians who had escaped to Britain far exceeded the number of émigrés from other occupied countries. Thus it was decided to provide Norway with the necessary weaponry and equipment in support of this aim.

As early as September, the Scandinavian Section of SOE, headed by Charles (later Sir Charles) Hambro, was recruiting Norwegian refugees who had endured the dangerous North Sea crossing in fishing boats to join the Norwegian or British forces. Those who were eager to actively engage the enemy and met the stringent requirements were trained as agents in espionage and guerrilla warfare. Courses were given in the use of explosives and small-arms tactics at special training schools in castles in England and Scotland and on country estates in the United Kingdom. Training and maneuvers of every kind took place under conditions of strictest security.

Once trained, the agents would then be landed by boats or by parachute back into Norway. Their mission would be to sabotage special objectives or attack enemy lines of communication. In short, Norway was to be a "thorn in the side of the Germans." Before long the first contingent evolved into the "Norwegian Independent Company No. 1." This was later to become known as "Company Linge," which derived its name from its first leader, former actor and Norwegian reserve officer, Captain Martin Linge, who served with the British Expeditionary Force in the earlier spring campaign.

Unlike the SOE leadership, the Milorg leadership in Norway did not yet believe that the country was ready for an active Military Resistance. An offensive policy consisting of raids and sabotage was contrary to their goal, which was the establishment of a centralized secret army prepared slowly and carefully in readiness for the day of liberation. They believed that the SOE's "over-hasty" mode of operation would lead to such strong German retaliation against the population that both the capacity and the will for resistance would be impaired. The idea of an active sabotage politic had to be weighed against the German reprisals that could be expected. The death penalty was imposed for sabotage, weapon possession, and for active support of the Resistance. These were critically important issues that had to be evaluated soberly and unhurriedly.[3]

In the summer of 1940, a national consciousness was already beginning to develop within Norway. Small individual groups assembled, mostly independently of one another, and consisting of members of voluntary defense organizations—men who had taken part in the spring military campaign, active sportsmen, members of the Scout movement, athletic clubs, and various youth organizations. The intention was to maintain a defense-minded awareness among the young, provide them with cautious field training, and follow General Ruge's appeal after the capitulation in North Norway to "wait, trust and be prepared."[4] The different resistance-minded groups were then to be organized into a system of cadres that would become activated only at the time of a large-scale invasion by the British—an invasion that many hoped and believed would occur in the near future. In the fall and winter of 1940, it was believed that the groups were numerous enough to be placed under a centralized leadership. By the end of the year, a Military Resistance organization—Milorg—was formed.

In December 1940, British leaders in the SOE issued a directive on Norwegian policy, which stated that it would support the Norwegian morale with the aid of raids, propaganda, and sabotage.[5] Norwegians working for SOE were told that all of that organization's resistance activities in Norway would be carried out under British leadership, and independently both of the Norwegian authorities in London and of the local Milorg leadership. In other words, members of the SOE, both in London and Stockholm, believed that it should conduct its work without interference from Milorg which they believed would put future SOE operations at grave risk. Like a number of the Norwegians in the Intelligence Service in the early phases of the Occupation, members of Milorg were overly talkative and had no previous training in clandestine work.[6]

Furthermore, the expectation of a British invasion—that never came—led to "over-hurried work" and a careless neglect of certain security measures. With the help of Norwegian collaborators, the Gestapo was soon aware of the Milorg activity, which led to a number of arrests in the summer and fall of 1941. These severe blows lent credibility to the allegation by certain British officers that Milorg lacked the ability to take simple security precautions. As might be expected, the distrust and the refusal of SOE to provide Milorg with information concerning their activities led to friction and misunderstandings between the two military organizations, despite their common goal, the liberation of Norway.

In early March 1941, the expectation of an invasion in the immediate future was strengthened by a British coastal raid against four ports in the Lofoten Islands in North Norway. Accompanying 500 British commandos were 52 Norwegian members of SOE, led by Captain Linge. Eleven herring and cod oil factories that supplied glycerine for the manufacture of German munitions were blown up. Additionally, an electric light plant and oil tanks containing 800,000 gallons were destroyed. More than 314 Norwegian volunteers were brought back to Britain, as well as 225 German and 12 Quisling prisoners.[7]

Although the British viewed the raid as an economic objective and militarily as a success, heavy German reprisals resulted, consisting of numerous arrests and the burning of innocent civilian homes. Moreover, much of the destruction in the raid was regarded by the Norwegian populace in the area as *their* property on which their livelihood depended, rather than as an enemy setback. This created even greater discord between the Norwegian authorities and SOE.

In June, the leaders of Milorg submitted a report to the King, which stated that "weapons are not wanted at the present time and that sabotage activities would only sharpen the enemy's attention and thereby repress our organization's work. Furthermore, widespread sabotage activities which the general population would have to suffer through would not create a favorable opinion within the population."[8]

It also outlined the need for governmental approval of Milorg, for the following reasons:

- Milorg believed that it would be easier to channel a "resistance feeling" among the population, and thereby gain their support for the work it was to do.

- Higher authority was necessary to deal with issues involving the use of sabotage, the execution of dangerous informers, and other critical matters of principle.

- Milorg needed official standing in its relationship with the Norwegian exile government in London and Great Britain. Without that recognition by its own government, the British SOE and SIS could legitimately avoid any contact with Milorg.

- Finally, to exercise military resistance, physical resources, such as weapons, equipment, and invasion troops were needed. And without the authority of the Norwegian government, Milorg could not expect Britain to provide those means.[9]

A copy of the report reached SOE, and in response, a directive of July 17, 1941, was issued. Its Scandinavian Section emphasized that all sabotage must be studied in detail in advance or be carried out under strict control. Poorly planned sabotage could only damage the Resistance Movement by lowering the people's morale as a result of the reprisals which would follow. *It was important to create as many problems as possible for the Germans and thereby force them to maintain as many troops in Norway as possible. For this strategic objective, sabotage was seen as a vital necessity.* SOE wanted the sabotage to appear "accidental" to avoid reprisals. It was to be carried out by special sabotage groups in Norway or those sent in by Great Britain. Transportation and communication facilities—ships, shipbuilding, road transportation, railroads, and electric power plant stations—were the most important targets.[10]

The Norwegian government did not know about the directive from the SOE. So to prevent a similar situation from occurring in the future, and to arrange for a greater Norwegian influence in Military Resistance work in Norway, it was decided to recognize Milorg as part of the Norwegian armed forces. In November 1941, it was placed under the Norwegian Army Command in Britain.[11]

In the week after Christmas, short-term hit-and-run British raids were resumed along the Norwegian coast. The first was against the villages of Reine and Moskenes in the Lofoten Islands, where a German armed trawler was sunk, 266 Norwegian patriots were evacuated, and 29 German prisoners taken prisoner along with a few Quislings. However, the British were ordered to withdraw when they intercepted a German radio signal indicating that a German force was being assembled at Narvik to counterattack the invaders.[12]

At the same time, a second Lofoten raid, supported by SOE commandos, took place on the coast at Måloy and Vågso, where Captain Martin Linge was killed while leading an attack on the German headquarters. The two towns were occupied and the entire German garrison killed or taken prisoner. After the combined Allied force returned to Britain, however, the Germans took heavy reprisals against the population and several neighboring villages. This only heightened the ill feelings between the Norwegian authorities and the SOE to fever pitch. Moreover, a number of Linge soldiers, disillusioned by the quick withdrawal, felt almost like mercenaries since the raid did not have the approval of the Norwegian government.[13] Furthermore, the Germans saw this as an opportunity to launch a propaganda attack on the Norwegian government-in-exile, accusing them of being under British rule with no influence whatsoever.[14]

On January 1, 1942, a special Norwegian Section within the SOE was established, headed by Colonel J. S. Wilson. Its purpose was to coordinate all SOE activities in Norway. And in February, as the result of talks between Norwegian Minister of Defense Oscar Torp and SOE's Sir Charles Hambro, the first meeting of the Anglo-Norwegian Collaboration Committee (ANCC) took place to establish top-level procedures for cooperation between SOE and the Norwegian Defense Command (FO).[15]

The main issue in the SOE-Milorg relationship was the question of their respective roles in the reconquest of Norway. The Norwegian position was that Milorg be fully activated only in case of a British invasion aimed at the liberation of Norway. SOE considered its own future operational function as one of supplying Milorg with the necessary weapon instructors, weapons, ammunition, equipment, and transportation of Norwegian agents. The ANCC also recognized the importance of limiting sabotage to essential targets and that all such actions be executed by SOE agents.

Not all of the Resistance groups in Norway held the same view on the issue of active Resistance and sabotage. In the spring and summer of 1940, the official Communist Party line in the occupied areas, especially around Oslo, favored cooperation with the German invaders. According to one Communist newspaper, the party line was roughly comparable to that of the French Vichy government after the fall of France in June. Some, however, particularly in the Bergen area, advocated active resistance against Germany from the outset of the Occupation. After the Norwegian Communist Party (NKP) was officially banned in August 1940, it operated as a resistance organization under cover names such as the League of Norwegian Patriots, the National Guard, and the National Front. Resistance activists often joined these Communist-organized groups without realizing the party affiliation. It was not until the spring of 1943, that the apparatus came forward as a Resistance organization under the party name.[16] In a directive to the Norwegian government in October 1941, party leader Peter Furubotn, a Bergen carpenter, acknowledged that the passive resistance politic was clearly an expression of opposition to nazification, but was of no real value in dealing with those more critical areas of war production and the labor force. The pioneer Communist was committed to "effective struggle methods which were organized sabotage in all its forms, and guerrilla struggles, etc."[17]

Communist sabotage operations did not begin until the summer of 1941, when the Soviet Union entered the war. A series of actions that took place in Oslo and East Norway at the turn of 1941-42 were unsuccessful and those involved were uncovered by the Gestapo. In the following August the so-called Osvald Group headed by Communist Spanish Civil War veteran Asbjorn Sunde successfully attacked the State Police Headquarters at Henrik Ibsengata in Oslo, but the action was followed by several arrests and executions. In a letter to the Norwegian Foreign Minister in London, the Home Front Leadership—the "Circle"—strongly emphasized that the "Home Front struggle at this point in time must remain weaponless," and that "actions against the State Police will be construed as examples of 'purposeless terrorist activity,' which a group of irresponsible Norwegians are carrying out."[18] Throughout the course of 1942, the Communists had established contact with the Linge Company from which they received weapons and training. Sabotage increased the following autumn, but most of the actions were of no particular military significance.

Unlike the SOE agents in France and the Low Countries, SOE saboteurs in Norway were not associated with networks because no such networks existed. Consequently, independent SOE teams were assigned to undertake specific assignments. Some embarked from Scotland; others from the Shetland Islands, on what came to be known as "the Shetland bus," a covert shuttle service that consisted of a fleet of fishing smacks that transported SOE agents and their cargo to and from Norway.[19] SOE sent equipment made up primarily of high explosives with primers and detonators and a variety of fuses and igniters for use in varied circumstances, together with a large quantity of incendiary bombs and hand grenades stored in concealed depots. Defensive weapons consisted of automatic pistols, knuckle dusters, rubber truncheons, and fighting knives.

Although Shetland was under British command, it was necessary to use Norwegian boats and Norwegian crews so as to pass unnoticed by German patrols along the Norwegian coast. Moreover, only Norwegians would have local knowledge of the coastal area or be able to land unnoticed in a Norwegian village. The boats carried no armament, and thus were totally defenseless against German air attacks and patrol boats. Of even greater concern was the weather, which was a more menacing enemy outside the heavily defended areas. Despite the drawbacks, 49 SOE agents were brought to Norway during the sailing season of 1941; an additional 21 were air-dropped during that period.[20] Tons of weapons, ammunition, and equipment were conveyed inland and stored in depots for use by local Milorg groups that were undergoing secret training in remote forest areas in preparation for an expected British invasion.

During the winter of 1941-42, the war situation changed dramatically for Germany with the entry of the United States into the conflict in December, and the severe setback to Hitler's *Wehrmacht* in the Russian winter offensive. Moreover, the British raids on the Norwegian coast simply reinforced Hitler's belief that the awaited all-out Allied invasion would take place in Norway. As early as the fall of 1941, Britain created a deception called "Plan Omnibus," suggesting that an invasion of Norway was being planned, to bolster Hitler's belief that Norway was the "zone of destiny." A number of false unrelated reports of troops being specially trained in Scotland and inspected by the King of Norway were fed to the Germans by using captured German agents and by placing advertisements in newspapers soliciting fishermen with knowledge of the Norwegian coast.[21]

On December 29, the Fuehrer told his naval Commander-in-Chief, Erich Raeder, that "he expected the British to make an 'all out attack with their fleet and landing troops… The German Navy must therefore use all its forces for the defense of Norway.' On the Fuehrer's insistence the attempt was planned and carried out."[22] Throughout the course of the year, Hitler increased the number of *Wehrmacht* troops from 100,000 at the end of January to about 250,000 in June.[23]

In 1942, Churchill actually favored an Allied invasion in North Norway, Operation *Jupiter*. American Chief of Staff George Marshall rejected the plan in favor of Operation *Torch*, the invasion of North Africa the following November. But as a plan to deceive the Germans regarding *Torch*, two fictitious plans were initiated in July, *Solo* 1 and *Overthrow*. The object was to create the impression of an invasion of either Norway or northern France.[24]

In spite of the courageous stand taken by the Civilian Resistance, and especially by the teachers' refusal to accept nazification of the schools, 1942 was a year of damaging defeats for the Military Resistance. With the help of the notorious Norwegian informer Henry Oliver Rinnan, the Germans infiltrated an "export" group that had been working with several Resistance organizations, sending refugees and volunteers across the North Sea. On February 23, 1942, the Germans seized a fishing vessel in Ålesund on the west coast, and 23 persons were arrested while preparing to sail to England. An additional 20 persons were arrested for aiding escapees, one of which was executed a few days later. Another was shot during reprisals in Trondheim later that year.[25]

In April, two SOE radio operators, Arne Vaerum, code-named *Penguin*, and Emil Hvål, code-named *Anchor*, en route to Stavanger and Oslo respectively, landed on the island of Sotra, where they made contact with a local merchant who was a member of a Milorg group. They were staying at the merchant's farm in nearby Telavag, a small fishing village just southwest of Bergen. Telavaag was an important transfer point for both SOE and SIS operatives. Both organizations sent agents to this juncture and picked them up after a mission was completed. Through an informer, the Gestapo was notified of the agents' presence. When they arrived at the farm, a shootout took place, in which Vaerum, the Gestapo chief, and his deputy were killed; Hvål was wounded and taken prisoner.

The reprisals by the Germans were disastrous. The wounded agent and 18 men from the boat in Ålesund bound for England, suspected of being members of Milorg, were tortured, then executed. *Reichskommissar* Terboven took revenge on the entire Telavåg population. The village was turned into another Lidice.[26] Every building was razed to the ground. The entire male population of 76 men and boys between the ages of 16 and 65 was sent to concentration camps in Germany, where most of them died. The rest of the population, 260 old men, women, and children, was interned in Norway.[27]

These were but the first of a number of crises that brought the Military Resistance to a temporary standstill by the summer of 1942. Numerous arrests took place, particularly in Bergen and Stavanger, resulting in severe setbacks to Milorg groups in West Norway. In East Norway, similar reversals occurred involving the arrest of Milorg leaders in Oslo, Drammen, Kongsberg, Horten, and Notodden. Many of those who avoided arrest were able to make their way to Sweden, with the result that the Military Resistance was drastically reduced. During December, the Gestapo struck hardest in the south in Kristiansand and throughout the region of Agder in what became known as "the black Christmas of South Norway," in which between 400 to 600 arrests took place.[28] Among those arrested was Major Arne Laudal, who had been responsible for building up the Milorg organization in South Norway to a force of 3,500 men.

The Gestapo's success can be traced to a combination of factors. Milorg was centrally located. Many were taken by surprise. Others made no attempt to escape, as they did not think the situation that serious, or else they realized that if they did escape, family members would have been taken as hostages. Furthermore, too many people knew about each other, and knew too much. Finally, they were unprepared for the torture the Gestapo was capable of, which resulted in the disclosure of much important information.[29] A special directive signed by Hitler announced that anyone who associated with British sabotage groups would be treated as bandits and not as soldiers, and would be subject to immediate execution. Nevertheless, active resistance continued.

On May 4, 1942, the first SOE sabotage action, Operation *Redshank*, took place against an industrial target in Norway. The operation involved a transformer station in Trondelag that was destroyed to stop production of the pyrite and concentrated copper from the heavily guarded Orkla mines. This mineral source provided the Germans with critical supplies of sulphur used in radar and wireless telegraphy equipment. The action halted any further output for a year.[30] This was followed in September by a combined operation unit of SOE commandos code-named *Musketoon*, which arrived with the *Knotgrass-Unicorn* team and blew up the power station at Glomfjord near a small village in northern Norway. The facility supplied electricity for a nearby factory that produced desperately needed aluminum for the Germans. The total output was used for the manufacture of *Luftwaffe* aircraft. However, during the evacuation, two commandos were shot and seven were captured and executed.[31]

In October, Operation *Kestrel* resulted in the destruction of a large part of the ore installation at Fosdalen in North Trondelag. These mines supplied the iron ore for the Herman Goering Works armament factories in Germany. The action reduced production by 75 percent over the next three months.[32]

In March 1942, the audacious Odd Starheim parachuted back into Norway, and with the help of five others, succeeded in seizing the 620-ton Norwegian coastal steamer, *Galtesund,* which was taken to Aberdeen, Scotland, thereby preventing the Germans from using it. In August, Starheim devised a plan, code-named *Carhampton*, to capture simultaneously a convoy of five German transport ships on the southwest coast of Norway. The following January, he set out once again for Norway by boat with a party of 40 men for Flekkefiord. However, after two unsuccessful hijacking attempts to seize the ships, the operation was abandoned and the team retreated into the mountains. In February, a second operation was planned against a titanium mine where the Germans were producing rare metals essential to their war effort. Starheim and his men would be joined by a new force, which would cross the sea from the Shetland Islands in motor torpedo boats. *Carhampton* would lie in wait in the woods behind the mines and blow up the road to prevent the Germans from sending assistance while the attack was being carried out by the motor torpedo boat force. A storm at sea forced back the MTBs and the assault on the mines was cancelled.[33]

Undaunted by this last abortive action, and unrelenting in his determination to strike another blow at the Germans, Starheim and his team, upon hearing that the *Galtesund's* sister ship *Tromosund* was to arrive at Flekkefiord the next day, set out to hijack the vessel. Starheim and his small crew boarded and successfully seized the coastal steamer and headed for Scotland. Both aircraft from Coastal Command and destroyers were sent out to escort the vessel to Aberdeen, but before they arrived, the ship was attacked by German aircraft and all on board were lost.[34]

UNTIL THE BEGINNING OF 1943, sabotage activity had been confined principally to hit-and-run raids in preparation for that major invasion of Norway that never came. And day after day, it was becoming increasingly obvious that the liberation would have to wait until the Germans had been defeated on other fronts. For the majority of the Norwegian people, the struggle was chiefly a response to the challenge of nazification, which passive resistance was successfully rejecting. Sabotage had no part in it. But withholding strategic and economic benefits from the Germans in preparation for the final liberation of the country could not be dealt with by passive resistance. Thus:

> *As 1942 drew to a close, while the ideological contamination had been rejected and Norway's soul had been saved, the body had increasingly been drawn into the German orbit in the service of the Axis war economy. Although Norwegians might spend their free time looking to the Allied victory, quite a number of them spent their working hours in activities which in various ways benefited the German war effort.*[35]

> *Short of letting the country's economy come to a standstill, where should the line be drawn between a reasonable level of economic activity to nourish the population, and providing economic aid to the enemy? For example, butter was rapidly becoming a scarcity, and demand grew for margarine. But the only available raw material for*

margarine in Norway during the occupation was fish oil, whose byproduct is glycerine, a very useful element in the manufacture of ammunition. So do you let the people go without their main source of fat, or do you let the Germans get their glycerine?[36]

These were dilemmas that did not lend themselves to easy solutions, especially in view of the fact that a large number of Norwegians worked at jobs that contributed to the German war economy.

While solutions to these questions were being sought within Norway, another and perhaps even more critical issue was being debated in London. This was the question of whether Allied bombing raids or sabotage should be the chief means of attacking military targets in Norway. There was unanimous agreement among the Norwegians that the cost in lives and property from the bombing would far exceed the number of victims of German reprisals from sabotage activity.

In July, for example, when it was discovered that an attack by 167 B-17 Flying Fortresses on the Norwegian Hydro factory in Heroya, near the densely built-up town of Porsgrunn, had caused heavy casualties among the civilian population, the exile Norwegian government lodged strong diplomatic protests.[37] The Norwegian government and the SOE leaders proposed sabotage as a better means of attacking industrial targets. But a number of American and British air force officers were not altogether convinced.[38] What was needed was an opportunity to prove that sabotage directed against a major enemy objective could be carried out successfully. That opportunity was close at hand.

13

The Vikings of Vemork

If you can meet with Triumph and Disaster
And treat those two imposters just the same;
If you can force your heart and nerve and sinew
To serve your turn long after they are gone,
And so hold on when there's nothing in you
Except the Will which says to them: "Hold On!"
Yours is the earth and everything that's in it,
And which is more—you'll be a Man my son!
—Rudyard Kipling (1865-1936) English author,
If…

Although most sabotage did not result in permanent or long-lasting effects, exceptions did exist. Throughout the course of the war one of the most daring, certainly the most prominent, and potentially the most important exception can be found in Norway itself. This was an operation, or more accurately, a series of actions, which established a lasting result that, had it failed, might well have made a significant difference in the final outcome of the European conflict.

High above the little town of Rjukan in the mountainous south central province of Telemark, some 75 miles west of Oslo, on an all-but-unapproachable plateau, stood the Norsk Hydro hydroelectric plant in the suburb of Vemork. It was here that the Germans were making use of a chemical fertilizer byproduct known as deuterium oxide or heavy water for what were vague plans for the possible production of an atomic bomb.

In August 1941, the British Secret Intelligence Service was informed by the Norwegian Underground that the Germans were demanding a significant increase in the heavy-water production at the Vemork plant. The intelligence source that provided the information was the Norwegian scientist, Leif Tronstad, also a member of the Resistance. To the authorities in London, the accelerated production of heavy water was a clear indication that the Germans were involved in the production of fissionable material. What the Allies needed was ongoing day-to-day intelligence from the plant concerning the amount of heavy water being produced, its purpose, and the speed of its transportation to Germany.

The man selected to provide London with this information was Einar Skinnerland, a 24-year-old native of Rjukan, who worked near the factory at the Moesvatn Dam, which served Norsk Hydro as a reservoir. He also spent much of his time concealing and distributing arms to farmers working for the Resistance in the surrounding region. Skinnerland left Norway with the group Odd Starheim led which seized the coastal steamer *Galtesund,* which was then taken to England. After arriving in London, he joined the Company Linge of SOE, and for the next 10 days he underwent intensive training in radio communications, parachute jumping, and a number of undercover skills. Just 11 days after being in England, he boarded a Halifax bomber on a return flight to Norway. Shortly after crossing the Norwegian coast, however, the pilot was unable to locate the drop zone, but the intrepid Skinnerland refused to turn back and jumped blind over the icy Hardanger Vidda wasteland. He landed safely and managed to make it home that morning for breakfast. No one had any knowledge of the part he played in the theft of the *Galtesund*, nor that he had spent his skiing vacation in England undergoing training as an undercover agent. The next day he contacted Dr. Jomar Brun, the plant engineer at the Vemork plant, who provided him with up-to-date intelligence on the German efforts to boost the yield of heavy water.[1]

It was now a matter of the highest priority that the production be stopped and the plant destroyed. After receiving microphotographs of blueprints, drawings, and other critical material brought by courier and concealed in tubes of toothpaste, the Allies studied ways of destroying the electrolysis equipment and the power plant producing it.[2] Bombing the factory was originally proposed, but because it was at the bottom of a deep narrow valley and the heavy water was situated on the bottom floor protected by several layers of concrete, the aircraft would have found the target difficult to locate, let alone hit. And even if the aircraft had been able to locate the factory, it was highly doubtful that bombing would have caused sufficient penetration to totally destroy the heavy-water cells.

A further deterrent was the German fighter defense. And finally, there was the danger of hitting the large quantities of liquid ammonia that were stored at the plant. If these were destroyed, the entire town of Rjukan would be wiped out. The only plausible solution was a ground assault against the machinery producing the heavy water. In the spring of 1942, Prime Minister Churchill ordered a full-scale attack of the Norsk Hydro plant by a raiding party of glider-borne British commandos. The mission was code-named *Freshman*.

To pave the way for the assault, an advance team of specially trained Norwegian SOE saboteurs who had first-hand knowledge of the Rjukan area was selected. The team was headed by the tall, pipe-smoking, Lieutenant Jens Poulsson and Knut Haugland, his second-in-command and the party's wireless operator. They were followed by Sergeant Claus Helberg, a classmate and close friend of Poulsson, and Sergeant Arne Kjelstrup, whose resilience and good humor were traits that not only commanded the respect of the others, but carried them through some of the darkest days of the Occupation. He still carried fragments of an enemy bullet that was lodged in his hip. After escaping from a Nazi-occupied hospital, he fled to Sweden. Being unable to find direct passage to England, he made his way there by way of the Soviet Union, Iran, South Africa, and the United States.[3]

For several months the four men underwent the most rigorous training courses that the British were able to provide. They were taught the use of small arms, dynamite, plastic explosives, booby traps, and numerous ways of silently killing a sentry. The wireless operator was trained in Morse code to send and receive 20 words per minute. Code-named Operation *Grouse*, the team's task was to parachute onto the Hardanger Plateau, northwest of Rjukan, establish a base of operations, undertake a reconnaissance of the area, and see that all was in readiness for a safe glider landing in the Skoland marshes, not far from the Vemork plant.

In early September, the group departed for Norway from the Wick RAF satellite airfield in Scotland. Twice they had to abort the mission because their Halifax bomber was unable to penetrate the dense fog and cloud cover over the North Sea. Finally, on October 18, they were air-dropped over the Hardanger Vidda onto a rough mountain plateau above the Songedal valley near Telemark. This was miles away from the

Skoland marshes where they were supposed to have been dropped. The Norwegian advisers who helped prepare the operation described the desolate wilderness as one of the most hazardous places in Europe.

> *Weather usually appalling, foggy and unpredictable, sudden air currents of gale force spring up during autumn; terrain inaccessible, mountain peaks with hundreds of dangerous glaciers and precipices, marshes, swamps, impassible streams, hardly any landing strips and dropping grounds.*[4]

It took the four-man team two days to recover the equipment that had been dropped by parachute and scattered by the severe winds that dominated the snow-covered, desolate terrain. Once the equipment had been found, a new snowstorm that had set in limited what any one man could carry. The most that one could expect to bear was 65 pounds. Yet before leaving England, each member of the team had been assigned 120 pounds. So every few miles they had to retrace their steps two or three times to the original starting point for another load. After several days of plodding through wet snow and slush, they found a sled half-buried in the snow on which they were now able to put their heavier equipment; what remained they carried in rucksacks. The sub-zero temperatures and the 4,000 feet altitude precluded a trek through the higher mountains and glaciers. Instead the team decided on a much longer, albeit danger-ous, course through winding valleys and lower elevations where lakes and marshes were unreliable because of the milder temperatures.

On two occasions, Poulsson's feet nearly froze after he fell through ice while crossing a stream. Later he developed a boil on his left hand that further limited his mobility. Despite this misfortune, he doggedly forged ahead through snow using one ski pole. Providentially, the party came upon isolated mountain huts where they would remain overnight. Their daily dwindling food ration—which was to last for at least a month—consisted of a slab of dried, powderlike meat loaf called pem-mican, a handful of groats (oatmeal), four biscuits, a little butter, cheese, some sugar, and a bar of chocolate.

Finally, on November 5, after 18 days of near starvation and col-lapse, they arrived at their base, an abandoned ski hut at Sandvatn near the Skoland marshes. Four days later, Haugland made his first radio contact with Colonel Wilson in London. Within the next several days, a suitable landing zone was selected some 20 miles south of Rjukan. It was here that the *Grouse* team would rendezvous with the *Freshman* raiding party.

On November 19, the *Grouse* teasm received the long-awaited code word *Girl*, which meant that the glider teams would arrive that night. At 1715 hours, two Horsa gliders towed by two Halifax bombers, each carrying 17 officers and men, took off from the Wick airfield in Scotland with enough explosives, weapons, and equipment to carry out a successful mission. The gliders were to be towed 400 miles, a distance well beyond any that had ever been towed before.

Two days earlier the forecast was clear skies and moonlight, but on the evening of their departure, the weather suddenly changed to rising winds and low hanging clouds. Shortly before midnight the *Grouse* team heard the droning of approaching aircraft near the designated drop zone, but the sound faded away and the gliders never appeared. The first Halifax had flown into thick, low lying clouds, some 35 miles from the drop zone. When the towline and glider had begun to cover with ice, the pilot decided to turn back, but as he did, the towline snapped. The glider descended into the fog and crash-landed on the snow-covered ground near Stavanger on the southwest coast of Norway. The second Halifax and glider crashed into a mountain farther south near Egersund. The crew members were all killed, but 23 of the commandos in the two gliders survived.

German ski patrols soon apprehended them. Some were taken to Gestapo headquarters in Stavanger and others to the Grini concentration camp outside of Oslo. Although all of them were wearing military uniforms when caught, and were therefore prisoners of war, three were poisoned or strangled to death, and the remaining 20 were shot. Their fate was not disclosed until after the war at the Nazi war crime trials. Those who were directly involved in the murders were hanged.[5]

Shortly after the glider disaster, British intelligence began making preparations for a second attempt to carry out the destruction of the Vemork facility. A new team of six Norwegian saboteurs, code-named *Gunnerside*, was given a short but detailed course in industrial sabotage at a secret location outside of London, where a dummy replica of the Norsk Hydro plant was constructed. The team was led by 23-year-old Joachim Ronneberg, who chose Lieutenant Knut Haukelid as his second-in-command. The others selected were Lieutenant Kasper Idland

and Sergeants Fredrik Kayser, Hans Storhaug, and Birger Stromsheim. The training was carried out under conditions resembling as closely as possible those they expected to encounter in Norway. The team was to be air dropped in the Hardanger Vidda, and from there make contact with the *Grouse* party. The operation was planned for Christmas Eve—when the Germans would least expect a raid—but because of severe weather the mission was postponed.

The unsparing winter of 1942-43—one of the worst in the nation's history—had also prevented supply drops from reaching the four isolated *Grouse* commandos. Aside from what little remained of the food they brought with them, and what they hoped to find in isolated hunters' huts, the half-starved and frustrated team managed to subsist on moss and reindeer meat, which included the ribs, brains, eyeballs, and the contents of the stomach. The *Freshman* tragedy was an inducement to move farther up the Vidda to avoid contact with German ski patrols. It was a real struggle for existence. After days, weeks, and now months of waiting, the mountains had become a mass of whirling snow amidst raw penetrating wind. When the weather became milder, the fog was as thick as gruel. From October until into February, conditions for skiing were hopeless.[6] The months of hunger, fatigue, and isolation prompted Jens Poulsson to later write:

> *Deep inside was uncertainty. What really was the purpose of all this? Why should we have to suffer in the mountains? Did we really have a chance to succeed and get away alive? Sometimes I felt like giving up. But I didn't. I never spoke about my doubts.*[7]

As the winter wore on, *Grouse* awaited instructions from London concerning the rendezvous with *Gunnerside*. In the meantime, there was plenty of work to keep them busy. One man would go out hunting for reindeer, another searched for wood, while still another would see that the wireless set was still operating. Food had to be cooked also. In the evenings after the sun went down, they laid in the dark and amused themselves by delivering lectures to one another, on "tact and good manners," for example, or "the art of shooting reindeer." They learned to value the small things in life. "A lump of sugar, a pat of butter or a crust of bread made us happy," Jens told us. We learnt what good comradeship meant. It was a time I'd be sorry to have missed."[8]

Finally, on February 18, 1943, after an aborted attempt the previous month, the heavily armed six-man *Gunnerside* team, dressed in white camouflage ski suits, parachuted into Norway to join forces with the four *Grouse* men, whose code-name was now changed to *Swallow* for security reasons. They landed on the Hardanger Plateau at the Skryken Lake some 20 miles northeast of where the advance *Grouse* party was supposed to meet them. However, on the first night of their arrival, the six commandos encountered a ferocious blizzard that forced them to remain in an abandoned hut for the next three days. The sudden change of climate from sea level and green fields in England to a harsh midwinter storm some 3,000 feet in the mountains brought on a climate sickness with symptoms of high fever and severe swelling of the glands in the neck.[9] After the storm abated, despite their weakened condition, the newcomers made preparations to locate their *Swallow* comrades.

As they were about to leave their hut, the six bearded commandos observed a man on skis coming across the lake and pulling a sled. As he approached the hut, he was seized, searched, and interrogated by Ronneberg. The man claimed to be a poacher who was hunting reindeer that he sold on the blackmarket. When asked if he was a member of the *Nasjonal Samling* Party, he answered that he was not, but that he was one of its supporters. The men were generally in favor of shooting the intruder to prevent him from reporting their whereabouts to the Germans, but Ronneberg was not. Even though he had declared himself in favor of the NS, the man appeared to be so frightened that Ronneberg was not sure that he even knew what he was saying; and that he was professing to be a Quisling sympathizer because he thought that the *Gunnerside* men might be Germans.[10] Ronneberg ordered the poacher to remain with them, and was given a toboggan to pull. He was later released after he signed a statement regarding his black-market activities and with a warning that if he betrayed the group, his illegal behavior would be reported to the Germans.

On February 23, as the men were about to descend a steep slope, they suddenly sighted two figures on skis in the valley below. Knut Haukelid soon recognized Lieutenant Helberg and Sergeant Kjelstrupk, both of whom he had trained with in England. Late that afternoon, the six *Gunnerside* newcomers and the two seasoned *Swallow* commandos reached the base camp where the two teams finally mobilized as one unit. Nine of the men were divided into two separate groups: a four-man demolition team to attack the Vemork plant and a five-man team to provide covering fire if necessary. Knut Haugland, the wireless operator, was to contact and remain with Einar Skinnarland in a mountain hut to help keep London informed of current developments. Before a final plan could be formulated for the assault, they had to select an approach to the target area. Moreover, it was critical that the latest intelligence on the strength and location of the German and Norwegian security guards at the factory site be obtained. Claus Helberg was selected to carry out a reconnaissance of the Rjukan valley and to rendezvous with a contact who would provide him with the latest intelligence at the plant.

On February 25, the nine white-clad, well-armed Norwegian commandos left their base to move to a hut closer to the factory complex from which the operation was to be launched, while Helberg set out to locate a feasible approach route. The plant was situated atop a 3,000-foot mountain on the far side of a gorge, which was cut at the bottom by the frozen Maana River. Normal access to the factory was provided by a narrow seven-foot suspension bridge, which crossed the steep ravine at one point. But since the bridge was heavily guarded by German sentries, that option was ruled out. Killing the guards would call attention to the attackers' presence by other Germans in the area, and provoke reprisals against the local civilian inhabitants.

Leif Tronstad proposed an alternative plan—a descent on the north side of the gorge, crossing the ice-encrusted riverbed, and climbing up some 600 feet on the opposite side to the narrow-gauge railway that was used to transport machinery from Rjukan to the factory. Earlier reconnaissance had indicated that the Germans had a guard of 15 men stationed in a hut in the middle of the yard between the buildings, but the railroad track was not guarded. The Germans no doubt believed that the seven-story colossuslike complex was so well protected by mountainous terrain and rivers that it would be too difficult for attackers to reach it.[13] Further exploration by Helberg confirmed aerial photographs of the Vemork area that revealed the growth of shrubbery and small trees jutting out from cracks in the precipice. This would enable the team to gain footholds as they climbed up the face of the vertical escarpment to the railway, which led to the plant containing the heavy-water cells.

On the dark and moonless night of February 27, 1943, at eight o'clock, the nine Norwegian saboteurs garbed in British battle dress and concealed by white camouflage suits, left their base camp for the heavy-water plant that they expected to reach some four and a half hours later. It was hoped that if the men were recognized as "British soldiers," the Germans would not take reprisals against Norwegian civilians in retaliation for the assault. Advancing in single file and well-armed with Tommy guns, pistols, knives, hand grenades, and explosives, the men climbed down the ravine, managed to cross the small ice-covered river, which was rapidly melting because of a sudden thaw during the previous 24 hours, and began the wearisome climb up the precipitous wall of rock which led to the railway line. It was movingly described by historian Dan Kurzman:

> *This was more than a wall; it was a test. A test not only of their sinews, but of their souls. Would they have the inner strength, the superhuman will to scale the wall inch by inch even if sapped of physical strength? This question, it seems, burned most brightly in the minds of the Grouse men, who still had not fully recovered from their long ordeal in the mountains. And to the fear of falling was added the fear of being detected and killed before they could complete their mission. But they were driven men, driven less by the desire to personally survive—most did not believe they would— than by momentous implications of failure. They had to succeed.*[14]

Feeling for foot and fingerholds among the bushes and stunted boughs that protruded from the face of the cliff and in the crevices of bare rock, the men silently clawed their way some 200 yards up to the crest of the ledge adjacent to the railway. Shortly after 11:00 p.m., the five-man covering team, consisting of Lieutenant Knut Haukelid, Lieutenant Jens Poulsson, Hans Storhaug, Arne Kjelstrup, and Claus Helberg proceeded in single file to a small shed about 500 yards from the railway gate entrance to the plant. They were followed by Lieutenant Joachim Ronneberg's demolition party, which included Fredrik Kayser, Kasper Idland, and Birger Stromsheim. For purposes of identification, either because of darkness or in confusion, the password "*Piccadilly*" was to be answered by the countersign "*Leicester Square.*"

At precisely 12:30 a.m., one half-hour after the change of sentries within the plant compound, Haukelid and Kjelstrup advanced to the fence gate, where they sheared the padlocked chain, and which Haukelid would later say, "barred the way to one of the most important military objectives in Europe."[15] Within seconds the assault force was within the compound and each man at his assigned post.

The demolition team moved along the inside of the fence to the electrolysis building where the heavy-water cells were located. Finding the steel door to the basement locked, Ronneberg and Kayser went behind the building, where they looked for a cable tunnel that they had earlier been told about, which would provide them access to the high concentration installation. At a nearby window, they were able to observe two rows of cells and a watchman in the room sitting at a desk. Walking alongside the wall, they saw a ladder that led down to the tunnel. After inching themselves into the narrow duct, they crept along amidst countless cables and pipes until they reached the door leading to the heavy-water compartment. Finding the door unlocked, Ronneberg cautiously turned the doorknob, clearing the way for Kayser who stepped in with his pistol aimed at the elderly Norwegian. "Raise your hands! If you resist, I will shoot you!"

While Kayser kept watch, Ronneberg placed the explosive charges on the 18 cylindrical heavy-water cells, when suddenly the silence was broken by a windowpane shattering. Despite the noise made by the broken glass, the humming of the generators muffled all other sound.[16] Caught off guard by this sudden interruption, the men were relieved to see Stromsheim and Idland trying to enter the room. Ronneberg immediately went to help them, but in removing a jagged piece of glass from the window frame, he severely lacerated his hand. Moving as quickly as possible, Stromsheim, who was also trained to deal with the explosives, went to assist his injured comrade.

Within minutes the demolition charges were in place and the fuses were set for two minutes, however, Ronneberg, while trying to stop the bleeding from his injured hand, attached two additional half-minute fuses just in case the others failed to ignite. After lighting the fuses, he turned to the watchman and told him he had 20 seconds to leave the building and take shelter. Then Ronneberg, Kayser, and Stromsheim hurried outside where they met Idland and waited. When the explosion occurred, it was as Haukelid would later write, "an astonishingly small, insignificant one. Certainly the windows were broken, and a glimmer of light spread out into the night, but it was not particularly impressive."[17]

It was several minutes before the Germans showed any signs of reacting to the blast. Both Poulsson and Haukelid of the covering party remained concealed between the power station and the electric light plant when a single unarmed German with a flashlight emerged from a guard hut and went over to a door leading to the plant. As he flashed the torch along the ground in the direction of the two saboteurs, Poulsson pointed his Tommy gun toward him, but was told by Haukelid not to fire as the German had no idea of what had happened. As he returned to the hut, he presumably attributed the indistinct blast to generator noise coming from the power plant or to the snow explod-ing a land mine.[18]

Doubtless the sound of the explosion was insulated by the basement's thick concrete walls. Nevertheless, the long, tortuous undertaking had finally met with success: 1,000 pounds of heavy water and 18 cells had been destroyed along with some vital machinery in the production plant. The nine saboteurs met some 300 yards outside the railway gate. None had encountered any opposition from the German guards. Except for Ronneberg's injured hand, all had come out unharmed.

It was not until the men had reached the bottom of the valley that the air raid sirens sounded. Now that they realized what had happened, the Germans were mobilizing their forces throughout the Rjukan area. "On the main road," Haukelid later wrote, "several cars rushed past. When the last of us crossed the road, a car came so close that we had to throw ourselves into a ditch."[19] From the other side of the valley on the railway line, the men observed electric torches scanning the area. The Germans had located the line of their retreat. However, the two teams were far enough ahead of the Germans that by the time the search operation got underway, they had reached the ridge leading to the Hardanger Vidda.

Once out of range, the nine men returned to where they had hid-den their skis and supplies. Now that their mission was completed, the *Gunnerside* and *Swallow* teams split up. And despite a search of the area by 2,800 members of the *Wehrmacht*, Lieutenant Ronneberg and four other members of his team skied an exhausting 250 miles to the safety of neutral Sweden. Lieutenant Poulsson headed for Oslo, but Sergeant Helberg remained in hiding in the Rjukan area for further underground activity. Lieutenant Haukelid and Sergeant Kjelstrup were also ordered to organize new resistance units. Knut Haugland remained behind with Einar Skinnarland in a mountain hut where the results of the mission were transmitted to London:

HIGH CONCENTRATION INSTALLATION AT VEMORK COMPLETELY DESTROYED ON NIGHT OF 27th-28th STOP GUNNERSIDE HAS GONE TO SWEDEN STOP GREETINGS.

In March 1943, one month after the raid on the Norsk Hydro plant, British experts made an assessment of the damage to the facilities that produced the heavy water. The results of that study revealed that production would be halted for at least two years. However, further disclosures indicated the Allies had miscalculated. Despite the destruction, the Germans were able to resume the production of heavy water within two months. By the end of June, the first supply of heavy water was being shipped to Germany.

By October, the Allied high command ordered a bombing raid on the heavy-water facility despite formal protests by the Norwegians, who rightfully feared the death of innocent civilians. On November 16, 147 B-17s of the American Eighth Air Force dropped over 400 tons of bombs on the facility. Of those bombs that were dropped, only a few actually hit the electrolysis plant, leaving the heavy-water cells virtually untouched. But in the nearby town of Rjukan 22 Norwegian civilians were killed in the raid. Nevertheless, the raid prompted the Germans to halt further production in Norway, and to transfer the heavy water across the Baltic Sea to Germany

On December 29, after London received information that the stores of heavy water were being dismantled, an urgent wireless message was sent to Einar Skinnarland in a mountain hut near Rjukan requesting verification of the proposed transfer. Confirmation was obtained from Rolf Sorlie, the former plant engineer at Vemork, and the intelligence was radioed to authorities in London, who ordered the demolition of the stores as soon as possible.

Knut Haukelid, who had remained in the mountains after the *Gunnerside* raid, was in charge of the mission. He was aided by Rolf Sorlie, the Rjukan contact, and Knut Lier-Hansen, a resourceful young member of the Resistance, who had served in the Norwegian army during the German invasion. He was later captured and escaped to Sweden, only to return to Rjukan, where he organized an underground unit of the Resistance while working at the Norsk Hydro plant. The canisters were to be sent by rail to Rjukan, and then on to Mael, where the train would be ferried across Lake Tinnsjo to the small village of Tinnoset; and then south to the embarkation port of Heroya, where they would be loaded on board a ship bound for Germany. But before they were moved, security in the plant vicinity was heightened by an additional detachment of SS troops that was brought into Vemork. This ruled out any further attempt by sabotage at the factory site. Hence, the attack would have to be made either on the train or on the ferry someplace between Rjukan and Heroya. Either possibility would inevitably involve the loss of civilian lives.

Unlike an officer who has but a small part to play in a larger military unit in wartime where a decision involving the loss of human lives involves only soldiers or possibly an enemy population, Haukelid was later to write that "in this case an act of war was to be carried out which must endanger the lives of a number of our own people—who were not soldiers. . . . I was the only person who had authority to make a decision. . . . As painful as it was to comply with that decision," Haukelid wrote, "our orders left no room for doubt as to what was intended. It was of vital importance to the result of the war that the Germans should not get the heavy water."[20]

After several days of soul-searching discussion, the decision was made to sink the ferry. The depth of the Tinnsjo was nearly 1,300 feet, and it was just possible that a number of the passengers might be rescued if the ferry was timed to explode not too distant from the opposite shore. Through a contact at the plant, the plotters were advised that the heavy-water shipment was to be moved during the week of February 13, 1944. The train was scheduled to leave Vemork on Saturday, and remain in Rjukan overnight, and then move on to Mael on Sunday, February 20, where it would connect with the ferry *Hydro* for the trip across Lake Tinnsjo. Two days before the ferry was to depart, Haukelid went aboard the vessel disguised as a worker to determine the best place for laying the charges. He also calculated the time for setting them in relation to when the blast was to take place.

Shortly after 1:00 a.m. on February 20, Haukelid, Sorlie, and Lier-Hansen drove to the ferry landing in a hired car. Armed with sten guns, pistols, and hand grenades, they climbed aboard the ferry and located a hatchway which led to the bilges. In a nearby compartment a poker game was in full swing. But upon entering the hatch the three saboteurs encountered a watchman standing in the doorway."[21] Lier-Hansen talked with the watchman to distract him while Haukelid and Sorlie went below the deck with their concealed sacks of explosives.

Creeping along the cramped and awkward keel, they were hunched over in about a foot of water that was standing in the bilge. Working feverishly, they connected detonators to two alarm clocks that were placed in a rib on the ship's hull. The charge consisted of 19 pounds of high explosive in the form of sausage links and concealed below the waterline. It was laid forward so that when the explosion occurred, the rudder and propeller would rise above the surface when the water began to flow in. The railway cars would roll off the deck, thereby creating the momentum that would pull the ferry down quickly. Haukelid had spent several hours calculating that when the charge exploded, it would blow about 11 square feet out of *Hydro's* side, causing the vessel to sink in less than five minutes.

After the charges were placed there was no time to spare, as the train was approaching the ferry. The three men made a hasty retreat without incident along the outer deck and down the gangway and to their car. Haukelid, along with two engineers from the Vemork plant left for Sweden to evade capture by the Germans; Sorlie returned to the mountains to join Skinnarland; and Lier-Hansen returned to Mael.

At 10:00 a.m. the train carrying the shipment of heavy water arrived at Mael, where it rolled on to *Hydro*. Shortly thereafter, it pulled away carrying 53 passengers. At approximately 10:45 a.m. the charges blew when the ferry was over the deepest point of the lake. As the bow was slipping beneath the waves, and the stern rising upwards, the freight cars carrying the precious cargo of heavy water plummeted onward into the lake. Twenty-seven passengers, including four German soldiers, were picked up by lifeboats from the nearby shore; the others went down with the ferry and the shipment of heavy-water canisters. The following day, the headline on every front page in Norway read:

RAILWAY FERRY HYDRO SUNK IN THE TINNSJO

The operation to halt the continued experimentation with heavy water had finally succeeded, an operation that would likely have led to the manufacture of an atomic bomb, and might have altered the outcome of the war. The price in human lives had been high. The English had sacrificed 34 men in the glider operation. The Allied bombing operation had cost the lives of 22 Norwegian civilians. Now for the third time the *coup de grace* on Lake Tinnsjo resulted in the loss of 26 lives, most all of which were civilian. But had the operation failed, the price could have been far greater. Clearly it was an achievement without peer in the annals of the Second World War.

The Stiffening of Resistance

The clandestine warrior harbors no great vision
that one day he will carry the war into the enemy's
country; he is fighting on his own territory, while his country's armies
have either been beaten or are fighting far away, perhaps overseas.
There are two sides to the war of resistance:
it is both a foreign and an internal war;
as such it may have to paralyze the administration, sabotage the economy
and destroy the communications of its own country
to prevent the enemy from using them.
—*Henri Michel,* The Shadow War

In 1943, Hitler's hope of an early end of the war was fast fading. The defeat of Rommel's German Afrika Korps in French North Africa had reopened the Mediterranean. This facilitated the Allied invasion of Sicily, which was a stepping stone to the Italian mainland. At sea, the U-boat danger was being significantly countered and a greater number of unopposed Allied convoys were crossing the Atlantic. In the air, American and RAF bombers were causing extensive damage to German industry. Severe defeats in Russia and the Mediterranean resulted in more than a million Germans killed or captured within the most recent year.

Yet even though the tides of war had turned on other fronts, Norway, like the other occupied countries of Europe, was not yet ablaze. But it was beginning to smolder. Besides the mission to destroy the German heavy-water production, other SOE operations were mounted against industrial targets to reduce the output of German war production. On January 25, 1943, in Operation *Cartoon*, a combined SOE Norwegian-British force successfully attacked the iron ore mines in Leirvik and blew up the factory that halted the transportation of 150,000 tons of ore. At the Arendal smelt works in Eydehavn, where ferrosilicon, a compound used in the manufacture of steel was being produced, the SOE team *Company* destroyed 2,500 tons, setting production back by six months. Additional sabotage action to reduce production of the Orkla pyrite was undertaken by the *Granard* team in February that involved mining a 5,800-ton supply ship, but this caused only minor damage.[1] One of the most successful attacks was an SOE raid at Stord just outside Bergen that paralyzed a factory producing concentrated sulphuric acid for the explosives industry. The plant was damaged so extensively that it took two-and-a-half years to bring production back to one-third of normal capacity.

A number of sabotage operations involved shipping and harbor installations in which the object was military rather than economic. These actions resulted in the immobilization of a number of ships— unwelcome proof to the Germans that more active troops were needed to defend the longest national coastline in Europe. Sabotage destroyed or severely damaged vessels, forcing the Germans to spend more time and effort in protecting their ships, shipyards, docks, and other maritime facilities. Max Manus, the illustrious "underwater saboteur," one of the most celebrated members of the SOE and a key figure in the renowned "Oslo Gang," performed a number of those operations, about which more will be said later. He was also one of the most sought-after members of the Resistance by the Gestapo.

Manus and his close friend, Gregers Gram, were air-dropped just outside of Oslo on March 12, 1943. Supplied with hundreds of pounds of explosive charges, their chief objective was to sink German shipping in the Oslo harbor. The charges consisted of limpet mines containing two and three-quarter pounds of plastic explosives designed to adhere to the side of a ship's hull with the aid of magnets. Within a month of their arrival in March, on the night of April 27, the first attack took place. The intrepid saboteurs entered the harbor by canoe wearing tweed jackets that concealed British battle dress to reduce the risk of reprisals in the event they were recognized or captured. The plotters managed to dodge the patrol boats, harbor guards, and searchlights by sheltering themselves behind a small island in the harbor.

The first objective was the 5,600-ton German transport steamer *Tugela*, and the second was the 3,800-ton Norwegian freighter *Ortelsburg*. They secured the limpets magnetically against the hull of each of the ships below the waterline and timed them to explode several hours later. Each mine was equipped with a firing pin that was held back by a spring kept taut by celluloid. When the acid in the timing device at the tip of the limpet ate through the celluloid, the spring was released, the firing pin dropped on the detonator cap, and the plastic was exploded.[2] The following morning at precisely 6 a.m., the two ships blew up seconds apart; the *Ortelsburg* sunk fast, the *Tuguela*, moored at the wharf, settled into the harbor mud with its afterdeck underwater.[3]

Particularly noteworthy and of special interest to Manus and Gram were the two large transport liners, *Monte Rosa* and *Donau*, which plied regularly from Oslo to Denmark, not only ferrying troops and war materiél to the Russian Front, but also carrying Norwegian boys drafted for forced labor in Germany and political prisoners to concentration camps. Manus and Gram worked closely with a secret Home Front intelligence organization called Sea Military Oslo (SMO), which sent reports to England of every ship that left a Norwegian harbor. The reports contained a copy of the ship's manifest and a list of the number and type of troops aboard. Through SMO, the two men were able to get jobs on the pier working as cable repairmen.[4]

The 26,000-ton *Monte Rosa* was scheduled to be in Oslo in June for a period of three days before departing. Manus and Gram prepared to sabotage the vessel and for almost four days before its arrival in Oslo harbor, the two men remained under the pier to avoid suspicion by the German harbor police. Ostensibly repairing cables under the jetty wearing greasy overalls over their British uniforms, they managed to conceal limpet mines and a small rubber boat that could be folded into a small package beneath the pier. Positioned on beams and planks, they waited amidst the filthy floating refuse and the huge rats, which ran back and forth along the steel girders.

On the late afternoon of departure, while lying on his back in the boat to avoid being seen, Gram paddled out to the *Monte Rosa* as best he could. After reaching the ship he attached the limpets to the hull, which were timed to detonate 20 hours later out at sea. However, because the vessel left port earlier than scheduled, it did not explode until it docked in Copenhagen. Although it was not totally destroyed, it was severely damaged. After repairs were made, the Germans converted the vessel into a hospital ship.[5]

It must be conceded that sabotage did not significantly reduce the economic exploitation of Norway. It did, however, require large numbers of troops, additional time, money, and effort on the part of the Germans to prevent the disintegration of their war economy. Moreover, despite the ongoing dispute over bombing from the air versus demolition by sabotage, there was no doubt that in certain cases the latter could be carried out with far greater accuracy and less loss of civilian life. Moreover, sabotage required a deftness impossible to achieve by bombing: in the case of one vital component in a factory that had to be destroyed, all other damage was pointless. And sometimes a well-placed stick of dynamite or plastic explosive could succeed where tons of high explosive had failed. The one disadvantage of sabotage was that it could lead to reprisals resulting in the execution of innocent hostages.

By the spring of 1944, reprisals were reduced—but not eliminated—after a dispute between *Reichskommissar* Terboven, the political head in occupied Norway, and General Falkenhorst, the military commander of the Occupation forces. The quarrel stemmed from the arrest of 10 of the leading men in Rjukan after the heavy-water raid at Vemork. Terboven threatened to have the men shot, but Falkenhorst later released them, claiming that British commandos carried out the raid and were therefore under military—not civilian—jurisdiction.[6] By creating the deception that sabotage was performed by British commandos and not Norwegians, German retaliation was often prevented. This was done by deliberately leaving British cigarette butts or pieces of British uniform or equipment at the sabotage site so that the Germans would think that the operations were carried out by troops parachuted in from Britain.

In October, the Chiefs of Staff to the Supreme Allied Commander (COSSAC) issued a directive concerning railroad sabotage in Norway, which stated that no actions were to be carried out without first receiving an order from the Allied High Command. This was but one of a number of basic considerations that would govern the success of the D-Day operation, the Allied invasion of Western Europe the following year. The call was for patience and self-restraint. The newly established Supreme Headquarters Allied Expeditionary Force (SHAEF) wanted to avoid a situation in Norway that might disrupt Allied operational plans elsewhere on the Continent. Norway's role in those plans was to serve as a cover for the Normandy landings (or more accurately, as the cover for the Pas de Calais landings that were the cover for Normandy in the Allied double-deception plan) in ensuring that the German garrison in Norway remain unreduced.[7] It was not until the D-Day landings in France in June of 1944 that the order to intensify railroad sabotage was given.

Nevertheless, several SOE teams did engage in railroad sabotage earlier, but most actions were either delayed indefinitely or could not be carried out because of geographic conditions. However, on October 10, 1943, one particular action, code-named *Feather 1*, consisting of seven SOE commandos, destroyed or put out of commission five locomotives at Lokken, Thamshavn, and Orkanger.[8] And on October 7, the Communist Osvald Group dynamited a German troop transport train at Mjondalen near Drammen in which two Germans and a larger number of Norwegians were killed.

Despite an official declaration denying the action on behalf of the 4,000 Norwegian civilians living in the Drammen district, the action resulted in the arrest of 60 hostages, from which the Gestapo executed five. In an evaluation of the action to authorities outside of Norway, the Circle stated:

> *We too condemn most severely the senseless acts of sabotage of which we have recently seen several examples—while at the same time strongly favoring all sabotage with a purpose, including acts of violence which genuinely damage the German war effort.*[9]

As was seen earlier, the summer and fall of 1942 were difficult times for Milorg, especially in the south of Norway. The five military districts were replaced by 14 smaller units. Although it now consisted of several thousand men, Milorg was mainly an army without weapons.[10] Furthermore, the Gestapo conducted numerous crackdowns, which resulted in an increase in the number of hostage shootings. Consequently, many of the leaders were either arrested or had fled to Sweden to avoid capture. Added to this was Milorg's strained relations with the Civilian Resistance leadership (the Circle), the SOE, and the Norwegian authorities in Great Britain.[11]

Throughout 1943 and the first half of 1944, within Milorg itself, the district organizations as well as the Central Leadership were slowly being reestablished and expanded under the capable leadership of a

28-year-old lawyer, Jens Christian Hauge. From a weak beginning in 1940, Milorg had grown out of a resistance conglomeration struggling to weather crisis after crisis as they waited for the final phase of the Occupation, namely, the liberation of their homeland. But in the meantime they were faced with the numerous activities that Occupation and Resistance involved—activities that were to contribute to a free Norway.

The reorganized Central Leadership (SL) established a number of departments that dealt with various resistance matters. A "passport office" created numerous false documents, stamps, and other legal forms that enabled persons to travel without the risk of being apprehended for routine questioning. A coding office decoded and put into code the SL's correspondence with Sweden, and to a lesser extent with London.[12] It was also in close contact with the clandestine National Police organization, whose duty it was to gather information on German agents, informers, infiltrators, and NS members.

Additionally, the "Police" worked with smaller groups that notified people who were at risk, smuggled messages in and out of prisons, engaged in intelligence work, and helped couriers and refugees get transportation out of the country.[13] Much of the work involving refugees was done by an organization known as "the Spider." This was a special export group responsible for hiding members of the Resistance wanted by the Gestapo, providing them with food and clothing, and getting them safely across the border into Sweden. This group also worked closely with the Milorg Central Leadership in the recruitment of members for Milorg.[14]

In London, the earlier disagreement over guidelines and forms of organizations for military activity in Norway was resolved between the Norwegian military authorities represented by the newly formed Norwegian Defense Command (FO) and the British SOE, which included the Norwegian Independent Company Number 1. Guidelines for future military resistance were finally established in May 1943, at a meeting in Stockholm, where Milorg leader Hauge met with representatives of the Defense Command. It was there that Milorg's further activities were fixed in accordance with the strategy determined by SHAEF. This meant that it would not have the authority to initiate any actions independently. Milorg members were to be trained, armed, and kept in a state of military preparedness for assistance to the Allied army of liberation.

This policy was officially stated in a document dated November 15, 1943, and submitted jointly by the Milorg Military Council, leaders of the clandestine police organization, and the civilian leadership. The report stated:

> *We are convinced that a policy of active assault on the enemy will bring disasters to the people and the country which will be out of all proportion to the military gains, and that it will disrupt and destroy the longer-range work of civil and military preparations which promise to be of the greatest importance to the nation* [15]

It further expressed the Home Front Leadership belief that the Norwegian people were totally unprepared to withstand the pressure of the large-scale terror and reprisals that would inevitably follow an offensive from Milorg.[16] Thus, until the spring of 1944, it was the expressed view that all sabotage was to be carried out by imported or specialist SOE groups sent from England and returned there.

Despite the restrictions placed upon Milorg by SHAEF as the Allied Supreme Command, the underground army grew significantly during 1943 and the first half of 1944. In large measure, this was due to a vigorous effort by the Milorg district leaders throughout the country and the diligent work of its Central Leadership under J. C. Hauge. The army now numbered 30,000 men.[17] Because of a serious shortage of weapons, however, instruction in their use was not yet possible. Milorg was still mainly an army without the means to fight. This, along with the policy of strict moderation imposed by the Allied High Command, was a situation that understandably created low morale within the Milorg rank and file.

In spite of the frustration and impatience for action by the more activist-minded members of Milorg, authorization to provide weapons and equipment could only be approved by the Norwegian government in London.[18] In the absence of that authority, any premature action might have jeopardized the plans for later operations and exposed the country to unnecessary reprisals and suffering. But the desire for active resistance was still strong in many quarters.

Acting independently and lacking the patience to follow the generally passive resistance line of the Home Front leadership and the Norwegian government in London, the Communists were unwavering in their efforts and continued to strike at targets of their own choosing. Throughout the course of the Occupation, they continued to denounce the more cautious restrictive policy of moderation as a manifestation of a corrupt capitalist society more interested in protecting Norwegian business and industry than in defeating the Germans. Although the Communists agitated for guerrilla warfare and sowed suspicion against the Western Allies, the government and the Home Front Leadership, there was never any danger of civil strife erupting between the Communist-controlled and the non-Communist resistance forces such as was the case in Yugoslavia and Greece, where internal conflicts forced the Allies to choose who they were going to support.[19] And in spite of Norway's basic opposition to Communism, as the war progressed, economic support was given to the Communist illegal press and their work in transporting refugees. On several occasions, their action groups received support from the Home Front. In fact, the amount of support given to the Communists amounted to more than went to any other organization except Milorg.

By the end of 1943 and the beginning of 1944, the central issue facing the Norwegian people and the main rallying point of the Norwegian Home Front was not the damage inflicted by armed action groups upon the German exploitation of Norwegian resources. Rather it was the announcement by Quisling that called for the exploitation of Norwegian men and women to work on behalf of the German war effort, and the action taken by the Resistance to prevent the Germans from forcing tens of thousands of Norwegian youth of military age to fight on the enemy's side on the Eastern Front.

The Mobilization Threat

Such men as these we will not be,

To live despised in story.

To copy these we will not seek,

Who trample under foot the weak,

And only live to kill and break,

And torture soul and body.

We would grow sturdy men and strong.

To this our humble station

A mind, a peace, a land belong

For childhood's cultivation.

—*Nordahl Grieg (1902-1943), "Song of the Norwegian Children"*

War Poems

Ever since the German invasion of Russia in June 1941, the threat of conscripting Norwegian youths to fight on the German side was uppermost in the mind of the Home Front. As early as January of that year, Quisling made an appeal to young Norwegians to volunteer for German military service to help promote the New Order in Europe. Approximately 2,000 Norwegians were recruited by *Reichskommisar* Terboven for service in Russia. Given the designation "Norwegian Legion," the unit suffered significant losses in January 1942, in the battle of Leningrad, only to be later demobilized in May 1943. Approximately 700 men continued to serve in German front-line service in a newly formed Norwegian SS Panzer regiment until the end of the war. In the fall of 1943, an SS Ski Battalion was formed to hunt down members of the Resistance on Norwegian soil.[1] The total number of Norwegians who served with the German forces is not known, but NS propaganda had succeeded in enlisting at least 5,000 volunteers for the Eastern Front.[2]

By the late fall of 1942, the French North African campaign had cost Hitler 150,000 men from some of the best German divisions. In the winter of 1942-43, the German disaster at Stalingrad resulted in the loss of 300,000 men. Moreover, the potential collapse of Italy and the Russian threat in the Balkans compelled Hitler to position as many divisions in Southern Europe as he had in the West. And toward the end of 1943 and the beginning of 1944, the war on the Eastern Front was going so badly for the *Wehrmacht* that German troops were in retreat. Thus, there was a great need for reinforcements to avoid total defeat.

On February 18, 1943, in the wake of the German capitulation at Stalingrad, Joseph Goebbels gave a speech in Germany calling for an all-out effort to activate larger numbers of men to combat the forces of Bolshevism in the East. The occupied countries of Europe were expected to aid in providing their respective labor forces. Within Norway, speeches and appeals organized by NS leaders were made that echoed the demand by the Nazi Propaganda Minister for a total mobilization of manpower in the struggle for the "new Europe."[3] On February 22, Quisling announced the "Total National Labor Effort," a law in which all able-bodied men between the ages of 18 and 55 and all women between 21 and 40 were required to register. The alleged purpose was to create an agricultural and forestry labor reserve, which could be used to increase the Norwegian food production and help to provide fuel by wood cutting. Certainly anything that would benefit the country would have the approval of the Norwegian people. But what if the registration was a deception to call up Norwegian youth for German military service?

A National Labor Service (AT) was nothing new in Norway. As early as the summer of 1940, the Administrative Council established the Labor Service as a voluntary organization to help in the country's reconstruction in the aftermath of the devastation caused by the German air and ground forces. However, as NS members gradually and discreetly became more and more involved in the AT and worked themselves into top positions, it was converted into a tool for the authorities. It was later made compulsory, in April 1941, after the NS came into power. In the summer, an ordinance was passed for conscripting workers into activities that the Germans considered "essential" or "important." But what was new about the situation in 1943 for most Norwegians was the additional number of occupations affected by the new "Labor Effort" law. Furthermore, it was beginning to be seen as a way of providing a labor reserve to bolster a floundering German Front in the East. Within two days of the announcement, *The London News*, the largest one of the most influential illegal papers in Oslo, published a directive that stated:

> *Those who are taken for national labor duty in agriculture, forestry, fisheries and transport shall do their duty to the full for the preservation of the country. All services which . . . imply obligations for the people to take part in military operations against the fatherland shall be refused. . . . Service outside the country's frontiers shall be refused.*[4]

Throughout the country, approximately 300,00 persons registered for the Labor Service, but initially the Home Front Leadership was uncertain as to how to react to the new mobilization law. According to the Hague Convention of 1907, an army of Occupation was given "the right to exact individual contributions and the performance of work from the population." Already 200,000 Norwegians had found employment in German undertakings. The question that concerned the Co-ordination Committee and the Circle was "what kind of work was being exacted from the population." The consensus throughout the country was that the workforce was only to be used in farming and other activities that were 100 percent Norwegian. But according to reports obtained from the NS administration, 35,000 men were to be called up in March for road and railway building for the next six months.[5]

When it was learned, however, that they were being mobilized in a labor unit of Organization Todt, which had charge of military installations in Norway, the Leadership Board reacted. In a letter to the Norwegian Prime Minister Johan Nygaardsvold in London, dated April 6, the board expressed the belief that the vast majority of those conscripted in the Labor Service would be enrolled in Organization Todt and that the new law was being used to direct a deadly blow to the Home Front. It was now clearly understood that the labor mobilization was a purely military initiative.

The Military Home Front was equally apprehensive. They saw the law as a sanction that could be a serious obstacle to the recruitment of men for Milorg. The Military Council issued a directive that those young men associated with military combat units should do everything in their power to evade mobilization short of leaving the country. In a

Home Front Leadership directive of April 13, a final decision was announced. "Not one person is to report to wherever they have been called, whether to an office, a department or work place. No one should show up for registration."[6] This directive was the start of a resistance offensive in which the Civilian Leadership took the initiative.

On April 20, in a bold act of sabotage using homemade bombs, the Communist action Osvald Group, led by Asbjorn Sunde, destroyed the conscription offices at Pilestredet 31 in Oslo that contained the registration records for the labor effort. Sunde was injured in the raid and three others were captured and later executed by the Germans. This marked the transition from a passive to an active resistance against attempts at forced mobilization.[7]

On May 8, resistance was further intensified by church leaders who sent a letter to Quisling that rejected the new statute. The letter, which was also sent to churches throughout the country, stated: "Since war exists between Germany and Norway, how could those men called to serve be forced to take part in actions with military goals that are in the best interests of the country that Norway is at war with? Faced with these choices, the church can no longer be silent."[8] Within five days those who had signed the letter were arrested and sent to Grini Prison.

At the end of May, 400 men from East Norway were called up for work in a German artillery regiment in Tromso in northern Norway, but only 71 men reported for duty. A member of the Circle secretly went to the induction center that happened to be a school in Oslo. His report, which was published in the illegal press, stated that one of the draftees was an agricultural worker. This indicated that the call-up was not intended to increase the food production in the country. On May 29, the Home Front sent the following message to the government in London: "The people who have been called up for mobilization are showing up in smaller and smaller numbers. In the period May 12 to 15, only 40 reported in Oslo. From May 18 to 19, only 25 percent showed up, and after that even fewer."[9] Within the next several months, it became increasingly obvious to the NS and German security forces that stronger measures were needed to counter the growing resistance, and particularly further acts of sabotage against the labor mobilization effort.

In mid-August 1943, Inspector Gunnar Eilifsen of the Oslo Police Department was arrested for refusing to take into custody some young girls who failed to report for labor service. The incident showed how little the NS could rely on the Norwegian police to enforce the new labor edict. Quisling met this act of defiance by passing a new "law" that placed the police under military law and by which Eilifsen was brought before a special Norwegian tribunal and condemned to death retroactively. The following day the entire Oslo police force was ordered to assemble on the police barracks grounds where the NS Minister of Police Jonas Lie and German security head General Rediess appeared. In a threatening speech, Rediess demanded a signed declaration of loyalty from all police officials and all of the rank-and-file members. Under threat of court martial and execution if they refused to sign, all but 14 submitted to the new edict. Throughout the country, 470 policemen were arrested for resisting the order, and 271 were sent to a concentration camp in Germany.[10]

In autumn, Quisling, in a demonstration of support for the German cause, offered to provide 50,000 Norwegians for service on the Eastern Front.[11] When Quisling's mobilization order was received at Terboven's office, it was immediately rejected. The reason: it was believed that the induction of 50,000 men would require an equal number to keep those drafted from fleeing to Sweden.[12]

In January 1944, another mobilization plan was suggested by the NS Minister of Justice, Sverre Riisnaes, to a German general in the *Waffen* SS that called for the compulsory induction of 75,000 Norwegian men (aged 18 to 23 years) and for their immediate transfer to training camps in Germany. Those who refused to report voluntarily would be forcibly taken by German civil and military commando units. To prevent a mass escape by Norwegian youths, border guards on both the Swedish frontier and along the Norwegian coastline would be increased substantially. Once mobilized, the Norwegian youth would be integrated with seasoned German troops of the *Waffen* SS to prevent them from deserting.[13]

Fortunately, a loyal Norwegian typist working in the NS Ministry of Justice came across a copy of the memorandum outlining the plan and passed it on to the Resistance leadership. Knowledge of the plan was then published in the illegal press, calling for a full boycott of the labor draft. When the government in London was informed, firm warnings were given over the BBC.

The directive has been given: Nobody is to show up for registration, not even the ones that are being told they will not be called to serve at this time. Soon our day will be here! Remember the last appeal that General Ruge gave his soldiers to stay prepared. If you are already in a German camp, there is no way for you to be a part of the liberation. Stay faithful towards your country, your king and your people. Refuse to be registered at any cost.[14]

In an effort to counter resistance to the labor draft, the NS party unleashed a stream of propaganda encouraging the youth to volunteer based on the false claim that to do so would shorten the war and bring about a swift return of their own government, albeit one dominated by members of the NS. Many of the youths were too young and inexperienced to deal with this German deception and were understandably confused by the subtle propaganda to which they were subjected. Though many of the boys dreaded the thought of being sent out of the country, they could do nothing about it.

Once again, however, it was the teachers throughout the country who provided the help and advice where it was needed most, in the families. They obtained the names and addresses of those youths liable for the draft and organized groups of parents. They provided them with copies of the directive and advised them to remain firm and unyielding in resisting the labor draft. Approximately 100,000 copies of the directive were circulated in Oslo and throughout the various districts. In addition, several sabotage actions took place against Labor Service offices in Oslo and at local centers in adjacent towns. The one in Oslo went awry from the start; the others met with varying success.

Yet despite the effort to resist the call-up, only about 30 percent followed the directive, and in some places support was considerably smaller. Only in a few of the mountain districts was the directive followed by almost everyone. In view of these setbacks, it was obvious that the announcement and circulation of the directive was insufficient inducement to discourage conscription. To make matters worse, the anti-draft campaign resulted in the loss of four members of one of the action committees. In the town of Notodden, where the district leadership conducted a strike against the Labor Service, a young man was sentenced to death by a special court and executed for influencing recruits to evade registration. Immediately thereafter, three Milorg boys in Oslo were arrested and executed for their part in an abortive action against the county records in the Akershus district.[15]

To many people, the Resistance was simply viewed as a source of additional anxiety and tribulation without really accomplishing anything. Clearly, stronger measures were called for to halt the conscription process and to boost morale among the general population, which was beginning to show signs of weariness and resignation.

Jens Christian Hauge, the head of the Milorg military staff, and those in the Home Front Leadership concluded that the 3,000 young men scheduled to report for registration would be more easily discouraged from doing so if they arrived only to find nothing but smoldering rubble. On May 18, the day before compulsory registration was to take place, Hauge contacted Gunnar Sonsteby, the leader of a small but extremely effective sabotage team known as the "Oslo Gang." He called for the destruction of the Labor Office at Akersgate 55 where the men were scheduled to register and where the card indexing machines that printed the draft cards were located.[16] Certainly, if anyone was capable of discouraging the Germans from pursuing their policy of mobilization and of dramatizing the effectiveness of the Resistance movement in the country, it was Sonsteby and the Oslo Gang.

The esteemed Resistance historian, Jorgen Haestrup, has said of Sonsteby that "nothing within the Resistance was foreign to him." He began resistance activity in the summer of 1940 delivering clandestine newspapers. Soon he was recruiting contacts for Milorg and recovering arms that had been hidden at the end of the military campaign. Later he joined the Norwegian Independent Company Number 1 (Company Linge) and was assigned as the SOE liaison for new agents in Norway. As liaison, he arranged for the reception of wireless operators dropped by parachute into various Norwegian towns and for the quartering of these men where they could live and operate their transmitters. He also provided them with the documentation they needed to operate "legally" within Norway.[17] Sonsteby built up a network of covert contacts and safe houses throughout the country, all the while evading the Gestapo by the use of disguises and numerous aliases. In November 1944, after receiving a specialized course of instruction in England, he returned to Norway as central control officer and chief of all sabotage operations in and around the Oslo region.

It was five o'clock in the afternoon when Sonsteby was called by Hauge. If the sabotage at the Labor Office was to succeed, the operation would have to be completed no later than eight o'clock, while there was still daylight. With the assistance of Gregers Gram, a member of the team, Sonsteby arranged for the preparation of the explosives. Through a contact at the Labor Office, a key to the outer door was obtained. At seven o'clock, Sonsteby met Gram, who had 15 pounds of plastic explosive concealed in a small suitcase hanging from the handlebars of his bicycle. Together the two men pedaled to Akersgate, where they were met by Max Manus, who provided cover outside the building in the event of any trouble. Since they had no time to prepare a detailed plan, they simply let themselves in and went to the second floor where Gram placed the suitcase in a corner and shouted to the 20 or so persons in the office to leave the building immediately as it was going to be blown up. The two-minute fuse was lit and by the time the people inside fled the building on the heels of the two saboteurs, the explosion occurred. Not only were the large presses on which the draft cards were printed destroyed, but the office itself was left in ruins.

Within the following week, it was soon discovered that another card-indexing machine had been requisitioned in downtown Oslo at Grensen 17 on the third floor of the Norske Folk insurance building. The earlier destruction had only delayed, but not thwarted, the draft registration. So once again Sonsteby was called to destroy the machine. On June 17, after two unsuccessful attempts to put the machine out of action, Sonsteby, along with Birger Rasmussen and William Houlder, two highly trained SOE agents and members of the Oslo Gang, along with a cooperative janitor, succeeded in demolishing the entire office and machine, thereby preventing the disposition of the draft cards. In a letter to SOE and Milorg authorities in Stockholm, a representative of the Home Front wrote: "I think I can safely say that the last few weeks of fighting has strengthened the position of the Home Front Leadership. People now feel that they have leaders that can make actions happen, and will not shun from using powerful means when necessary."[18]

The sabotage operations were enough to discourage the vast majority of young men from registering for the draft despite the grave personal risk for failing to do so. When the police began to round up and arrest those youths of eligible age they found in the streets, thousands left home and went into hiding with relatives and friends in the country, or in the forests or mountains. Many had been Scouts and made use of their training by settling in tents, huts made from branches and brush, or improvised shelters from whatever means were available. It was estimated that about 3,000 young men were situated in the woods of the outlying Oslo area, 1,500 in Lower Telemark, and hundreds in other districts in the built-up areas of East Norway.[19] It was in these secluded camps that they were to become popularly known as the "lads in the forest."

Throughout the summer months the youths relied on relatives and friends to provide them with food and other necessary provisions. These were supplemented by supplies from small business firms, shop-keepers, and farmers. However, these arrangements were dangerous because over time the camps would be exposed to infiltration by informers and *agents provocateurs*. A survey of the location of the individual camps was made and joint efforts were undertaken to provide them with food. But these efforts could not go on indefinitely without the risk that German troops would soon seek them out.

In some of the camps, groups organized by Communists were pressing for the formation of partisan detachments with the expectation of receiving arms and equipment. Now that the Allied forces had landed on the Continent, it was believed that arms would immediately be made available to the Resistance. The weapons provided to underground forces, however, were limited to those in actual battlefront areas, which, for the present, meant France. Milorg was still extremely ill-equipped and would remain so well into the coming winter. At a leadership meeting of Milorg, it was decided that only those lads deemed most suitable for training be taken into cells that Milorg was establishing. The remainder would be dispersed throughout the rural countryside. Farmers were called upon to help the lads with work and room and board, thereby granting them access to household ration cards for food and clothing. Throughout the summer, "export" organizations arranged new routes for the transportation of more than 1,500 of these young men to Sweden where Norwegian "police troops" were receiving limited training under Norwegian military command.[20]

By mid-summer, NS authorities issued an order to all *lensmenn* (sheriffs) to intensify the search for the lads in the forest. This prompted the Resistance to issue a warning to all NS rural police officials that stated, among other things:

> *This directive is not to be understood as a recommendation but as an order from the highest authority in time of war. The leadership of the Home Front demands in the name of the Norwegian people that the sheriffs refuse any complicity in the persecution of our youth. Any sheriff who misjudges who they are that constitute Norway's sole lawful authorities and his own lawful superiors, must be prepared to take the consequences. The war has now entered its final phase, and the Home Front does not shrink from using the stronger measure in this conflict, where the future of the entire nation is at risk. Sheriffs who infringe this directive may expect the same fate as police inspector Lindvik and sheriff Horgen [Both of these men had been liquidated for the arrest of some of the lads]. We repeat: No Norwegian youth is to be arrested because he does his duty to his fatherland.*[21]

In one last effort to acquire the Norwegian manpower for service on the Eastern Front, the Germans used food as a political weapon to force conscription. Henceforth, the head of the household would no longer be able to obtain ration cards for the entire family; each member would have to appear at the rationing office in person. Those who failed to register would be refused ration cards. Without them, those who took to the forests and mountains would have no means of obtaining food and would be starved out.

As a countermeasure, Resistance authorities called upon London and Stockholm to print sufficient numbers of ration cards, but because the government was unable to obtain the proper paper for printing, the cards could not be supplied. It was now clear to the Resistance leadership that their only recourse was to steal the rationing cards. To accomplish this, a simple but daring plan was devised by Alf Sanengen, the head of the anti-Labor Service action committee by which Sonsteby and members of the Oslo Gang would intercept the consignment of ration cards while en route to the post office.

On the morning of August 9, Sonsteby, assisted by five other members of the Oslo Gang, hijacked the truck carrying the shipment of cards. The driver and guard were threatened at gunpoint and told to drive to a heavily congested area in downtown Oslo where it met a receiving party in another van in front of Skippergate 17. Within 10 minutes, and in the midst of people going to work, one and a half tons of newly printed ration cards were transferred from the printers' truck to the van, which was then driven outside the city and into hiding. A total of 70,000 food ration books and 30,000 tobacco cards were now in the possession of the Home Front. Despite a reward in the amount of 200,000 tax-free kroner offered for information leading to the arrest of those responsible, no one was willing to assist the NS authorities.

Soon thereafter, the Home Front Leadership contacted the NS Supply Minister and offered to return most of the cards if the order was rescinded that no ration cards be issued to those who refused registration of the labor draft. Thirteen thousand ration cards were held by the Resistance to supply those young men who were still in hiding, but with the easing of restrictions, the camps were eventually eliminated. The offer was unconditionally accepted, and after a written agreement was negotiated between the Minister and the Home Front Supply Service, all the rationing offices throughout the country were instructed to issue rationing cards to everyone without exception.[22] The NS authorities made no further attempt during the Occupation to use the food supply as a weapon to enlist Norwegian youth in the German mobilization effort.

To both the Resistance leadership and the population as a whole, the struggle against the conscription of Norwegian youth was a major victory. To the Germans, the Home Front directives, echoed by London BBC broadcasts and duplicated in the illegal press—underscored by sabotage operations and boldly endorsed by the "lads in the forest"— were convincing proofs that the mobilization effort was a total fiasco. Its failure was perhaps best expressed by *Reichskommissar* Terboven himself: "Quisling's old standing demands of peace, sovereignty, military honor, and mobilization have finally been buried."[23] Apart from the failed attempt two years earlier by the Germans and their Norwegian collaborators to implement the nazification program into the churches and schools—a struggle that was solely civilian in nature—no other issue so united the Civilian and the Military Home Front Leadership as the specter of compulsory mobilization. The fight over conscription was a continuation of that struggle—a struggle that succeeded in preserving the soul of a nation.

Moondrops for Milorg

Look for me by moonlight
Watch for me by moonlight
I'll come to thee by moonlight
Though hell should bar the way!
—*Alfred Noyes (1880-1958) "The Highwayman"*

The victory over mobilization by the Resistance leadership provided both the confidence needed to continue the struggle and the courage to make use of the means necessary to ensure success in the future—means that were now becoming readily available to the Home Forces.[1] Shortly after the D-Day landings in Normandy in June 1944, SHAEF sent a directive to SOE/Norwegian Defense Command that stated: "No Allied military offensive operations are planned for this [Norwegian] theater; therefore no steps must be taken to encourage the Resistance Movement as such to overt action, since no outside support can be forthcoming."[2] Nevertheless, sabotage operations on a limited scale by specially trained units of Milorg—not Milorg as a whole—were authorized to hinder the withdrawal of German forces from Norway for use against the Allied advance on the Continent.

After the June invasion on the Continent, planning and an extensive build-up of Milorg forces took place to enable them to successfully carry out their objectives. SOE instructors with arms, ammunition, and heavy equipment were sent from Great Britain by Shetland-based boats to the west coast of Norway. Within Norway itself, arms were manufactured in a number of clandestine workshops. Probably the most famous gunsmith in the country was Bror With, better known by his cover name, "Granat Larsen." In 1944, Larsen designed a homemade Sten gun, and then, with the help of a number of others, produced over 1,000 Sten guns. Where agents and larger numbers of provisions were required in the interior of the country, or where the coastline was heavily fortified, airdrops were undertaken. Most of these clandestine air operations were the responsibility of SOE, but a number were also organized by the SIS.[3]

The first recorded airdrop took place on the night of February 13-14, 1941, when SIS agent Sverre Midtskau jumped from an RAF slow-moving Whitley Mark V twin-engined bomber, which in the early phase was the only available type with sufficient range and load capacity for dropping supplies. Eleven months later, the first completed SOE drop took place when agents Odd Starheim and Andreas Fasting returned in a Whitley to Vest Agder in the south of Norway. Starheim was sent to reorganize Operation *Cheese* after having managed to evade the Gestapo and flee the country some seven months earlier. Fasting was organizing intelligence Operation *Biscuit*.

As they crossed the Norwegian coast, heavy mist caused the pilot to veer slightly off course. They discovered this when German anti-aircraft guns on an aerodrome directly below them opened fire. Caught in the crossbeams of searchlights and tracer bullets, the Whitley turned sharply to the northwest. Soon after the cloud cover dispersed, the landscape became visible and the container that held their skis was released from the bomb racks. Both agents waited for the signal light to turn green, at which time they jumped from the aircraft. Their parachutes unfurled and they landed in a snowdrift on a high mountain plateau.

This was the start of an activity that was to last until the end of the war in which more than 1,200 recorded sorties were undertaken, of which over 700 were successful.[4] In November 1942, the Whitley was replaced by the Short Stirling and the large four-engined Handley Page Halifax bomber which was adapted for parachuting agents and packages through a hole in the floor of the rear fuselage and containers from the bomb racks. Two special-duty squadrons, Numbers 138 and 161, operating from the RAF airbase at Tempsford, England, were responsible for all airdrops until early 1944 when the air activity was extended to other airfields: East Norwich, Newmarket, Rivenhall, Great Dunmow, Tarrant Rushton, Shepherds Grove, and Wethersfield. Some of these stations were far enough from Norway that intermediate landings had to be made at Kinloss, Wick, Lossiemouth, and Peterhead in Scotland.[5] A mission across the North Sea would often involve a round trip of 1,500 miles and a total flying time of 12 hours.

In all the countries of occupied Europe, with the possible exception of Czechoslovakia, airdrops in Norway presented the greatest difficulty.[6] Operations were often conducted under extremely hazardous conditions. Unlike the air taxi service in France where agents and supplies were landed by Lysanders (as well as other types of aircraft) on small fields that served as landing grounds, all air transport operations in Norway involved parachuting agents as well as containers and packages to the Milorg forces, most of which were in southern Norway and near the Swedish frontier. The mountains and heavily forested regions not only made landing an aircraft impossible, but also made flying at lower altitudes extremely dangerous.

During late autumn and the winter months, bad weather posed a constant threat. In the so-called dark season, long winter flights frequently involved snow, heavy cloud cover, ice, and fog, which forced a number of flights to return without completing their mission. There were other dangers: interception by enemy aircraft, flak from anti-aircraft batteries, failure to locate the drop zone (DZ), failure to receive the proper recognition signal from the reception committee on the ground, and the unintended agent and supply drops which occurred far from their landing zones, thereby subjecting them to possible capture by the Germans.

Operational flying was mainly confined to moonlit periods. Moonlight made navigation a great deal easier despite the barren landscape, which often consisted of remote valleys and plateaus. Moonlight was needed to read maps and to locate the drop zone for parachuting. Since the only contact with the reception committee was visual, moonlight facilitated the pilot's recognition of lights on the ground to identify the DZ from the air. Various places were reconnoitered for drop zones by agents in the field and referred to the Home Forces district staff for approval. The location had to be relatively flat and easily identifiable from the air. No high mountains or hills could be in the vicinity, and although facilities for storing supplies were imperative, on many occasions provisions had to be carried long distances from the reception area.

On the evening of a drop, the BBC Norwegian language news programs would end with a list of coded personal messages including the one referring to the particular operation that was "on" for that night. The message consisted of an apparently meaningless phrase like "the little white rabbit has returned to his hutch," that would be understood by ground personnel in the district where the drop was to be undertaken. Resistance forces maintained a 24-hour radio watch, and frequently messages had to penetrate through heavy jamming to a portable wireless set in a barn or attic where the agent in charge was carefully listening for the correct phrase.

The most common method of marking a drop zone was to line up three lights in a row, 100 yards apart. A fourth light was situated 50 yards from the three lights. This light was used for flashing an agreed-upon identification letter in Morse code to the aircraft.[7] This method was not entirely foolproof. It was an easy matter to home in on the wrong lights, and on several occasions drops were made far from the intended area. One RAF dispatcher recorded but one of a number of problems inherent in such operations:

> *Run to target from South end of Lake Oieren. A very poor reception seen as A/C approached. At this point the bomb aimer accidentally switched red and then the green light on, and before the dispatcher could stop them, the four agents had jumped.*

> *They went out 6-8 miles NW of target between the bottom tip of the lake and Trogstad; the aircraft was traveling at 180 miles per hour, but all parachutes were seen descending steadily from 2500 ft. away from the reception. Lights were very badly handled, only being switched on as A/C ran over.*

> *Consequently, three runs were necessary and then made with difficulty. Men jumped quickly on light signal, but without instructions from dispatcher. OK in three runs. 1st run—10 containers and 3 packages; 2nd run—4 packages; 3rd run—2 packages. When the lights were on they were good, and correct letter was flashed well. Air Transport Operation Report by F/O Corley-Smith 138 Sqn. 3/3/45.*

The reception committee generally consisted of eight to twelve men, but there might well be more or fewer. Picking up agents from a drop was not a problem, but removing a typical aggregate of 18 containers, each weighing up to 440 pounds, required a well-organized effort. Each container was about six feet in length, made of steel and lined with thick rubber to protect their contents upon impact. Each had three inner canisters shaped like medium-sized dustbins. They were equipped with handles and could also be partitioned. It was important to conceal them under trees or in the snow as quickly as possible. It was not unusual for parachutes to fill with wind and drag containers over a wide area before the ropes tangled and collapsed the parachute. This exposed the ground personnel to great risk in locating, retrieving, and transporting the containers. On one occasion a reception committee rode the containers down the mountainside like toboggans.[8]

Frequently ground personnel had to endure considerable strain and hardship waiting for an aircraft that was either delayed or failed to appear at all because of unreliable maps, mechanical problems, or encounters with flak or enemy aircraft. It is difficult to imagine how it was for those who knew the Occupation and what it was like to wait, sometimes for hours on end, for an aircraft that might not come or that came and went because the ground signal was unrecognizable. It was not uncommon for a new member of the reception team to ask, "Do you think they'll come tonight?"

In 1943, equipment was developed that enabled the aircraft to establish ground-to-air communication. The "S" phone was an ultra-high frequency radio telephone used during dropping operations, which at relatively short distances enabled the reception team to converse with the approaching aircraft so that even in unfavorable weather conditions the aircraft could be led to the reception point to carry out successful droppings. It was relatively secure as its transmissions could not be picked up by enemy direction finders more than one mile away. The device was strapped to the ground receiver's chest, and was so directional that the operator had to face the path of the aircraft with which he was communicating. Even with heavy ground mist, it was possible to lead the aircraft to the reception point, and with the aid of an "S" phone make sure that it was the right aircraft, before lighting the torches in the reception area. Another homing device on the aircraft was the "Rebecca" receiver, which was capable of picking up signals from a corresponding "Eureka" transmitting from the ground. The latter emitted a radio beacon in the form of a blip on the receiving screen, enabling the pilot to navigate with great accuracy.

Unfortunately, neither the "S" phones nor the Eurekas were sufficiently understood by many reception teams, who found them unwieldy and therefore failed to use them. But where they were used systematically, they were of the utmost value.[9] The Eureka used to direct the SOE *Gunnerside* team, which was dropped to destroy the heavy-water plant at Vemork, worked well. For some unknown reason, however, the Rebecca aboard the aircraft that delivered two earlier missions into Norway was not able to home in on the Eureka's signals. In that operation, the chief concern was keeping the batteries charged because the team's hand generator caused a good deal of trouble.

The air operation code-named *Pommel 12,* a moondrop to Milorg District 13, is an example of an ordinary mission to the Home Forces, which took place during the night of February 22-23, 1945. That night, 66 sorties were flown to Norway, 15 of them to Nordmarka north of Oslo.

At 1842 hours on February 22, Flying Officer Allan took off in his Short Stirling from the RAF airdrome Great Dunmow, followed exactly half an hour later by another Stirling. Both aircraft set course for a miniscule spot on the map, a frozen lake called Grasdalsputten. A reception committee of 17 Milorg men were anxiously awaiting their arrival. Through the BBC, they received the coded message that a drop could be expected that night. Their Eureka transmitter was turned on and when the first aircraft was about 25 miles away from the lake, the signal came in loud and clear on the Stirling's Rebecca receiver. At about 2300 hours, the reception committee heard the drone of an aircraft in the distance. Since it seemed to be heading straight for them, they rushed to light their torches. But before reaching the drop zone the aircraft turned away and disappeared. The men heard a lot of air activity, but the Stirling did not come back.

Then suddenly another aircraft approached. Again the torches were lighted and again they suffered the disappointment of seeing the aircraft turn away without dropping any supplies. When a third aircraft approached, the torches were lighted again, and this time the pilot recognized the reception committee. He lowered his flaps to slow down the air speed and noticed the Morse letter "J" being flashed repeatedly. From a height of 700 feet, 17 containers fell from the Stirling. A quick turn-around and then another run to drop three packages, but to no avail— the hatch was frozen solid and would not open. A third run was made and the dispatcher managed to get a single package out.

On the ground, eight of the containers went through the ice and had to be hauled up. With each one weighing about 400 pounds, this was not an easy job. Even in a temperature of 20 degrees below zero, the men were sweating. As they worked, they frequently glanced around: Have the Germans heard the aircraft? Are they possibly on their way here? But this was not the time to hesitate; and after awhile all the containers had been collected, the parachutes rolled together, and the torches put away. Everything was loaded onto sledges, dragged a couple of hundred meters to a ditch, and hidden there. Then all traces of the night's activity were erased and the men from Milorg slipped quietly away. Both Stirlings returned safely to Great Dunmow during the night and another special-duty operation was completed. For the men in Norway, the receipt of about 80 Lee Enfield rifles, 40 Sten guns, 9 Bren guns, 5 revolvers, 30,000 rounds of ammunition, plus explosives and other equipment meant added capability of hitting the enemy where and when he least expected it.[10]

One of the more chilling airdrop experiences involved SIS wireless operator Olaf Reed Olsen, who was sent back to southern Norway to organize Project *Aquila*, an intelligence operation in the Kristiansand area. At 0145 hours on the morning of April 20, 1943, after two previous jump cancellations due to severe winds, Olsen was seated at the edge of the hole in the afterpart of the Halifax preparing to be dropped northwest of Drammen. It was the last night of the full moon before the summer months, when agents could no longer be dropped into Norway.

While circling the drop zone, the unusually strong wind shifted the plane from side to side. The pilot advised the agent that he was not to jump for the following reasons: first, there was a 30-mile wind force, and that was 15 miles too much; second, he could not find a stretch of open marsh which should have been there according to the map—all he could observe were mountains and forests everywhere; third, he dared not fly too low below because of the violent gusts of wind; and he was unable to reduce speed to less than 160 miles, compared to the normal 115-120 miles, because he would lose steering control in the violent air currents.[11]

Nevertheless, Olsen was determined to jump, and after 15 minutes of discussion with the Polish pilot, who thought it madness, he was given the go-ahead, a green light: "Action station," the dispatcher called out. Olsen flung his legs into the hole. Then red light—"Go!" Once out of the plane, the wind struck Olsen in the face, twisted him around, and flung him back, causing him to strike his head against the rear wheel of the Halifax, causing him to lose consciousness for a short period. When he came to he saw the rear turret of the plane and the rest of the craft silhouetted against the sky. He then realized that he was hanging from the plane! Either from fear or pain or both he fainted again; when he regained consciousness he was still hanging and was being tossed up and down at a furious pace. He lost consciousness a third time, and when he recovered he looked up and saw that, through what must have been a miracle, the parachute was open, and he was descending to the ground; but the cords had gotten entangled in the material dividing the "umbrella" into several sections. The wind then carried him into the densely wooded Eiker Forest into a cluster of fir trees; around him branches broke up and a large bough struck him in the face, knocking him unconscious again. When he came to he managed to cut away the parachute straps holding him to the tree with his commando knife and collapsed in a foot and a half of snow when he realized he had dislocated his knee. "Never, never," he vowed, "would anyone make me do another parachute jump, indeed, at that moment I never wanted to see a plane again."[12]

Nevertheless, one year later on May 6, 1944, Olsen, along with fellow wireless operator Lars Larsen, found himself being air dropped once again between Drammen and Kongsberg. In that year, he had set up wireless stations in Kristiansand and Oslo, was granted two months leave during which time he was married in Toronto, Canada. The men's assignment on this day was to set up an additional intelligence network—Projects *Makir 1* and *Makir 2*—along the coastline between Stavanger and Kristiansand, the latter being the location of the largest German naval base in southern Norway. The intelligence they acquired provided the Allies with information on submarine bases, coastal defenses, and convoy movements. These stations remained in operation until October 1944.

In late October 1943, United States Army Air Force personnel stationed in England were sent to the RAF airfield in Tempsford for training in clandestine operations. The training involved RAF supply drop procedures to European resistance groups, including the Norwegian Home Forces. Upon completion, those trained were transferred to the Harrington airfield, which was to remain their base until the end of the war. The aircraft used were converted B-24 Liberators. Some of the machine guns and the complete ball turrets were removed to lighten the aircraft. The hole left by removing the turrets was converted into a hatch for dropping agents and packages. Much new equipment was installed, including the Rebecca transmitter which, with the Eureka receiver on the ground, greatly helped to locate the drop zone.[13] By May 1944, the unit was ready for operations to Scandinavia.

One American squadron consisting of six run-down Liberators on loan from the Eighth Air Force was under the leadership of Norwegian-born Colonel Bernt Balchen. This unit carried out a total of 64 missions to Norway from July to September 1944, after which it was withdrawn from service. The Eighth Air Force took over operations. The American missions were referred to as Carpetbagger Operations and classified as "Clandestine night operations in support of underground forces in occupied lands." A total of six B-24s were lost on missions over Norway.[14]

In October, the Office of Strategic Services (OSS), the American counterpart to the SOE, requested that a number of B-24s scheduled for Scandinavia be increased from four to ten. Approximately 60 percent of the flights were made during daylight or non-moon periods. British Stirling aircraft could not fly above 62° degrees north latitude in the Trondheim area, due to range limitations, whereas the American Liberator could.[15]

In December 1944, a Norwegian Special Operations Group (NORSO) being trained in the mountains of Scotland was being considered to undertake sabotage activity against railroads, tunnels, and bridges north of Trondheim in the Trondelag district. NORSO was a specialized unit of the OSS consisting of stranded Norwegian seamen and Americans of Scandinavian descent who were fluent in Norwegian and trained to operate deep behind enemy lines. The mission, code-named RYPE, was headed by Major William E. Colby, who in the later cold-war period was director of the Central Intelligence Agency (CIA). The team was assisted by a select British-trained Milorg sabotage team, code-named *Woodlark*, operating on the Swedish frontier.

On February 3, 1945, NORSO ordered an advance RYPE party to locate a dropping zone for the main party that was to arrive during the next full-moon period to reconnoiter targets along a railroad line in northern Norway. The line contained a number of tunnels, which were to be attacked with explosives. In Stockholm, Milorg was notified that the reception party should flash "F" for Fred. The BBC message to alert the reception party would be *Kaalrabiren er lekker*—the turnips are delicious. In case the airdrop was to take place during a non-moon period, Milorg was told to send an experienced Eureka operator from Stockholm so that the aircraft, upon receiving the signal, could home in on the reception party for a successful drop.[16]

On the evening of March 24, four British Stirlings carrying a British-sponsored team of 16 Norwegian paratroopers, code-named *Waxwing*, was sent to interdict a railway north of the RYPE operational area.[17] Later that same night, four B-24s took off from Kindloss airfield, near Inverness, Scotland, at 20-minute intervals.

At approximately 0130 hours, the four planes were met by a reception committee of five Norwegian skiers smuggled in from Stockholm. Four stacks of wood arranged in an upside-down "L" configuration were torched, enabling the B-24 Liberators to see the drop zone. As the wood was lighted, signals were transmitted and the reception was about to take place. A question-and-answer password had been agreed upon by Milorg through Stockholm for the final recognition between RYPE and the reception party. RYPE would ask, "Is the fishing good here?" The reception party would answer, "Yes, especially in the winter."

However, one of the members of the reception committee answered, "Here the fishing is no damn good." He was instinctively responding to a Scandinavian superstition: if you tell a stranger that the fishing is good, he will deplete your fishing hole, leaving you nothing. An American who could not speak Norwegian, drew his pistol, but the Norwegian realized his mistake and immediately corrected himself.[18]

Colby later reported that a ground mist and the slow removal of equipment and personnel from the four planes caused some unexpected problems. One container went through the ice in the lake where the drop zone was located. Another came apart in the air, and scattered three packages with four rucksacks that included a radio and batteries, a container of Bren guns, a package of skis, and two packages of rucksacks. The reception committee provided a horse and sled to assist in gathering the scattered equipment. Container dumps were placed in the woods and covered with white chutes and snow to prevent detection from the air.[19]

Throughout the course of the Occupation, a considerable number of Allied aircraft were lost on these special operational missions. No less than 20 Short Stirlings crashed in Norway, and although the greatest losses were sustained by the RAF, the American Eighth Air Force was also heavily hit. Some of these never reached their drop zone, are listed as missing in action, and are assumed to have come down in the sea either on their way to or from Norway. The total loss of crews in connection with missions to Norway came to some 200.[20] Fortunately, many of the Allied airmen parachuted to safety and managed to cross into Sweden, thanks to help received from the Resistance. Some, however, were captured and spent the rest of the war as prisoners in Germany.

Altogether, 245 agents were dropped in Norway. Milorg and other groups received a total of about 12,500 containers and 3,000 packages. As much as 70 percent of the supplies were dropped in the last nine months of the war. The drops included about 22,000 Lee Enfield rifles, about 7,000 Sten guns, 7,000 US-manufactured carbines, 7 million rounds of ammunition, and about 3,000 light machine guns of the Bren type for use against armor, the Piat (projector infantry anti-tank), and the American bazooka.[21]

Now that the Resistance had military instruction, training, arms, ammunition, and equipment, it was able to mobilize a secret army of thousands of well-trained and well-equipped men. Milorg forces were growing in strength and numbers, and bases were being established in mountain and forest districts throughout the country. The sabotage operations that had now been authorized by the Allied Supreme Headquarters, albeit limited in scope, were enough to provide the needed boost in morale at a time when many were experiencing a growing impatience and sense of frustration. For the Home Front forces, the waiting was almost over.

The Home Front Offensive

Carry on! Carry on!

Fight the good fight and true;

Believe in your mission, greet life with a cheer;

There's big work to do, and that's why you are here.

Carry on! Carry on!

Let the world be the better for you;

And at last when you die, let this be your cry:

Carry on, my soul! Carry on!

—Robert Service (1874–1958) Canadian poet and essayist

Although the SHAEF June directive sanctioned specialized Milorg units to sabotage selected targets directly related to the German war effort, direct confrontation with the Germans was to be avoided. Upon instruction from London, the Home Forces were authorized to attack sources of power, shipping traffic, and selected industrial targets to hinder an eventual German withdrawal from Norway. On June 26, 1944, Milorg received the following memorandum from the Norwegian Defense Command (FO): "Gasoline and oil are now targets with high priority. From now on both gasoline and oil should be attacked, both stored resources and those under transportation at any given opportunity."[1] In the following weeks, one special-action Milorg unit carried out 10 separate attacks against gasoline and fuel oil facilities. On August 18, Milorg mounted an operation against the Norsk fuel oil tank factory at Son south of Oslo, blowing up 7,000 tons of petrol and 4,000 tons of diesel fuel.[2] On September 25, members of Milorg District 13 demolished 63 oil tank cars on a side track.[3] And on October 12, about 50,000 gallons of lubricating oil, a large store of grease, and a considerable quantity of special gear oil were burned when the Oslo Gang destroyed the vacuum oil storage depot.[4] These and similar operations were part of a systematic plan to deprive the Germans of vitally needed fuel to support their U-boat campaign.

High on the list of industrial sabotage were ball bearings, chemical products, weapons production, transformers, machines, and machine parts and storages, and workshops. In short, any product or facility considered "war-important" was a potential target. An important action was the attack on the Swedish Kullager Ball Bearing Company in Oslo in which 50 tons of ball bearing storages were destroyed. Without ball bearings, the armament industry would slow to a halt. Equally important was the explosives industry, a major part of German war production in Norway—explosives being necessary for the construction of fortifications, naval bases, and so on.

Chief among those who led a series of attacks that paralyzed factories and other war-producing facilities was the Oslo Gang. Its leader, Gunnar Sonsteby, although not directly associated with Milorg, served as a liaison officer between members of the SOE Norwegian Independent Company (NORIC) and the Milorg Central Committee.[5] As the operational leader of the Home Forces, Sonsteby became more and more involved in the day-to-day activities of the Military Resistance, especially sabotage activity. Conversely, Jens Christian Hauge and the civilian leaders were not involved in the detailed planning, but were concerned with what operations should be given priority.

During the summer of 1944, Sonsteby was advised to undertake an operation against the Lysaker Chemical Plant, a major producer of sulphuric acid, an important ingredient in the production of explosives. On June 28, after two reconnaissance visits to the factory and with the help of local Milorg men, Sonsteby and Birger Rasmussen entered the factory area by cutting a hole through the fence a good distance from the sentries. They headed directly for the two acid tanks where they placed explosive charges fitted with a "pencil" time fuse. This pencil-like tube contained a glass cylinder filled with acid. Applying pressure on the knob broke the glass, spilled the acid, which then attacked a thin copper wire. When this was eaten through, it released a hammer, which struck the detonator and set it off, igniting the charge. The charges were set for 10 minutes. A similar action took place at Verpen, some 35 miles west of Oslo, which involved both Oslo Gang members and Milorg men. Both charges were set to explode simultaneously. To avoid reprisals against the civilian population, pieces of British uniform and equipment were left at the scene so that the Germans would think the sabotage had been done by troops parachuted into the area. The deception worked.[6]

On the night of August 13, Max Manus was in command of a sabotage operation at the Korsvoll Bus Depot in Oslo. This was a huge building, half of which the Germans had requisitioned for use as an aircraft factory and hangar for 25 Messerschmidt fighter planes and 150 airplane engines that were being serviced. The structure was situated in a densely populated residential area, which discouraged its destruction by bombing from the air.

At 0130 hours Manus, Sonsteby, and four others drove to the building and entered it by picking the lock. They restrained the Norwegian night watchman, who gave no resistance. As the six men passed through the Norwegian section of the depot, they encountered women washing down the buses. After Sonsteby explained that they were black marketeers who were using the depot cellar to store food for the Resistance, the women went casually about their business with little concern for the trespassers. They then descended into the cellar after cutting through three wire fences that barricaded the German side of the building. The signal was then given to drive the car that contained the explosives into the building.

The men carried 270 pounds of plastic and 70 pounds of ordinary dynamite in each of five separate suitcases down to the cellar, where they were stacked one on top of the other with four-minute fuses protruding from each satchel. At 0200 hours, the fuses were detonated, the night watchman and cleaning women let out, and within minutes an explosion occurred and the building was ablaze. With the exception of a number of scorched fuselages, which the Germans removed, the aircraft and parts were completely destroyed.[7]

A month later, the team undertook a raid to blow up the imposing Kongsberg arms-producing factory some 50 miles southwest of Oslo. Milorg leader Jens Christian Hauge instructed Sonsteby to destroy the four Bofors anti-aircraft guns that were at the plant ready for delivery, a 15" field gun being repaired, and two large boring-and-drilling machines whose destruction could hinder arms production for the rest of the war. SOE and Norwegian authorities in London granted authorization. Through a reliable contact in the factory who was a member of

Milorg, the team was familiarized with the factory area, and operational plans were finalized. On the night of September 17, Sonsteby, Birger Rasmussen, and the Kongsberg Milorg leader, Oscar Beck, retrieved 250 pounds of plastic explosives that Milorg had received from England in one of the arms drops. An additional 115 pounds had been smuggled into the factory earlier by the Milorg contact. By cutting through a chain-link fence, the three men entered the building after the night watchman had passed. The explosives were taken to the assembly area where the large guns were located. The charges were set to go off on a four-hour delay, but because the fuses were white and clearly visible between the charges and detonators, they had to be camouflaged. A number of boards were used to cover them to avoid discovery by a watchman or passerby. The explosions had an excellent effect, causing extensive damage to the structure of the building as well as to the armament and machinery inside.[8]

Authorization to attack the railways in Norway on a larger scale was not granted to Milorg until December 1944. The escalation was brought about after heavy pressure from activist circles in Norway and after prolonged debate, both at home and abroad. Earlier in the year, SHAEF sanctioned a limited number of attacks in the hope that railroad sabotage would force the Germans to send troops by sea, providing convenient targets for the Royal Navy and the RAF.[9] Independent SOE railway sabotage units, the Oslo Gang, and some Communist groups took part in these actions.

The Norwegian Orkla mines were of critical importance to the Germans after they had lost their supplies of pyrite from Sicily after the Allied invasion there. This sulphuric mineral was essential to the German war effort, and London wanted the railway to the mines severed. Norwegian SOE saboteurs had repeatedly attacked the locomotives that drew the ore trains from the mines to the coast. In one attack, five engines were disabled, only one of which was repairable. At the end of August, Sonsteby and his team received orders from London to mount an attack on the engine at the Thamshavn railway in Oslo where it was being repaired.

At midnight on September 12, after a careful reconnaissance of the factory using drawings and diagrams provided by contacts within the plant, Sonsteby, Rasmussen, and Johan Tallaksen cut through the barbed-wire fence and evaded the sentries, gaining access to the interior of the building. They secured a large magnetic charge consisting of eight pounds of plastic explosive to a girder under the locomotive and attached two three-pound charges attached to the power supply unit. They lighted the fuses, and within two minutes after the men ran from the building, the explosion occurred, reducing the locomotive to a useless mass of twisted iron.[10]

AT CHRISTMASTIME 1944, the Allied drive across France, Belgium, and Holland had bogged down. The Germans had broken through the Allied lines in Belgium. It was the Battle of the Bulge and the Americans were experiencing severe losses. The bombardment of London and Antwerp by the V-1 rocket and the more recently developed V-2 dispelled the notion that the war would soon be over. Norway was entering the sixth year of the war and there was a growing desperation among the people. What was needed was a large boost in morale.

An opportunity came on January 16, 1945, when the German troop transport *Donau* was anchored at the Oslofiord jetty. On this occasion, Max Manus had the able assistance of Roy Nielsen. He replaced Gregers Gram, who had been shot the previous November in a trap two cleverly trained Germans posing as deserters had set. Once again, the "underwater saboteur" managed to foil the German guards by hiding beneath a freight elevator located on the pier. A hole had been drilled in the elevator floor that made a straight drop into the water beneath the jetty. With the help of a sympathetic electrician who worked on the pier, Manus and Nielsen dropped through the hole and beneath the jetty and into an inflatable rubber boat on the ice. Manus cracked the ice while Nielsen paddled the boat toward the German vessel. Once alongside, 10 limpets were sucked onto the *Donau's* hull from the forward hatch to the afterhatch. The limpets were timed to explode two hours later.

On the other side of the pier was another troop transport, the 7,000-ton *Rolandseck*. The one remaining limpet was attached to the hull next to the engine room. The charges were set on a nine-hour delay. Just before entering the open sea, the limpets on the *Donau* exploded. The captain turned the ship back toward the shore and managed to run it aground before she sank at the stern. The number of men killed is not known, but there were 1,250 troops on board headed for the Western Front, 250 airmen, and the ship's crew. The cargo consisted of 450 horses and several hundred cars and cannon. Later the *Rolandseck,* which had 500 troops aboard and carried 250 horses, sleighs and cars, sank at the pier.[11]

To prevent the Germans from transferring further divisions from Norway to the Continent for use against the Allies, Milorg, in conjunction with units of the SOE, carried out nearly 30 attacks on railroads and bridges on a larger scale. The importance of hindering the transfer of German troops to the Continent became increasingly obvious to the Allies after the Germans mounted the Ardennes counter-offensive in mid-December. While there is disagreement on the effects that sabotage had on *Wehrmacht* withdrawals from Norway, SHAEF maintains that instead of shipping out four divisions per month, the Germans were only able to do less than one. According to their records, four divisions were pulled out in 1944 and seven in the last year of the war.[12]

One of the most successful railway sabotage raids occurred on January 13, when the Jorstad Bridge north of Trondheim was demolished in an action by four *Woodlark* SOE veterans of Company Linge and four men from Milorg. More than 70 Germans were killed and about 200 wounded in the operation. In addition, 20 railroad cars, five of which contained horses, went down into the river.[13]

Clearly the largest coordinated attack on the railroads was launched by about 1,000 Milorg saboteurs on March 14, 1945—Operation *Concrete Mixer*—that involved blowing up the north-south railway line that straddled both sides of the Oslofiord. The action involved the simultaneous destruction of four principal rail lines, numerous bridges, lengthy stretches of track, junctions, and signal boxes throughout the country. The operation demonstrated to the Germans that Milorg possessed real military potential.

Sonsteby and the Oslo Gang were an integral part of *Concrete Mixer* that involved the destruction of the Norwegian State Railways headquarters in Oslo and the German transport office, actions intended to cause mass confusion, paralyze the interaction of the rail coordinates, and hinder the transportation of German troops to the Continent.

At 2130 hours, Sonsteby and his team gained entrance to the railway office by duplicated keys provided by the caretaker who was their contact. Carrying four suitcases of explosives of 50 pounds each, the men entered the smaller building, which led to a passageway that brought them to a larger complex, where they took a German sentry by surprise. After recovering from the shock, he started to create an uproar, which left the men no choice but to shoot him with a silenced machine pistol. Within five minutes the charges were set in place, and after the men made a quick departure, the building collapsed from the explosion, killing the German guards inside.[14]

For all practical purposes, sabotage activity ended in the spring of 1945. At the end of April, as it was becoming increasingly clear that the end of the war was not far off, the Norwegian Ministry of Justice in London was concerned with the postwar task of bringing to justice those traitors and others who had collaborated in a treasonable manner with the Germans during the Occupation. Of particular importance to the Resistance were the archives of the *Nasjonal Samling* (NS) Police Department and NS Department of Justice. These archives contained the records of all NS members who either played a prominent part in collaborating with the enemy or were suspected of specified crimes beyond the mere fact of party membership.

When it was learned that NS officials intended to destroy the files, the Oslo Gang was entrusted with the job of salvaging them for use in the postwar legal proceedings. With the assistance of a contact in the NS Department of Justice and a sympathetic caretaker at the Police Department, Sonsteby's gang and several members of Milorg organized a coup to coordinate the two actions. On May 2, the team presented themselves as members of the police to gain access inside the building. Once inside, a departmental secretary who worked for the Resistance provided the men with important papers that had been prepared for them in advance. Several gang members dressed as police officials arrived at the two offices. Soon by rearrangement, a delivery van drove into the courtyard of the one building where several other members hurried inside to remove a huge safe containing two tons of incriminating files. After rolling the safe down the stairs and then up into the van, they drove to the Department of Justice building where they collected another half-ton of records. These files were later to provide the legal basis for bringing to trial after the liberation those who gave aid and comfort to the enemy.[15]

IN THE LATE WINTER AND EARLY SPRING OF 1945, the question of how the war would end in Norway was a matter of grave concern to the Norwegian government and the Home Front leadership. Once it was generally recognized that an Allied invasion of Norway was no longer considered a possibility, it was only reasonable to expect that freedom would only be regained with the final defeat of Germany in all of occupied Europe. Milorg had grown to about 40,000 men, most of whom had now been well-trained, equipped, and armed. The country was divided into 23 self-contained districts, all of which had radio contact with England.[16] Norwegian SOE instructors dispatched from Britain and Sweden established bases, which consisted of specially selected men situated in camps deep in the forest and in the mountains. But as late as May, about 350,000 German forces were still in Norway, and there was uncertainty as to how the Germans there would react to the prospect of capitulation. They might refuse to surrender, in which case the Allied armies would have to fight their way into the country. Resistance groups would then, presumably, have an active role to play in assisting the invading forces in the final liberation.

Another possibility was that the Germans might decide to evacuate Norway early in order to shift their forces to more critically needed areas in Europe. In that case, measures would have to be taken to prevent a possible repetition of the "scorched earth" policy undertaken in Finnmark and North Troms by German forces in October 1944, just before the forceful evacuation there. The deliberate destruction had included all means of communications, infrastructure, and practically all buildings, including approximately 11,000 homes and 350 large fishing vessels. And no provisions of any kind were allowed to remain for the 40,000 inhabitants who were forcibly evacuated and driven southward. In anticipation of a repetition of such a policy, Milorg would act to protect installations such as power stations, harbor installations, communications, and public utilities from German destruction.

Shortly after the scorched earth tactic in Finnmark, detailed anti-demolition plans were made in London and circulated to Milorg district leaders who were called upon to obtain intelligence concerning enemy preparations for demolition, which would then be sent to the Resistance Central leadership. Company Linge officers in Norway, acting with specially designated units of Milorg, were shown how to operate master switches which could be placed in factories for the purpose of creating blackouts when German demolition teams went into action. Spare parts, along with diagrams and sketches of machinery and plant equipment, were hidden so that any damage could be readily repaired. If Norwegians were forced to carry out any demolition work, dummy or comparatively harmless charges would be installed.[17]. In January 1945, SOE members of the Royal Norwegian Navy were secretly sent to 13 ports to organize an intelligence service that would give early warning of any German plans to carry out demolitions.[18]

As of April, all railroad sabotage was ended and all other types of action were reduced to a minimum. Milorg's responsibility in the final months of the war was now the protection of Norwegian lives and property. Organized jointly by Special Force Headquarters (SFHQ) and Milorg leadership, parties were instructed to go into action only on orders from London or if the Germans started demolition. Missions were planned at nine major hydroelectric stations in the Kongsberg and Upper Telemark region where many of the country's industrial plants were located. Plant guards who supported the Resistance were able to plant weapons and ammunition inside. Plans were also made to attack German troops in the vicinity of the factories; local port officials were also prepared to frustrate German plans to destroy wharves and harbors by replacing demolition charges with dummies. And railroad workers were instructed to ensure road and rail access and communication with Sweden to facilitate the return of Norwegian police units in training there to aid in actions against the enemy. In all of these cases, the role of the Resistance would be critical.

The Liberation & After

Let our object be our country, our whole country,

and nothing but our country. And by the blessing of God,

may that country itself become a vast and

splendid monument, not of oppression and terror,

but of wisdom, of peace, and of liberty,

upon which the world may gaze with admiration forever.

—Daniel Webster (1782-1852), American orator and statesman

As early as January 1943, a military conference was held at Casablanca to determine the most effective way of attacking Germany in Europe. It was there that the Chief of Staff to the Supreme Allied Commander Designate (COSSAC) was ordered to prepare an outline plan for the liberation of Western Europe, in which the opening of the Second Front—OPERATION OVERLORD—was given the highest priority. Later in August of that year, COSSAC proposed an alternative plan that dealt with the reconquest and liberation of the occupied countries in the event the German military machine showed signs of a general weakening before the launching of OVERLORD. This reserve plan, code-named RANKIN, involved Norway, and consisted of three variants: *Rankin A, Rankin B, and Rankin C.*

Rankin A recommended an invasion of the occupied countries that would require sending an expeditionary force to liberate Norway. Yet the large number of land, sea, and air supplies that were needed would create too great of a logistical problem. Strategically, since Norway was so far north and distant from any rapid route that led into the heart of Germany, this was considered a highly unlikely alternative.

Rankin B dealt with a voluntary German withdrawal from certain areas of its northwest perimeter, which could mean a retreat from part or all of Norway. COSSAC recommended sending a brigade into North Norway and a division into South Norway to secure the necessary naval and air bases and assist the Norwegian Army in the country's recon-struction, and to secure the disarmament of the German military forces.

Rankin C was based on a complete breakdown of German military strength and unconditional surrender. Allied forces would occupy as soon as possible suitable areas to secure compliance for surrender and for reconstruction work in the occupied countries.[1]

In all three variants the plans would involve small-scale operations against a much-weakened enemy. As one of the participants later wrote, "At first, COSSAC planned to send forces to Norway as mentioned under *Rankin B* 'as soon as the situation permits' and, together with the Norwegian Army based in the United Kingdom, take control of Norway, and secure the disarmament of the German military forces."[2]

In the summer of 1943, COSSAC assigned responsibility for the liberation of Norway to the Scottish Command in Edinburgh, under Lieutenant-General Sir Andrew Thorne. In a directive issued in October by the newly constituted Supreme Headquarters Allied Expeditionary Force (SHAEF), which had now replaced COSSAC as the top Allied planning authority for the reconquest of Western Europe, it was Thorne's responsibility to plan for the liberation in accordance with *Rankin C*. In November at a joint consultation meet-ing between the Scottish Command and the Norwegian Defense Command (FO), a Norwegian Military Mission was organized and attached to Force 134, the name given to the Allied liberation force in Norway under Scottish Command.

As the Allied plan for the liberation of Norway unfolded, however, the Norwegians found it highly unsatisfactory. The troops earmarked for South Norway were a Norwegian brigade in Scotland, a British division, and an American infantry regiment supported by a Norwegian-American infantry battalion, all of which were considered insufficient by the FO to meet the challenge of a vastly larger enemy force. In addition, it would take between six weeks and three months after the German surrender before the entire force was landed on Norwegian soil.[3] Nor were any Allied troops to be deployed to North Norway. This was not only militarily, but also politically, objectionable to the FO. Without the presence of British and American forces in the north, the FO feared that Norwegian territorial integrity in the region would not be guaranteed vis-à-vis possible Soviet intentions.

Throughout the course of 1944, General Thorne's Force 134 was continually faced with the problem of how to obtain a quick Allied presence in Norway at the time of the German surrender. In the fall, *Rankin C*—now renamed *Apostle*—was based on the assumption that a drastic reduction in German forces in Norway would occur due to a mounting German need for more troops on the Continent. This projection did not prove correct. In fact, in the fall, German forces were increased by a division that entered the country through Finland.[4] Later, a supplementary plan—code-named *Doomsday*—concentrated on an Allied landing in the cities of Stavanger, Kristiansand, and Oslo. The plan called for the reception of two separate Special Air Service forces, each consisting of 400 men—a Royal Air Force Regiment and Norwegian commando troops.[5]

Meanwhile, in a visit to London in the summer of 1944, Milorg leader Jens Christian Hauge met with General Thorne representing SHAEF. Hauge submitted a directive to the Allied High Command and the Norwegian government which, after it was approved, was called the "September Directive." Essentially, the document outlined Milorg's protective role in conducting a peaceful and orderly surrender and disarmament of German forces in the country, should there be a total and simultaneous surrender on all fronts. Accordingly, the Home Forces responsibility would involve the following provisions:

> *The disarmament of both Norwegian and German Nazis was to be done by the Wehrmacht.*
>
> *Peacekeeping was to be done in cooperation with the new Norwegian state police.*
>
> *Protection of the infrastructure, communications and other public buildings.*
>
> *Arrests of the NS leaders and the German and Norwegian Nazi officials in the police force.*
>
> *Taking charge of the police stations, barracks, prisons, prison camps and all German and NS controlled offices.*
>
> *The confiscation of archives from the NS party, the Gestapo and the occupational government.*[6]

If the orderly and peaceful alternatives should fail, the liberation would most likely take place in circumstances dominated by a German collapse. Should that occur, Milorg's main task would be the prevention of widespread scorched-earth tactics.

In December, the unexpected German counter-offensive in the Ardennes left no doubt in the mind of the Allies that the disintegration of German forces on the Continent was still a long way off. Consequently, all available resources in the Western Theater of operations must be concentrated on an offensive against the German heartland.

In the spring of 1945, Norwegian authorities had a growing concern about how the Germans in Norway would react when they were finally defeated on the Continent. If the *Wehrmacht* should continue to fight, what would compensate for the lack of Allied assistance to Norway that had now been earmarked for the Continent? The forces at the disposal of General Thorne for the liberation consisted solely of Norwegian troops. Altogether there were about 28,000 men in the armed forces, including a brigade in Scotland numbering 4,000 men, and about 14,000 fully-trained police troops on Swedish soil, many of whom had fled to Sweden to resist the Quisling mobilization. They could be used as light infantry forces to assist, if necessary, in the final liberation. In addition, the navy could provide 8,000 men and 52 ships, and the Norwegian Air Force had 2,600 men and about 80 aircraft of various kinds.[7]

Finally, there were the Home Forces, which consisted of 40,000 well-trained, well-armed, and equipped men. The *Wehrmacht*, however, still had 13 divisions in Norway, which amounted to about 350,000 troops, along with elements of the *Kriegsmarine* and *Luftwaffe* believed to be capable of waging a continuous struggle to the bitter end.

In April, King Haakon appealed directly to Churchill requesting Allied forces if the Germans continued to resist in Norway, but the Prime Minister refused on grounds that all available troops and ships were needed on the Continent. A similar request was made to Sweden (which, since the summer of 1943 had "revised" its "neutrality" policy from a pro-German stance to a pro-Allied one) to exert additional pressure on Germany or, if necessary, to intervene militarily in case the Germans should decide to prolong the war.[8] This appeal was also rejected. Both Churchill and the Swedish government believed that the

Germans in Norway would surrender peaceably unless provoked or pressured too early.[9]

From the Norwegian standpoint, the consensus was clear. Despite the substantial increase in the amount of military arms and equipment provided Milorg since the beginning of the year, the Home Front wanted nothing to jeopardize a peaceful end to the Occupation, and would do nothing unless it was in conjunction with an Allied invasion. On April 27, the Home Front leadership (HL) submitted a letter to Norwegian Prime Minister Johan Nygaardsvold, expressing its concern that the Allies might dictate too many severe surrender conditions to the Germans in Norway. A concern for fewer casualties and less destruction in the event of a less-than-peaceful end to the German Occupation signaled growing uncertainty by the HL. Still uppermost in their mind was the memory of Finnmark and Troms and the possibility that the country could become another theater of war. Consequently, the Norwegian government was opposed to anything that might provoke the Germans to prolong the war. Norway would have nothing to gain and everything to lose in a struggle in which the odds were about 10 fully trained soldiers of the *Wehrmacht* to one Milorg man.

According to a report from a contact in the German General Staff at Lillehammer, support was mounting within the German military command for a peaceful end to hostilities. But this did not necessarily mean that the *Wehrmacht* leadership intended to agree to unconditional surrender. They wanted a guarantee from the Allies that they were not to become prisoners of war of the Russians. They also wanted their troops to be given an "honorable retreat."[10]

On the other hand, that same contact reported that *Reichskommissar* Terboven and a hard core of senior officers at a Nazi Party meeting in Oslo on April 20, Hitler's birthday, reported to the Fuehrer that "Norway shall be held." It was Terboven's intention to make Norway a final bastion where top Nazi leaders could seek refuge. He put forth a plan to launch a major raid against the Home Front forces in Nordmarka, just north of Oslo, but the head of the Gestapo in Norway, *Oberfuehrer* Fehlis, halted the operation with the help of SS Chieftain Heinrich Himmler, who now claimed for himself, because Hitler had committed suicide on April 30, 1945, the dictatorship of the Third Reich.[11]

To the people of Norway, the anxiety and strain of waiting during the last days of the war was almost too much to bear since they had no idea what to expect from the occupying forces. However, at the end of April, the Home Front Leadership received a message from the Swedish Red Cross that Himmler offered an unconditional surrender to Great Britain and the United States, but that it was incomplete since Himmler had not offered it to the Soviet Union. Nevertheless, the news was encouraging since it suggested the likelihood of a united German surrender. But as a brake on any premature victory celebrations by the general populace, the Home Front Leadership issued the following instructions to the people:

1. Avoid gathering in crowds. Do not participate in any demonstrations of any kind. Do not act in a threatening manner towards the Germans or the NS.

2. Correctly distribute the news that is transmitted by London radio. Make notes; do not rely on memory; stop rumors and false news.

3. Do not relax on ordinary precautions. Remember, the Gestapo works until the bitter end.

4. Follow the directives that are given by the government, the High Command and the Home Front Leadership for every new situation.[12]

5. DIGNITY—CALM—DISCIPLINE

On May 3, three days after Hitler committed suicide, his successor, Grand Admiral Karl Doenitz, summoned Terboven and the *Wehrmacht* Commander in Norway, General Franz Boehme, to a meeting in Flensburg on the Danish frontier. Doenitz made it clear that he wanted an end of the war on all fronts. On May 5, German forces capitulated in the Netherlands, northwestern Germany, and Denmark. But since the Allied Powers would only accept terms of unconditional surrender, it was still uncertain as to how General Boehme would react. The Germans in Norway were still undefeated and in full possession of their strength.

On May 7, Boehme gave orders to his troops to remain on their guard until confirmation of Doenitz' surrender directive arrived from the *Wehrmacht* High Command headquarters (OKW) at Lillehammer.

Moreover, he still pressed for certain conditions for his army. He insisted that the Germans were to disarm themselves and that any attempt
by Norwegian or Allied forces to disarm German soldiers would be met
with violence. The Norwegian HL and the Allied High Command
agreed that disarmament would be overseen by the OKW. Nor was
Boehme willing to relinquish control of the Oslo State Broadcasting
Station since the Germans were still in power. That same day, the
Home Forces transmitted a directive from American General Dwight
D. Eisenhower to General Boehme advising him to contact SHAEF by
radio. This was to give Boehme the opportunity to announce the surrender of his troops. The German commander waited until the next
day, May 8, to respond, when he simply announced that he was awaiting the arrival of the Allied Armistice Commission.

Meanwhile, the Home Front forces mobilized and assumed guard
duties at all municipal buildings and key locations throughout the country. Despite a certain amount of confusion and uncertainty, the Home
Front Leadership contacted the *Wehrmacht* headquarters to assure them
that the mobilization meant no danger to the German troops, but was
simply a guarantee for the preservation of law and order.[13]

Later that evening, British Brigadier Hilton and the other members of the Armistice delegation drove to Lilllehammer where the
demand for German surrender was delivered. All *Wehrmacht* forces were
ordered to withdraw from their fortifications and from all major
Norwegian cities. They were then told to assemble at key locations for
a general demobilization within the next two weeks. The transfer of
power that followed was done peacefully without any major incidents.
Both the German and the Norwegian Home Forces conducted themselves with disciplined solemnity.

Not all of the German and Norwegian NS officials were so acqui-
escent when faced with their day of reckoning. Several hours before
midnight on May 8, *Reichkommissar* Terboven and SS
Obengruppenfuherer Wilhelm Rediess blew themselves up in a bunker at
Skaugum estate, the previous residence of the Crown Prince, which
Terboven had taken over at the time of the Occupation. The NS
Minister of Police, Jonas Lie, along with Sverre Riisnaes, NS Minister
of Justice, and Henrik Rogstad, the NS head of the State Police, barricaded themselves in a farm in Baerum, just west of Oslo. After a com-

pany of Milorg surrounded them, Lie and Rogstad took their own lives, but Riisnaes surrendered.[14]

In an attempt to avoid detection, General Boehme and Gestapo Chief Fehlis dressed SS and Gestapo personnel in *Wehrmacht* uniforms and concealed them in detention camps with ordinary German soldiers. Most of them, about 2,700 Germans, were later apprehended and their cases investigated by Allied and Norwegian authorities. Fehlis himself committed suicide on May 10 when, together with 73 other Gestapo members, he was discovered by Home Front forces in Telemark.[15] And in anticipation of what they might expect in postwar legal proceedings against enemy collaborators, other Quisling authorities took their own lives as well.

In the wake of the German capitulation, Vidkun Quisling still considered himself the legitimate head of state. Yet despite orders from Norwegian authorities to turn himself in to the Oslo police station at Mollergaten 19, the former Norwegian "Minister-President" persisted in efforts to negotiate his case with the Home Front Leadership. But after being told he would be forcibly arrested if he resisted further, he surrendered on May 9 together with a number of his ministers.

The first contingent of Allied troops consisted of both British and Norwegian paratroopers arrived at the Gardermoen airfield just north of Oslo on May 9. And on May 11 two brigades of the British First Airborne Division and a brigade of the Special Air Service (SAS) landed at Oslo, Kristiansand, and Stavanger. In the first part of June, an American regiment and two additional British brigades were brought in as reinforcements to oversee the disarmament and withdrawal of the German troops.

The Commander-in-Chief of the Norwegian forces, Crown Prince Olav, arrived in Oslo on May 13, together with the chief military commander in Norway, General Thorne, the heads of the three armed services, and the Norwegian government delegation. The return of the Crown Prince clearly marked the end of rule by the Resistance leadership. On May 14, in a meeting with the government delegation at the Royal Palace, led by Defense Minister Oscar Torp, the Home Front transferred authority back to the exiled Norwegian government.

Throughout the cities, towns and villages, jubilant crowds gathered to celebrate the end of Occupation. The climax to the celebrations came amidst much rejoicing on June 7, when His Majesty King Haakon VII returned to Norway exactly five years to the day that he had left for England. Norwegian flags that had been banned for the past five years now appeared on porches, were draped from buildings, and waved by people everywhere. After five long oppressive years, Norwegian Resistance in the Second World War had come to an end and Norway was once again free.

It is estimated that approximately 40,000 Norwegians were arrested for political reasons or "threatening manners" toward the Occupation forces during the war. Close to 9,000 were held in German work camps and prison camps throughout the Continent. According to official sources, 2,091 members of the Resistance lost their lives during the five-year occupational period: 366 were executed, 162 were killed in open conflict with the Germans, 93 died attempting to cross the North Sea to England; 130 died in Norwegian prisons, many as the result of torture or by committing suicide. In addition, those whose health had been ruined because of torture or cruel and unusual punishment in prison will never be known.

In concentration camps in Germany, the death toll of Norwegian political prisoners was 1,340, of which 610 were Jews.[16] The total number of Jews deported from Norway was about 800, most to Auschwitz, a smaller number to slave-labor camps in Germany. Only 23 of those deported survived. Some 900 Jews, about half the Jewish population, evaded arrest and internment. With the aid of the Resistance, they managed to flee to Sweden.[17]

Throughout the course of the Occupation large numbers of foreign prisoners of war were brought to Norway and formed into slave-labor battalions by the *Organisation Todt*, to build roads, rail lines, and various German construction and military projects. At the time of liberation, the number of laborers totaled 100,000. About 83,000 were Russians. Among the other nationalities, Poles and Serbs comprised the largest groups. A majority of the prisoners were seriously weakened by sickness and malnutrition, which resulted from inhumane conditions in cold and hostile climates. Approximately 17,000 East European Slav prisoners died from hunger, disease, and German brutalities during the war.[18]

As early as May 8, thousands of NS Party members and enemy collaborators were taken into custody and placed in prisons and concentration camps previously occupied by members of the Resistance. Names were taken from lists compiled by the Home Front, the newly organized police force, and other groups. Within two months the number of prisoners rose to 14,000.[19]

In the feverish atmosphere that prevailed in the early postwar period, many of the NS Party members who were seized were later released. Only those suspected of specified crimes or who played a prominent role in the NS Party were retained in custody. Although the mere fact of party membership was not enough to warrant arrest, this directive was not followed everywhere in the heated climate of the period. Unlike the retribution exacted from collaborators in most other occupied countries, particularly in France where thousands were summarily executed in the weeks before and after the liberation, the climate in Norway was calmer and far more disciplined.

Nevertheless, public resentment and hostility towards collaborators withheld during the five years of Occupation was now given vent throughout the country. Within the Grini Prison on the outskirts of Oslo, where the largest number of collaborators were housed, the inmates were exposed to overcrowding, food shortages, and unsanitary conditions, problems that were soon corrected after the first several months. During the first weeks following liberation, there were sporadic incidents of physical abuse and humiliation by prison guards, most of whom had little or no experience or training in dealing with prisoners. Since many of the guards were made up of Home Front Forces, some of whom were former inmates themselves during the Occupation, the maltreatment of prisoners came from what the guards had learned from the German and NS police. These incidents were dealt with appropriately by the authorities wherever the identity of the offender and the facts of the offense could be established.[20]

Resentment and bitterness toward collaborators was expressed in a social boycott. NS party members were suspended from their government jobs, and most private business firms acted in like manner. The employer who retained members of the NS party in his employ risked the loss of the remainder of his staff. The same attitude was adopted by many private clubs and associations toward those who had not taken a "sufficiently patriotic stand" against the Germans and the NS. Extenuating circumstances to justify collaborationist activity were viewed as acts of national disloyalty. Newspaper accounts that condemned the abuses of power, torture, and the cruelty by the NS, along with protests that denounced the "appalling leniency in the treatment of arrested collaborators," all contributed to a climate sharply critical of the legal proceedings. Defense lawyers were accused of delaying tactics by invoking unnecessary formalities or technicalities. Those who advocated moderation were viewed as "silky" or "velvety," that is, overly permissive in their attitude toward the collaborators.[21]

Women who had fraternized with the German soldiers were reproached as "German tarts"; and although they had not violated any criminal laws, many were publicly censured and humiliated by those whose unrelenting hostility was not so easily appeased. There were instances in which a number of them had their heads shaved; others were disgraced by being paraded through the streets where they were scorned in other ways. Large numbers of them were placed in protective detention for their own safety. Later they were released as the antagonistic feelings diminished.

The most notorious of all the Norwegian traitors was Henry Oliver Rinnan—cover name—"Lola," who was described by one author as the "devil's apprentice."[22] Rinnan was a master of deception and a valuable asset to the Gestapo. At his trial he admitted responsibility for the murder of hundreds of Norwegians by the Gestapo, and was personally convicted of 13 murders. At the end of the war, it was revealed that he had 70 male and female Norwegians working for him, and was given an expense budget by the Gestapo commandant in Trondheim, Gerhard Flesch, that amounted to 300,000 kroner—$75,000—per year, which was used to help finance the destruction of numerous underground groups. Rinnan's life ended with his back to a granite wall facing a firing squad after the Norwegian Supreme Court denied an automatic appeal.[23] Ten members of the opprobrious "Rinnan Gang" were sentenced to death, eleven to hard labor for life, and numerous others to long terms of imprisonment.

Certainly the most celebrated postwar trial in Norway was that of Vidkun Quisling, the self-proclaimed President-Minister who had allied himself with the German aggression both before and throughout the Occupation of Norway. A number of people believed that because of his treasonable activity, Quisling should be tried before a military tribunal and shot summarily. Nevertheless, in accordance with Norwegian criminal procedure, Quisling was granted the same rights of defense as any other offender. According to a well-known Swedish attorney who attended the proceedings and later published a book about them, the trial was distinguished by "objectivity, simplicity, concentration and dignity."[24]

The trial began on August 20, 1945. The following major accusations were brought against him:

- His self-proclamation as head of the Norwegian government immediately following the German Occupation on April 9, 1940

- His revocation of the order for mobilization on the day of the German invasion

- His call for volunteers to enter the war in support of Germany

- His formation of a "government" on February 1, 1942, when he was elevated to the office of Minister-President by the unconstitutionally enacted "Act of State" by a packed NS Supreme Court

- His complicity in the deportation of the Jews which resulted in the loss of hundreds of their lives

- His responsibility for the death sentences passed on patriotic Norwegians

During the course of the proceedings, documentation was brought forth from records obtained from German naval archives and the diary of Alfred Rosenberg concerning a visit by Quisling to Berlin as early as December 1939, involving a meeting he had with Hitler and Grand Admiral Raeder. It was at that meeting that Raeder's idea of acquiring German naval bases in Norway germinated and Quisling proposed his own plan for attacking Norway. Evidence was also brought forth supporting the charge that he received financial support from Hitler in the latter's planned attack.

To Quisling, who never stopped believing that he had the best interests of Norway at heart, his plea of "not guilty" to all charges was backed by a most pathetic monologue that lasted several hours and clearly showed he had receded into an illusory world of his own. He concluded by saying: "If my activities had been treasonable—as they have been said to be—then I would pray to God that for the sake of

Norway a large number of Norway's sons will become such traitors as I, but that they will not be thrown into jail."[25] The judgment of the Court was "guilty on all major counts," and the sentence was death. After the Supreme Court rejected an appeal, he was taken to Akershus Castle, and on October 24, 1945, he was executed in the courtyard by firing squad.

Of a total of 30 death sentences passed on Norwegian collaborators, 25 actually took place. The crimes consisted of hideous acts of torture, killing prisoners or informants, of causing the death of their own countrymen under aggravating circumstances.[26]

Ultimately, more than 90,000 cases of collaborationist activities were investigated, but only about 46,000 persons were found guilty of wartime offenses. Of these, 18,000 received prison sentences and 28,000 were fined and/or deprived of voting privileges for 10 years. In about 5,000 cases, the offense was so insignificant that no charge was made. Of those who were sent to prison, only 4,500 were for more than three years and 600 for more than eight years. Generally speaking, the trend toward greater leniency increased in the years after the war. By the summer of 1948, under a system of reprieve, the sentences of most of the collaborators were reduced by one-half. There were 80 cases of life imprisonment or death sentences commuted to imprisonment for life. For this group the average time served was about nine years.[27] The last execution took place in the autumn of 1948.

In the transition from war to peace, the task turned to reconstruction and the postwar future. For Norway that meant the reestablishment of the pre-war constitutional government with one significant difference: henceforth, the former neutralist posture that determined the course of Norwegian foreign policy shifted to one of alliance, a change that was based upon a re-evaluation of defense policies, but also on the experiences of the Resistance struggle.

Conclusion

In a section of the Norwegian Resistance Museum in Oslo there is a display that reads: *In the skies above London, in the African Desert, in the ruins of Stalingrad and on the Normandy beaches, Norway was given back to us.* True enough. One can hardly deny that the outcome of the Second World War was decided by the foresight of the Allied political and military leaders, the economic capabilities, and the military strategies, tactics, and logistics that were applied to the task of a total global war. Thus is total war defined by the military historian who views the Second World War in a conventional sense; in which the conflict was fought by conventional forces in clearly defined engagements and skirmishes. For the traditional military historian, the psychological impact of the occupation on a people who lived under Nazi rule is of little, or at most, of secondary importance.

Conversely, the Resistance historian is deeply concerned with the impact of the war on the ordinary men and women within the occupied countries who were forced to live day in and day out under barbaric rule, many of whom risked their lives by taking up the gauntlet in defense of the principles and ideals of Western Civilization. As the renowned Danish Resistance historian Jorgen Haestrup has noted, World War II was a total war that was fought in another sense and just as real as it was global. In his words, the war "was not only a subject for those directly engaged militarily, but a tragedy with profound moral, psychological and political aspects which affected millions outside the military fronts in daily life, outlook, future and existence."[1]

In German-occupied Norway, donning the armor for one meant living alone for months at a time in a hut in the wilderness as a wireless operator providing intelligence to London. For another, it meant keeping the hope of freedom alive by running the risk of circulating an underground newspaper to undermine Axis propaganda with the knowledge that the struggle had not ended, but rather was being intensified. For still others, it meant being air dropped under cover of darkness to train and supply local resistance groups in the arts of sabotage.

It could mean risking the loss of one's life at sea as a merchant seaman. Those were just *some* of the more dangerous challenges that faced the men and women of the Resistance. But equally militant in the struggle to preserve and defend those principles and ideals that make life worth living were the parents, teachers and religious leaders who were willing to suffer hunger, disease, imprisonment, torture and even death rather than submit to nazification indoctrination. By standing up to the barbarian within their own cities, towns, and villages, it was these people who provided the moral stamina that the country needed at a time when it was most needed. But Norway also found in those who were subjected to danger, hardship, and suffering a source of spiritual strength for the more passive, but increasingly convinced, sympathizers. All of these and the like-minded among them, both individually and collectively, had a profound effect upon morale. The Resistance mentality that was forged by the Home Front and supported by the Norwegian exile-government in London provided the nation with a sense of purpose and a national will, which enabled that Scandinavian kingdom to resist the barbarism that was Nazism in what was not only the darkest, but the most laudable period in that nation's history.

Sources & Bibliography

Archives

Norse Hjemmefrontmuseum (Norwegian Resistance Museum), Oslo Universitetsbibliotek, Oslo.

Memoirs, special studies, and general works

Adamson, Hans Christian and Klem, Per, *Blood on the Midnight Sun*. New York: W. W. Norton and Company, 1964.

Andenaes, Johs., Riste, Olav, and Skodvin, Magne, *Norway and the Second World War*. Oslo: Engers Boktrykkeri A/S, 1966.

Astrup, Helen, and Jacot, B. L., *Oslo Intrigue: A Woman's Memoir of the Norwegian Resistance*. New York: McGraw-Hill Book Company, Inc., 1954

Baden-Powell, Dorothy, *Operation Jupiter*. North Yorkshire, England: Magna Print Books, 1982.

Buckley, Christopher, *Norway, the Commandos, Dieppe*. London: His Majesty's Stationery Office, 1952.

Churchill, Winston, *The Gathering Storm*. Boston: Houghton Mifflin Company, 1948.

Cookridge, E. H., *Set Europe Ablaze*. New York: Thomas Y. Crowell Company, 1967.

Cruickshank, Charles, *SOE in Scandinavia*. Oxford: Oxford University Press, 1986.

Dawidowicz, Lucy S., *The War against the Jews*. New York: Bantam Books, 1976.

Dear, Ian, *Sabotage and Subversion: Stories from the Files of the SOE and OSS*. London: Arms and Armour Press, 1996.

Derry, T. K., *A History of Modern Norway: 1814-1972*. Oxford: Oxford University Press, 1973.

_____, *The Campaign in Norway*. London: His Majesty's Stationery Office, 1952.

Egner, Arne, Stenersen, Sten, et al., *Slipp Over Norge* (Supplies over Norway). Oslo: A/S Sem & Stenersen, 1982.

Faeroy, Frode, *Frigjoringen* (Liberation). Oslo: Norges Hjemmefronmuseum (Norwegian Resistance Museum), 1994.

Foot, M. R. D., *Resistance: European Resistance to Nazism 1940-45*. New York: McGraw-Hill Book Company, 1977

Gallagher, Thomas, *The X-Craft Raid*. New York: Harcourt Brace Jovanovich, Inc., 1971.

Gjelsvik, Tore, *Norwegian Resistance: 1940-1945*. Montreal: McGill-Queens University Press, 1979.

Haestrup, Jorgen, *Europe Ablaze: An Analysis of the History of the European Resistance Movements 1939-1945*. Odense, Denmark: Odense University Press, 1978.

Hansson, Per, *The Greatest Gamble*. New York: W.W. Norton and Company, Inc., 1967.

Hauge, E. O., *Salt Water Thief*. London: Gerald Duckworth & Co. Ltd., 1958.

Haukelid, Knut, *Skis against the Atom*. London: William Kimber and Co. Ltd., 1954.

Heimark, Bruce, *The OSS Norwegian Special Operations Group in World War II*. Westport, Conn., Praeger, 1994.

Hoff-Jenssen, Jorgen, *Avisa: Den Illegale Avis i Kristiansund N. 1943-45* (*News:* The Illegal News in Kristiansund North, 1943-45). Fetsund, Norway: 1975.

Howarth, David, *The Shetland Bus.* London: Thomas Nelson and Sons Ltd., 1951.

_____, *We Die Alone.* New York: Macmillan Company, 1955.

Howarth, Patrick, *Undercover: The Men and Women of the SOE.* London: Phoenix Press, 1980.

Hoye, Bjarne, and Trygve, Ager M., *The Fight of the Norwegian Church against Nazism.* New York: The Macmillan Company, 1943.

Johnsen, Berit Eide, *Motstandsbevegelsen Pa Agde, 1940-1945* (Resistance Movement in Agder, 1940-1945). Kristiansand: Trykk Edgar Hogfeldt AS, 1992.

Johnson, Amanda, *Norway, Her Invasion and Occupation.* Decatur, Ga.: Bowen Press Printers, 1948.

Kersaudy, François, *Norway 1940.* New York: St. Martin's Press, 1987.

Koht, Halvdan, *Norway: Neutral and Invaded.* New York: The Macmillan Company, 1941.

Kraglund, Ivar, *Kampen For Det Frie Ord* (The Fight against the Mobilization Threat in Norway, 1943-44). Oslo: Norges Hjemmefrontmuseum, 1998.

_____, *Sikringstjenesten, 1940-1945* (Security Work, 1940-1945). Oslo: Norges Hjemmefrontmuseum, 1990.

Kraus, Rene, *Europe in Revolt.* New York: The Macmillan Company, 1942.

Kurzman, Dan, *Blood and Water: Sabotaging Hitler's Bomb.* New York: Henry Holt and Company, Inc., 1997

Larsen, Karen, *A History of Norway*. New York: Princeton University Press, 1948

Larsen, Stein Ugelvik, Hagtvet, Bernt, and Myklebust, Jan Petter, ed. *Who Were the Fascists? Social Roots of European Fascism*. Bergen: Universitetsforlaget, 1980

Macintyre, Captain Donald, *Narvik*. New York: W.W. Norton and Company, Inc., 1959

Manus, Max, *9 Lives Before Thirty*. Garden City, New York: Doubleday and Company, Inc., 1947

_____, *Underwater Saboteur*. London: William Kimber and Company Ltd., 1953

March, Anthony, *Darkness Over Europe: First Person Accounts of Life in Europe During the War Years, 1939-1945*. Chicago: Rand McNally and Company, 1969.

Masterson, J. C., *The Double-Cross System in the War of 1939-1945*. Yale: Yale University Press, 1972.

Mendelsohn, Oskar, *The Persecution of the Norwegian Jews in World War II*. Oslo: Norges Hjemmefrontmuseum, 1991.

Michel, Henri, *The Shadow War: European Resistance, 1939-1945*. New York: Harper and Rowe Publishers, 1972.

Moen, Petter, *Petter Moen's Diary*. New York: Creative Age Press, 1951.

Moland, Arnfinn, *Kampen Mot Mobiliserings Trusselen I Norge, 1943-44* (The Fight against the Mobilization Threat in Norway, 1943-44). Oslo: Hjemmefrontmuseum, 1987.

_____, *Milorg 1941-43: Fremvekst, ledelse, og organisasjon* (Milorg, 1941-43: Growth, Leadership and Organization). Oslo: Hjemmefrontmuseum, 1991.

_____, *Sabotasje I Norge Under 2 Verdenskrig*. (Sabotage in Norway during World War II). Oslo: Hjemmerfrontmuseum, 1987.

Moulton, J. L., *The Norwegian Campaign of 1940*. London: Eyre & Spottiswoode, 1966.

Olsen, Oluf Reed, *Two Eggs on My Plate*. Chicago: Rand McNally and Company, 1952.

Ottosen, Kristian, *Theta, Theta*. Bergen: Universitetsforlaget, 1983.

Peillard, Leonce, *Sink the Tirpitz*. New York: G. P. Putnam's Sons, 1968.

Petrow, Richard, *The Bitter Years*. New York: Morrow, 1974.

Public Record Office, *SOE Syllabus: Lessons in Ungentlemanly Warfare in World War II*. St. Edmundsbury Press, Suffolk, Great Britain, 2001.

Rings, Werner, *Life with the Enemy 1939-1945*. Garden City, New York: Doubleday and Company, Inc., 1982.

Riste, Olav, and Nokleby, Berit, *Norway 1940-45: The Resistance Movement*. Oslo: Nor-Media A/S, 1970.

Royal Norwegian Government Information Office, *Before We Go Back: Norway's Fight Since April, 1940*. London: His Majesty's Stationery Office, 1944.

Shirer, William L., *The Challenge of Scandinavia* Boston: Little Brown and Co., 1955.

———, *The Rise and Fall of the Third Reich* New York: Simon and Schuster, 1960.

Salmon, Patrick, ed. *Britain and Norway in the Second World War*. London: His Majesty's Stationery Office, 1995.

Schofield, Stephen, *Musketoon*. London: Jonathan Cape, 1964.

Sonsteby, Gunnar, *Report from No. 24*. New York: Lyle Stuart, Inc., 1965.

Stafford, David, *Camp X*. New York: Dodd, Mead & Company, 1986.

Steinbeck, John, *The Moon Is Down*. New York: The Viking Press, 1942.

Sveri, Elisabeth, *Kvinner I Norsk Motstandsbevegelse, 1940-1945* (Women in the Norwegian Resistance). Oslo: Norges Hjemmefrontmuseum, 1990.

Taylor, Telford, *The March of Conquest*. New York: Simon and Schuster, 1958.

Terraine, John, *The Right of the Line: The Royal Air Force in the European War 1939-1945*. Herefordshire, Great Britain: Wordsworth Editions Limited, 1985.

Ulstein, Ragnar, *Etterretningstjenesten 1940-1945* (The Intelligence Service, 1940-1945). Oslo: Norges Hjemmefrontmuseum, 1994.

_____, *The North Sea Traffic: Flight to War*. Bergen: Sjofartsmuseum, 1992.

Undset, Sigrid, *Return to the Future*. New York: Alfred A. Knopf, 1942.

Wilmot, Chester, *The Struggle for Europe*. Herefordshire, Great Britain: Wordsworth Editions Limited, 1997.

Worm-Muller, Jacob, *Norway Revolts against the Nazis*. London: Lindsay Drummond, 1941.

Journal articles and editorials

"Battle of Europe: German Saddle Burrs," *Time*, January 26, 1942.

Bronner, Hedin. "War Poems: A Norwegian Secret Weapon," *American Scandinavian Review*, 36 all issues 1948.

"Chaos," *Newsweek*, September 29, 1941.

"Ferment of Conquest: Nazi Woes Increase in Norway and Other Occupied Countries," *Newsweek*, September 22, 1941.

"Germs of Revolt: Unrest Sweeps Occupied Europe," *Newsweek*, August 11, 1941.

"Nazi Headache: Norway Seethes with Sabotage in Face of Gestapo Crackdown," *Newsweek*, May 12, 1941.

"Reich Commissioner Josef Terboven Tells Norwegians What's What," *Newsweek*, March 10, 1941.

"Trondheim and Tirpitz," *Newsweek*, March 23, 1942.

Haugland, John, "Norway Lives for the Hour of Revolt," *The New York Times Magazine*, March 28, 1943.

*E*nd Notes

Chapter 1: Neutrality of the Dove

1. German and Scandinavian Exhibits, 1800-1945 (Norsk Folkemuseet Oslo: 1998), 1ff.

2. T. K. Derry, *The Campaign in Norway* (London: Her Majesty's Stationery Office, 1952), 5.

3. *Ibid.*

4. Karen Larsen, *A History of Norway* (New York: Princeton University Press, 1948), 11-12.

5. *Ibid.*

6. J. L. Moulton, *The Norwegian Campaign of 1940* (London: Eyre & Spottiswoode, 1966), 122-23

7. *Ibid.*

8. *Ibid.*

9. William L. Shirer, *The Challenge of Scandinavia* (Boston: Little, Brown and Company, 1955), 30.

10. *Norway Year Book, 1938*, as cited in Derry, *Campaign in Norway*, 6, 11.

11. The source for the details of the Norwegian Homeland Defense is the report compiled by *Undersokelseskommisjonen av 1945* (Investigation Commision of 1945), Municipal Department, 11, S. 67. This information was obtained from the Norges Hjemmefrontmuseum (Norwegian Resistance Museum), Oslo.

12. Derry, *Campaign in Norway*, 7

13. *Ibid.*, 36.

14. Moulton, *Norwegian Campaign*, 126.

15. Derry, *Campaign in Norway*, 7.

16. Olav Riste and Magne Skodvin, *Norway and the Second World War* (Oslo: Engers Boktrykkeri A/S, 1966) 11.

Chapter 2: The Cunning of the Serpent

1. Halvdan Koht, *Norway: Neutral and Invaded* (New York: The Macmillan Company, 1941), 14.

2. *Ibid.*, 15. "The Norwegians were reassured in a Reichstag speech in October 1939, by a statement to the effect that neutral Norway had declined Germany's offer of a non-aggression pact solely because 'she did not feel threatened in any way.' Six months later the Wehrmacht struck." Werner Rings, *Life with the Enemy, 1939-1945,* trans. J. Maxwell Brownjohns (Garden City, N.Y.: Doubleday and Company, Inc., 1982), 12.

3. Koht, *Norway: Neutral and Invaded*, 15.

4. William L. Shirer, *The Rise and Fall of the Third Reich* (New York: Simon and Schuster, 1960), 673.

5. Riste and Skodvin, *Norway and the Second World War*, 28.

6. The "phoney war" refers to the period after the European Allies (Great Britain and France) declared war on Germany in September 1939 when a lull followed. Hostilities broke out on a large scale in the spring of 1940 with the Germany invasion of the Low Countries.

7. *Ibid.,* 33.

8. *Ibid.,* 34.

9. *Ibid.,* 35

10. *Ibid.,* 38-39.

11. *Ibid.,* 13-14.

12. Winston Churchill, *The Gathering Storm* (Boston: Houghton Mifflin Company, 1948) 531.

13. *Ibid.,* 544 ff.

14. *Ibid.,* p 547.

15. *Ibid.,* 561-63.

16. Shirer, *Rise and Fall of the Third Reich,* 680-82.

17. *Ibid.,* 695.

18. Moulton, *Norwegian Campaign,* 127.

19. Captain Donald Macintyre, *Narvik* (New York: W.W. Norton and Company, Inc., 1959), 20.

20. Shirer, *Rise and Fall of the Third Reich,* 695.

21. *Ibid.*

Chapter 3: Norway at War

1. Koht, *Norway: Neutral and Invaded,* 67.

2. *Ibid.,* 68.

3. *Ibid.,* 76.

4. Jacob Worm-Muller, *Norway Revolts against the Nazis* (London: Lindsay Drummond, 1941) 13.

5. Koht, *Norway: Neutral and Invaded,* 84.

6. Telford Taylor, *The March of Conquest* (New York: Simon and Schuster, 1958), 124.

7. Winston Churchill, *The Rise and Fall of the Third Reich.* (New York: 1960, 601

8. *Ibid.,* 603.

9. *Ibid.,* 613.

10. Taylor, *March of Conquest,* 128-29.

11. *Ibid.*

12. *Ibid.*

13. François Kersaudy, *Norway, 1940* (New York: St. Martin's Press, 1987), 108-09.

14. Koht, *Norway: Neutral and Invaded,,* 99

15. *Ibid.,* 100-101.

16. Churchill, *Gathering Storm,* 642.

17. Taylor, *March of Conquest*, 132.

18. Moulton, *Norwegian Campaign*, 131.

19. *Ibid.,* 213.

20. Cited in Derry, *Campaign in Norway*, 169.

21. *Ibid.,* 164.

22. *Ibid.,* .194.

23. *Ibid.*

24. *Ibid.,* 194-195.

25. Churchill formed Independent Companies made up of volunteers shortly after the German invasion of Norway. Their essential feature was the ability to operate as self-contained units, in which the local population was expected to play a large part, for guerrilla warfare. In Norway, however, the local population was too small and too scattered for serious cooperation.

26. Moulton, *Norwegian Campaign*, 237.

27. *Ibid.,* 228.

28. Churchill, *Gathering Storm*, 652.

29. Derry, *Campaign in Norway*, 220.

30. As cited in T. K. Derry, *A History of Modern Norway: 1814-1972* (Oxford: Oxford University Press, 1973), 382.

Afterthoughts on the Campaign

1. Macintyre, *Narvik*, 24.

2. Moulton, *Norwegian Campaign*, 295.

3. Derry, *The Campaign in Norway*, 230-31.

4. Moulton, *Norwegian Campaign*, 259.

5. Derry, *The Campaign in Norway*, 231.

6. Moulton, *Norwegian Campaign*, 260.

7. Patrick Salmon, "British Strategy and Norway, 1939-40," *Britain and Norway in the Second World War,* ed. Patrick Salmon (London: HMSO, 1995), 4.

8. Riste and Skodvin, *Norway and the Second World War,* 54.

9. Koht, *Norway: Neutral and Invaded,* 4.

Chapter 4: Under Nazi Rule

1. Anthony March, *Darkness Over Europe: First-Person Accounts of Life in Europe During the War Years 1939-1945* (Chicago: Rand McNally and Company, 1969), 27.

2. Rings, *Life with the Enemy,* 154.

3. Worm-Muller, *Norway Revolts against the Nazis,* 11.

4. *Ibid.*

5. Koht, *Norway: Neutral and Invaded,* 130. In point of fact, any strategic advantage the Germans might have gained by seizing Norway was nullified by Churchill, who was able to preserve the balance of power in the North Atlantic by leasing bases in Iceland, Greenland, and Newfoundland. And because of this, the Germans had to tie down even more divisions there to prevent the Allies, with the active assistance of the inhabitants, from occupying the country themselves; Dorothy Baden-Powell, *Operation Jupiter* (North Yorkshire, England: Magna Print Books, 1982), 15.

6. Baden-Powell writes: "Von Falkenhorst totally disapproved of the leaflet which had been issued to the men under his command informing them that Norwegians could be 'won over by friendliness and small attentions of flattery. Norway was, after all, a civilized European country, not some Pacific island inhabited by naked savages.'" *Ibid.,* 17-18.

7. Olav Riste and Berit Nokleby, *Norway, 1940-45: The Resistance Movement* (Oslo: Nor-Media A/S, 1970) 11.

8. Worm-Muller, *Norway Revolts against the Nazis,* 129-31.

9. Amanda Johnson, *Norway, Her Invasion and Occupation* (Decatur, GA.: Bowen Press Printers, 1948), 209.

10. Koht, *Norway: Neutral and Invaded,* 131.

11. Johnson, *Norway, Her Invasion and Occupation*, 210.

12. The shutting off of imports from Great Britain and transoceanic countries appears graver when one contemplates that during prewar days, nations like the United States, Canada, and Argentina brought Norway about 80 percent of her bread, and that she produced less of the things necessary for living than any of the other occupied countries, except perhaps the British Isles. *Ibid.*, 211-12.

13. *Ibid.*, 219.

14. *Ibid.*, 212.

15. Worm-Muller, *Norway Revolts against the Nazis*, 32. Many people, including at least half of the members of Parliament, would have been prepared to accept a *fait accompli* if Germany had occupied the ports only and left the rest of the country unmolested; Baden-Powell, *Operation Jupiter*, 13.

16. Worm-Muller, *Norway Revolts against the Nazis*, 33.

17. *Ibid.*, 135-36.

18. For a fuller analysis of the Council of State negotiations, see Worm-Muller, *Norway Revolts against the Nazis*, 50-66. The author writes: "The NS Party had been granted a grace period for acquiring substantially more popular support and control over the life of the community, so that it might become a usable partner for the occupying authority." See also Tore Gjelsvik, *Norwegian Resistance: 1940-1945*, trans. Thomas K. Derry (McGill-Queens University Press, Montreal, 1979).

19. "The NS Party had been granted a grace period for acquiring substantially more popular support and control over the life of the community, so that it might become a usable partner for the occupying authority." Tore Gjelsvik, *Norwegian Resistance: 1940-1945*, trans. Thomas K. Derry (McGill-Queens University Press, Montreal, 1979), 13.

Chapter 5: The Civilian Reaction

1. Oluf Reed Olsen, *Two Eggs on My Plate* (Chicago: Rand McNally and Company, 1952), 19ff.

2. Olav Riste and Nokelby, *Resistance Movement*, 15.

3. *Ibid.*

4. Henri Michel, *The Shadow War: European Resistance, 1939-1945* (New York: Harper and Rowe Publishers, 1972), 245.

5. Worm-Muller, *Norway Revolts against the Nazis*, 47-48.

6. *Ibid.*

7. *Ibid.*

8. Jørgen Haestrup, *Europe Ablaze: An Analysis of the History of the European Resistance Movements, 1939-1945* (Odense, Denmark: Odense University Press, 1978), 77.

9. Author interview with Jørgen Jenssen, 12 September 1998.

10. Author interview with Jørgen Jenssen.

11. "Although the morale of the German army did not actually reach breaking point, there were many signs that the soldiers in Norway had a different mentality from those in Germany. The Gestapo, therefore, tried to control them and the relations between the Army and the Gestapo grew worse. The following story told to Worm-Muller by a good friend illustrates these relations. His friend was sitting in a nearly empty restaurant in Oslo. Near some German officers was a Nazi sympathizer who broke into the conversation of the officers, saying something to them. Suddenly one of the officers stood up and shouted, "Get out, you damned Gestapo." The Norwegian became very confused and stammered. "I am a Norwegian; I am not Gestapo," but the officer simply replied, "Get out, you bloody Gestapo." Worm-Muller, *Norway Revolts against the Nazis*, 109-11.

12. John Steinbeck, *The Moon Is Down* (New York: The Viking Press, 1942), 110. One young woman living in Kristiansund was warned by her mother not to look at the Germans on the street for fear that her expression of contempt would provoke an unpleasant confrontation. "Besides," she added, "you destroy yourself if you hate too much." Interview with Nanna Jenssen, Sept. 12, 1998.

13. Grieg, while exiled in England during the Occupation, was greatly admired for accompanying coast patrols, raiders, and commando parties on missions while he wrote of his people's devotion to Norway and their longing for freedom. He never expected any sacrifice from others that he was not ready to make himself. He was killed during a raid while flying over Potsdam, Germany, in December 1943; Hedin Bronner, "War Poems: A Norwegian Secret Weapon," *American Scandinavian Review* 36 (1948): 226-27.

14. Riste and Nokleby, *Norway: The Resistance Movement*, 16.

15. Gjelsvik, *Norwegian Resistance*, 13.

16. *Ibid.*, 16.

17. *Ibid.*, 16-17.

18. *Ibid.*

19. *Ibid*, 36.

20. According to statistics compiled by the National Socialist German Workers Party (NSDAP) between the years 1940-42, membership of the Quisling Party rose from 3,000 to 37,000, and in 1943 it reached a peak of 43,000; see *Who Were the Fascists? Social Roots of European Fascism,* ed. Stein Ugelvik Larsen, Bernt Hagtvet, Jan Petter Myklebust (Bergen: Universitetsforlaget, 1980), 601-669.

21. Gunvald Tomstad, a member of the Resistance, feigned membership in the NS to act more effectively as an Allied agent. His perception of NS members enabled him to successfully deceive the German authorities; see Per Hansson, *The Greatest Gamble*, trans. Maurice Michael (New York: W. W. Norton and Company, Inc., 1967), 60-61.

22. Gjelsvik, *Norwegian Resistance*, 36.

23. Riste and Nokleby, *Norway: The Resistance Movement*, 19.

24. Worm-Muller, *Norway Revolts against the Nazis*, 77.

25. Rene Kraus, *Europe in Revolt* (New York: The Macmillan Company, 1942), 467.

26. Worm-Muller, *Norway Revolts against the Nazis*, 77-78.

27. Gjelsvik, *Norwegian Resistance*, 38.

28. *Ibid.,* 14.

29. *Ibid.,* 25.

30. *Ibid.,* 30.

31. Kraus, *Europe in Revolt*, 471.

32. Worm-Muller, *Norway Revolts against the Nazis*, 98.

33. Bjarne Hoye and Ager M Trygve, *The Fight of the Norwegian Church Against Nazism* (New York: The Macmillan Company, 1943), 164.

34. *Ibid.,* 165-66.

35. *Ibid.,* 18.

36. According to Gjelsvik, *Norwegian Resistance: 1940-1945*, p. 19-20: "Due to weak leadership in the police organization, Jonas Lie succeeded in frightening more than 60 percent of all police officials and 40 percent of the rank and file into joining the party, and that without direct threats of dismissal."

37. Hoye and Trygve, *Fight of the Norwegian Church*, 168-69.

38. Riste and Nokleby, *Norway: The Resistance Movement*, 27-28.

39. Gjelsvik, *Norwegian Resistance*, 39.

40. Ibid., 18-19.

Chapter 6: The Ideological War I—The Church Front

1. Hoye and Trygve, *Fight of the Norwegian Church*, 47.

2. William L. Shirer, *Rise and Fall of the Third Reich*, 238.

3. *Ibid.,* 240. In 1940, Norway had a state church, the Evangelical Lutheran Church.

4. Hoye and Trygve, *Fight of the Norwegian Church*, 9.

5. *Ibid.,* 11.

6. *Ibid.,* 14.

7. *Ibid.*, 19.

8. *Ibid.*, 156.

9. *Ibid.*, 153.

10. Johnson, *Norway, Her Invasion and Occupation*, 241-42.

11. Hoye and Trygve, *Fight of the Norwegian Church*, 37.

12. *Ibid.*, 67.

13. *Ibid.*, 68.

14. Johnson, *Norway, Her Invasion and Occupation*, 104.

15. Hoye, and Trygve, *Fight of the Norwegian Church*, 85.

16. *Ibid.*, 83-84.

17. *Ibid.*, 85.

18. *Ibid.*, 96.

19. *Ibid.*, 132.

20. *Ibid.*, 126-27.

21. Johnson, *Norway, Her Invasion and Occupation*, 256.

Chapter 7: The Ideological War—The School Front

1. Johnson, *Norway, Her Invasion and Occupation*, 80.

2. *Before We Go Back* (Royal Norwegian Government Information Office, London: HMSO, 1944), 36-37.

3. Johnson, *Norway, Her Invasion and Occupation*, 266.

4. *Ibid.*, 264.

5. *Ibid.*, 266-67.

6. Worm-Muller, *Norway Revolts against the Nazis*, 102-03.

7. *Ibid.*

8. Gjelsvik, *Norwegian Resistance*, 60.

9. Hoye and Trygve, *Fight of the Norwegian Church*, 71-72.

10. Gjelsvik, *Norwegian Resistance*, 61.

11. Johnson, *Norway, Her Invasion and Occupation*, p 270.

12. Gjelsvik, *Norwegian Resistance*, 61.

13. Johnson, *Norway, Her Invasion and Occupation*, 271.

14. Gjelsvik, *Norwegian Resistance*, 64.

15. *Ibid.*, 56.

16. *Ibid.*

17. *Ibid.*, 115-17.

18. Johnson, *Norway, Her Invasion and Occupation*, 282.

19. *Ibid.*

Chapter 8: The Struggle for a Free Press

1. Haestrup, *Europe Ablaze*, 219.

2. Ivar Kraglund, *Kampen For Det Frie Ord* (The Fight for the Free Word) (Oslo: Norges Hjemmefrontmuseum, 1998), 6.

3. *Ibid.*

4. *Ibid.*, 7.

5. *Ibid.*, 14

6. Haestrup, *Europe Ablaze*, 220-21.

7. Kraglund, *Fight for the Free Word*, 6-7

8. Hans Luihn, *De illegale avisane* (The Illegal News), cited in Kraglund, *Kampen For Det Frie Ord* (Fight for the Free Word), 13. Luihn has suggested there were 200 newspapers. Haestrup's estimate was closer to 500 newspapers. He maintains that various newspapers had only a short life span, and that others appeared at irregular intervals, and often, with varying editors. Some newspapers merged with others. Haestrup, *Europe Ablaze*, 224.

9. Kraglund, *Fight for the Free Word*, 9.

10. *Ibid.*, 11.

11. *Ibid.*, 7.

12. *Ibid.*, 15.

13. *Avisa,* 11 October 1944.

14. Kraglund, *Fight for the Free Word,* 15.

15. *Ibid.,* 8.

16. *Avisa,* 11 October 1944.

17. Kraglund, *Fight for the Free Word,* 20.

18. *Ibid.*

19. *Ibid.,* 16-17.

20. Gjelsvik, *Norwegian Resistance,* 107.

21. Kraglund, *Fight for the Free Word,* 25.

22. *Ibid.*

23. *Ibid.,* 21.

24. The prison experiences of Petter Moen were documented in a diary that he compiled in prison from February to September 1944. The diary was written with a pin taken from a blackout curtain and pricked on prison toilet paper. As each roll was completed, it was put into a ventilator and blown under the floor of his cell. Moen was later drowned on a German prison ship that struck a mine and sank during a storm near the Swedish coast. The diary is considered a Norwegian classic of the Occupation period. *Petter Moen's Diary,* trans. Bjorn Koefoed (New York: Creative Age Press, 1951).

25. Gjelsvik, *Norwegian Resistance,* 144-45.

26. *Ibid.,* 134.

27. *Ibid.,* 143-44.

28. Kraglund, *Fight for the Free Word,* 32.

Chapter 9: The Illegal Press in Kristiansund

1. Much of the information for this chapter came from the unpublished notes of Jorgen Hoff-Jenssen and John M. Hansen, compiled in 1945 immediately at the end of the Occupation. The material was arranged and edited in 1975 by Jorgen Hoff-Jenssen.

2. Adamson and Klem, *Blood on the Midnight Sun*, 270-71.

3. *Ibid.*

Chapter 10: Anglo-Norwegian Intelligence

1. The elderly were in the vanguard because they knew what it was like to live under foreign domination, while younger people had been born in freedom. One had to do without something to appreciate its value; Baden-Powell, *Operation Jupiter*, 80-81.

2. Ragnar Ulstein, *The North Sea Traffic: Flight to War,* trans. Ellinor Melvaer, Ase Marie Hoel, and Gunnar Hay Hoel (Bergen: Sjofartsmuseum, 1992), 7.

3. Olsen, *Two Eggs on My Plate*, 62.

4. *Ibid.,* 62-63.

5. Gjelsvik, *Norwegian Resistance,* 72.

6. Haestrup, *Europe Ablaze*, 173.

7. Ragnar Ulstein, *Etterretningstjenesten* (Intelligence Service), *1940-1945* (Oslo: Norges Hjemefrontmuseum, 1994), 5-6.

8. *Ibid.*

9. *Ibid.,* 12.

10. *Ibid.,* 10-11.

11. *Ibid.,* 14.

12. *Ibid.,* 22-23.

13. Olsen, *Two Eggs on My Plate*, 59.

14. Ulstein, *Intelligence Service*, 13.

15. Haestrup, *Europe Ablaze*, 393-94.

16. Ulstein, "Norwegian Intelligence," *Britain and Norway in the Second World War,* 132.

17. *Ibid.*

18. Haestrup, *Europe Ablaze, 173.*

19. Ulstein, "Norwegian Intelligence," *Britain and Norway in the Second World War,* 26.

20. Olsen, *Two Eggs on My Plate,* 240.

21. Berit Eide Johnsen, *Motstandsbevegelsen Pa Agder, 1940-1945* (Resistance Movement in Agder, 1940-1945) (Kristiansand: Trykk Edgar Hogfeldt AS, 1992), 24.

22. Ulstein, *Intelligence Service,* 26.

23. E. O. Hauge, *Salt Water Thief,* trans. Malcolm Munthe (London: Gerald Duckworth & Co., Ltd., 1958), 51.

24. Hansson, *Greatest Gamble,* 38.

25. Johnsen, *Resistance Movement in Agder,* 37-38.

26. *Ibid.,* 58.

27. Hitler's preoccupation with Norway was rooted in his belief that the Allies would, at some undisclosed time, invade that country (Operation Jupiter). He therefore maintained a garrison in Norway, which eventually grew to 300,000 men. This put a strain on manpower, since these troops could have been more effectively used in some other theater of operations. The records of German military authorities in Norway support the fact that the Germans took these Allied plans seriously, although they were a deception for the invasion of Normandy. Einar Grannes, "Operation Jupiter: A Norwegian Perspective," *Britain and Norway in the Second World War,* 109-118.

28. Ulstein, "Norwegian Intelligence in the Second World War," *Britain and Norway in the Second World War,* 139.

Chapter 11: Theta: The Bergen Connection

1. Much of the material in this chapter was drawn from Kristian Ottosen's autobiographical work, *Theta, Theta* (Bergen: Universitetsforlaget, 1983). Additional information was obtained from a taped author interview with Mr. Ottosen at his home in Oslo in September 1998, and from written correspondence to the author in February 1999.

2. For a comprehensive account of the mission to seek and destroy the Tirpitz, see Thomas Gallagher, *The X-Craft Raid* (New York: Harcourt Brace Jovanovich, Inc., 1971), 89-166.

3. Pauline Hall (1890-1969) had a prominent career as composer, critic, and music promoter. This is the English version of the Norwegian poem, "Fangens aftensang" (Prison Vespers).

4. Nuremberg Documents, PS-1733, NOKW-2579, NG-226. The "Night and Fog" decree was issued by Hitler in December 1941, and promulgated by Wilhelm Keitel, head of the Armed Forces High Command (OKW). Keitel believed that the decree would be a deterrent to anyone who might otherwise be "suspected" of resistance because those apprehended would disappear without leaving a trace and no information would be given concerning their whereabouts or their fate. The number of foreign nationals who vanished into "Night and Fog" was never established, but certainly the number exceeded several thousand.

Chapter 12: The Politics of Sabotage

1. E. H. Cookridge, *Set Europe Ablaze* (New York: Thomas Y. Crowell Company, 1967), 1-18.

2. Baden-Powell, *Operation Jupiter*, 65, 70.

3. Arnfinn Moland, *Sabotasje I Norge Under 2 Verdenskrig* (Sabotage in Norway during World War II) (Oslo: Norges Hjemefrontmuseum, 1987), 3.

4. Gjelsvik, *Norwegian Resistance*, 72.

5. Moland, "Milorg and SOE," *Britain and Norway in the Second World War*, 143.

6. *Ibid.* 142.

7. Christopher Buckley, *Norway, the Commandos, Dieppe* (London: HMSO, 1952), 181-82.

8. Moland, *Sabotage*, 3.

9. Arnfinn Moland, *Milorg, 1941–43: Fremvehot, ledelse og organisasjon* (Milorg, 1941-43: Growth, Leadership and Organization) (Oslo: Norges Hjemefrontmuseum, 1991), 12-13.

10. Moland, *Sabotage*, 4.

11. Gjelsvik, *Norwegian Resistance*, 74.

12. Buckley, *Norway, the Commandos*, 194

13. Joachim Ronneberg, "The Linge Company and the British," *Britain and Norway in the Second World War*, 154.

14. *Ibid.*

15. Riste and Nokleby, *Norway: The Resistance Movement*, 50.

16. Gjelsvik, *Norwegian Resistance*, 123.

17. Moland, *Sabotage*, 4.

18. *Ibid.,* 5.

19. For the complete story of the North Sea shuttle service, see David Howarth's *The Shetland Bus* (London: Thomas Nelson and Sons, Ltd., 1951).

20. Riste and Nokleby, *Norway: The Resistance Movement*, 48-49.

21. J. C. Masterman, *The Double-Cross System in the War of 1939-1945* (Yale: Yale University Press, 1972), 86.

22. The Fuehrer Naval Conference, December 29, 1941, as cited in Chester Wilmot, *The Struggle for Europe* (Herfordshire: Wordsworth Editions, Limited, 1997), 93.

23. Einar Grannes, "Operation *Jupiter:* A Norwegian Perspective," *Britain and Norway in the Second World War*, 112.

24. Masterman, *Double-Cross System*, 109.

25. Riste and Nokleby, *Norway: The Resistance Movement*, 51.

26. Lidice was a small Czechoslovakian village not far from Prague that was dynamited in June 1942, in savage retaliation for the assassination of the diabolical Reichs-protector, Reinhard Heydrich, by Czech SOE agents who came from Britain. The entire male population was massacred and the women and children were carted off to concentration camps where many died.

27. Riste and Nokleby, *Norway: The Resistance Movement*, 52.

28. Berit Eide Johnsen, *Resistance Movement in Agder*, 22.

29. *Ibid.*

30. Moland, *Sabotsje,* 7.

31. Stephen Schofield, *Musketoon* (London: Jonathan Cape, 1964), 147.

32. Moland, *Sabotsje,* 8.

33. Hauge, *Salt Water Thief,* 144, 154.

34. *Ibid.,* 157-58. It is believed that Starheim drowned with the entire ship's company in March 1943. According to his biographer, the young saltwater thief's body drifted onto the western shore of Sweden on the little island of Tjorn near Gothenburg three weeks after the *Tromsund* was attacked. After the war his body was removed from Swedish soil and returned to Farsund, the little fishing village of his youth.

35. Riste and Nokleby, *Norway: The Resistance Movement,* 56.

36. *Ibid,* 58.

37. Haestrup, *Europe Ablaze,* 440.

38. On the relative merits of bombing vs. sabotage as a means of attacking the Germans in the occupied countries, see Patrick Howarth's *Undercover: The Men and Women of the SOE* (London: Phoenix Press, 1980), 301-03.

Chapter 13: The Vikings of Vemork

1. Dan Kurzman, *Blood and Water: Sabotaging Hitler's Bomb* (New York: Henry Holt and Company, Inc., 1997), 58.

2. *Ibid.*

3. *Ibid.,* 65.

4. As cited in Cookridge, *Set Europe Ablaze,* 322.

5. Kurzman, *Blood and Water,* 96-109.

6. Knut Haukelid, *Skis Against the Atom,* trans. F. H. Lyon (London: William Kimber and Co., Ltd., 1954).

7. As cited in Kurzman, *Blood and Water,* 124.

8. Haukelid, *Skis Against the Atom*, 84.

9. *Ibid.*, 73.

10. *Ibid.*, 75.

11. *Ibid.*, 89.

12. *Ibid.*, 91.

13. *Ibid.*, 90.

14. Kurzman, *Blood and Water*, 146-47.

15. Haukelid, *Skis Against the Atom*, 95.

16. *Ibid.* 96.

17. *Ibid.*, 98.

18. *Ibid.*, 98-99.

19. *Ibid.*, 100.

20. *Ibid.*, 162-63.

21. *Ibid.*

22. *Ibid.*, 167.

23. *Ibid.*

Chapter 14: The Stiffening of Resistance

1. Moland, *Sabotage*, 10-12.

2. Max Manus, *9 Lives Before Thirty* (Garden City, New York: Doubleday and Company, Inc., 1947), 161.

3. *Ibid.*, 169-73.

4. *Ibid.*, 242-43.

5. *Ibid.*, 246-53.

6. Haukelid, *Skis Against the Atom*, 108-09.

7. H. P. Willmott, "Operation Jupiter and Possible Landings in Norway," *Britain and Norway in the Second World War*, 104.

8. Moland, *Sabotage*, 11.

9. Gjelsvik, *Norwegian Resistance,* 127-28.

10. Riste and Nokleby, *Norway: The Resistance Movement,* 50.

11. Moland, "Milorg and SOE," *Britain and Norway in the Second World War,* 22.

12. "Milorg and SOE," *Britain and Norway in the Second World War,* 30.

13. "Milorg and SOE," *Britain and Norway in the Second World War,* 26.

14. "Milorg and SOE," *Britain and Norway in the Second World War,* 30.

15. Riste and Nokleby, *Norway: The Resistance Movement,* 67.

16. Riste and Nokleby, *Norway: The Resistance Movement,* 68-69.

17. Gjelsvik, *Norwegian Resistance, 126.*

18. Riste and Nokleby, *Norway: The Resistance Movement,* 69.

19. For a more in-depth study of the causes underlying civil strife between Communist and non-Communist resistance groups, particularly in the Balkans, see Patrick Howarth's *Undercover: the Men and Women of the SOE,* especially chapters 5 and 6.

Chapter 15: The Mobilization Threat

1. Arnfinn Moland, *Kampen Mot Mobiliserings Trusselen I Norge, 1943-44* (The Fight against the Mobilization Threat in Norway, 1943-44) (Oslo: Norges Hjemmefrontmuseum, 1987), 1-3.

2. Gjelsvik, *Norwegian Resistance,* 131.

3. Moland, *Fight against Mobilization,* 5

4. Gjelsvik, *Norwegian Resistance* , 93;

5. Moland, *Fight against Mobilization,* 10.

6. *Ibid.*

7. *Ibid.,* 11.

8. *Ibid.*

9. *Ibid.,* 13.

10. Riste and Nokleby, *Norway: The Resistance Movement,* 72.

11. *Ibid.*

12. Riste and Nokleby, *Norway: The Resistance Movement,* 73.

13. Gjelsvik, *Norwegian Resistance,* 131-33.

14. Moland, *Fight against Mobilization,* 21.

15. Gjelsvik, *Norwegian Resistance,* 151-52.

16. Gunnar Sonsteby, *Report from No. 24* (New York: Lyle Stuart, Inc., 1965), 109.

17. *Ibid.,* 19, 21, 42.

18. Moland, *Fight against Mobilization,* 22.

19. Gjelsvik, *Norwegian Resistance,* 154-57.

20. In November 1943, the Swedish government authorized a restricted form of military training for Norwegians who might later be used to preserve order in Norway. About 14,300 refugees took part. Gjelsvik, *Norwegian Resistance,* 117.

21. *Ibid.,* 159-60.

22. Sonsteby, *Report from No. 24,* p. 131-33.

23. Gjelsvik, *Norwegian Resistance,* 161.

Chapter 16: Moondrops for Milorg

1. Toward the end of the war, the Home Front Forces was the official term used for all organized resistance groups responsible to the Central Committee of the Home Forces in Oslo.

2. Riste and Nokleby, *Norway: The Resistance Movement,* 75.

3. Arne Egner, et al., *Slipp Over Norge* (Supplies over Norway) (Oslo: A/S Sem & Stenersen, 1982), 51.

4. *Ibid.*

5. *Ibid.*

6. Charles Cruickshank, *Special Operations Executive (SOE) in Scandinavia* (Oxford: Oxford University Press, 1986), 6. See

also Mark Seaman, "Special Duty Operations in Norway," *Britain and Norway in the Second World War,* 169.

7. Egner, *Supplies by Air,* 51-52.

8. Cruickshank, *SOE in Scandinavia,* 6.

9. Haestrup, *Europe Ablaze,* 399.

10. Egner, *Supplies by Air,* 53.

11. Olsen, *Two Eggs on My Plate,* 1952, 131-33.

12. *Ibid.,* 134.

13. Egner, *Supplies by Air,* 55.

14. *Ibid.,* 51.

15. Bruce H. Heimark, *The OSS Norwegian Special Operations Group in World War II* (Westport, Conn.: Praeger, 1994), 61.

16. *Ibid.,* 68.

17. *Ibid.,* 72.

18. *Ibid.,* 72-73.

19. *Ibid.,* 78.

20. Egner, *Supplies by Air,* 52.

21. *Ibid.*

Chapter 17: The Home Front Offensive

1. Moland, *Sabotage,* 16.

2. *Ibid.,* 24.

3. *Ibid.*

4. *Ibid.*

5. NORIC was the Norwegian Section of the Special Operations Executive. In the second half of 1944, SOE worked in close cooperation with Milorg. Sonsteby, *Report From No. 24,* p. 106.

6. *Ibid.,* 128.

7. *Ibid.,* 136-38.

8. *Ibid.*, 142-48.

9. Cruickshank, *SOE in Scandinavia*, 242.

10. Sonsteby, *Report from No. 24*, p. 138-41.

11. Manus, *9 Lives before Thirty*, 303-08.

12. Moland, *Sabotage*, 26.

13. *Ibid.*, 27.

14. Sonsteby, *Report From No. 24*, 172-74.

15. *Ibid.*

16. Norges Hjemmefrontmuseum (Norwegian Resistance Museum) (Trykk: Centraltrykkeriet Grafisk Service AS, 1982), 39.

17. Cruickshank, *SOE In Scandinavia*, 249.

18. *Ibid.*, 249-50.

Chapter 18: The Liberation & After

1. Paal Frisvold, "Planning the Liberation: The Norwegian Contribution," *Britain and Norway in the Second World War*, 197.

2. *Ibid.*, 197-98.

3. *Ibid,* 199-200.

4. Frode Faeroy, *Frigjoringen* (Liberation) (Oslo: Norges Hjemmefrontmuseum, 1994), 11.

5. *Ibid.*, 11-12.

6. *Ibid.*, 21.

7. Johs. Andenaes, Olav Riste, and Magne Skodvin, *Norway and the Second World War* (Oslo: Engers Boktrykkeri A/S, 1966), 120.

8. Sweden's pro-German neutrality can be explained in part by Hitler-Germany's military rule in Europe and the fear of being drawn into the war. Historians in both Sweden and Norway have also described conflict patterns that have negatively affected Swedish-Norwegian relations, including the dissolution of the Swedish-Norwegian union in 1905; a traditional Swedish

"big brother" mentality; different foreign policy orientation; and Norwegian Resistance to a Swedish leadership role in cooperation with the Nordic countries. Faeroy, *Liberation*, 14.

9. *Ibid.*, 13.

10. *Ibid.*, 29.

11. *Ibid.*, 30.

12. *Ibid.*, 19.

13. *Ibid.*, 36.

14. *Ibid.*

15. *Ibid.*

16. Riste and Nokleby, *Norway: The Resistance Movement*, 89.

17. Lucy S. Dawidowicz, *The War Against the Jews* (New York: Bantam Books, 1976), 503.

18. Faeroy, *Liberation*, 39.

19. Andenaes, Riste, and Skovden, *Norway and the Second World War*, 123.

20. *Ibid.*, 125-26.

21. *Ibid.*

22. Hans Christian Adamson and Per Klem, *Blood on the Midnight Sun* (New York: W. W. Norton & Company, 1964), 228.

23. *Ibid.*, 271-72.

24. Andenaes, Riste, and Skovden, *Norway and the Second World War*, 128.

25. *Ibid*, 129.

26. *Ibid.*, 148.

27. *Ibid.*, 145.

Conclusion

1. Haestrup, *Europe Ablaze*, 495.

Index

Notes:

- Page numbers in *italic* indicate maps, photographs, or other illustrations.

- Page numbers such as "232n6" indicate that information may be found on page 232, in endnote 6.

- Page numbers such as "*plate 1*" indicate photo pages.

Bergen (Norway)

   Communist Party line, 145

   German military assault April 1940, 17, 21, 26

   German military objectives, 29

   illegal press, distribution of early bulletins, 90

   military defense, problems of, 5, 6

   Milorg, Gestapo actions against, 148

   proposed Anglo-French invasions, 12–13, 15

   school strikes, 80

   teachers sent to concentration camps, 81

   Theta (Norwegian transmitting station), 124–138

Berggrav, Eivind, 46, 69, 72, 75–76

Bethouart, Antoine, 35, 37

Bismarck (German battleship), 120–121, 129

Bluecher (German heavy cruiser), 17, 18, 42

Blytt, Sidden, 135, 136

Blytt, Sigurd Gran, 125

Bodo (Norway), 36, 37, 38, 48

Boehme, Franz, 212, 213, 214

Bonte, Friedrich, 26, 27

Brauer, Kurt, 17, 19, 20

British Army, 32–33, 38, 142

British Royal Navy, 6, 27–28, 39, 43, 121–122

British Secret Intelligence Service (SIS), 112, 115, 122, 123, 139, 187. *See also* SPECIAL OPERATIONS EXECUTIVE (SOE, BRITISH INTELLIGENCE)

Brun, Jomar, 153

Brunsvig, Paal, 97

Bulgaria, 120

Bulletin, The, 92

business leaders, and formation of R-Group, 57

C

"The Café" (*Theta* headquarters), 125,

127, 135, *plates* 2–5

Carhampton plan, 149–150

Casablanca (Morocco), 207

Chamberlain, Neville, 12, 13, 16

Chariot (two-man torpedo), 130–131

Cheese (Norwegian transmitting station), 120–122, 187

Chiefs of Staff to the Supreme Allied Commander (COSSAC), 170, 207, 208

Christiansen, I. E., 46

Churchill, Winston, 11–12, 15, 31, 35, 36, 38, 43, 129, 139, 147, 154, 210

"Circle" *(Kretsen)*, 66–67, 171, 177, 178

civilian casualties in Norway

   attributable to heavy-water sabotage efforts, 163, 166

   during German invasion, 41

clandestine newspapers. *See* ILLEGAL PRESS

clergy, churches, and church leaders

   bishops' letter of protest to Stancke, 70

   bishops resign, 75

   boycott of Nazi-controlled Oslo radio, 71

   conscription efforts, opposition to, 178

   Free Church Manifesto, 76

   Joint Christian Council for Deliberation, formation of, 69

   maltreatment following bishops' resignation, 76

   ministers as substitute teachers, 84

   Nazi preachers, using Bible as propaganda tool, 72

   Oath of Silence abolished, 70

   pastoral letter to congregations condemning NS regime, 70–71

   pastors and clergymen resign, 76

   refusal of NS demand for "holy war" proclamation, 71–72

   religious radio programming, attempts to control, 69–70, 71

   response to Quisling's decrees

Thorne, Andrew, 207, 208, 209, 210, 214

Thorsen, Bjarne W., 125, *125*, 126, 127, 130, 135

Tinnoset (Norway), 164

Tjorn Island (Sweden), 247n34

Tomstad, Gunvald, 121, 122, 238n21

Toronto (Canada), 111, 135

Torp, Oscar, 144, 214

torture. *See* ARRESTS, IMPRISONMENT, INTERROGATION, AND TORTURE

trade unionists, and formation of R-Group, 57

Trident (British submarine), 130

Tripitz (German battleship), 129–131

Tromosund (Norwegian steamer), 150, 247n34

Tromso (Norway), 34, 38, 131, 178

Trondelag (Norway), 149

Trondheim (Norway), 147
  boycott of German propaganda films, 60
  German military assault April 1940, 17, 26, 30
  German military objectives, 29, 31
  Jorstad Bridge, sabotage, 203
  military defense, problems of, 6
  NORSO, sabotage activities, 195
  Prinz Eugen, docking for repairs, 130
  proposed Anglo-French invasions, 12–13, 15
  Resistance demonstrations at cinemas, 60
  school strikes, 80
  shipping point for trade with Great Britain, 9
  teachers transported to concentration camp, 82

Trondheim Student Association, 64

Trondheimsfiord (Norway), 129, 130, 131

Tronstad, Leif, 152, 159

Truant (British submarine), 21

Tugela (German steamer), 168–169

U

U-boats. *See* SUBMARINES

Ungdomsfylking (Youth Service Association), 73–74, 84

United States, 129, 146

University Student Association, 84–85

Utne, Leif, 125, 126

Utne, Rolf, 125, 127, 132, 137, 138

V

V-1 and V-2 rockets, 202

Vaernes airfield (Trondheim), 26, 32

Vaerum, Arne, 147–148

Vagan (Norway), 105

Vågso (Lofoten Islands), 144

Vaihingen an der Enz concentration camp, 138

Varanger Peninsula (Norway), 113

Varangerhalvoya (Norway), 113

Veiten (Gestapo headquarters, Bergen), 132

Vemork (Norway), 152

Venlo (Holland), 137

Vermork (Norway), 152, 164

Verpen (Norway), 199

Vi vil oss et land (We want a country), 91–92

volunteers join Ruge's fighting forces, 30

W

Warburton-Lee, Captain, 27, 28

warnings of German military activity, 14–16

Warspite (British battleship), 28, 29

Waxwing team, 195

weapons
  arms, ammunition, and heavy equipment supplies for Milorg, 186, 196

Wehrmacht (German army)
  Aandalsnes, attack on, 33
  and Gestapo, deterioration of relationship during Occupation, 237n11